Fourth International Workshop on Natural Language Processing for Social Media 2016

Held at the Conference on Empirical Methods in Natural Language Processing (EMNLP 2016)

Austin, Texas, USA
1 November 2016

ISBN: 978-1-5108-3153-7

SocialNLP@EMNLP2016 Chairs' Welcome

It is our great pleasure to welcome you to the Fourth ACM Workshop on Natural Language Processing for SocialMedia – SocialNLP'16, associated with EMNLP 2016. SocialNLP is an inter-disciplinary area of natural language processing (NLP) and social computing. We hold SocialNLP twice a year: one in the NLP venue, the other in the associated venue such as those for web technology or artificial intelligence. There are three plausible directions of SocialNLP: (1) addressing issues in social computing using NLP techniques; (2) solving NLP problems using information from social media; and (3) handling new problems related to both social computing and natural language processing. Through this workshop, we anticipate to provide a platform for research outcome presentation and head-to-head discussion in the area of SocialNLP, with the hope to combine the insight and experience of prominent researchers from both NLP and social computing domains to contribute to the area of SocialNLP jointly. The submissions to this year's workshop were again of high quality and we had a competitive selection process. We received 32 submissions from Asia, Europe, and the United States, and due to a rigorous review process, we only accepted 6 as long oral papers and 7 as short oral papers. Thus the acceptance rate was 40 percent. We are delighted to have Prof. Cristian Danescu-Niculescu-Mizil, from Cornell University, as our keynote speaker. We also encourage attendees to attend the keynote talk presentation. The valuable and insightful talk can and will guide us to a better understanding of the future. Putting together SocialNLP 2016 was a team effort. We first thank the authors for providing the quality content of the program. We are grateful to the program committee members, who worked very hard in reviewing papers and providing feedback for authors. Finally, we especially thank the Workshop Committee Chairs Prof. Annie Louis and Prof. Greg Kondrak.

We hope you join our community and enjoy the workshop!

Organizers
Jane Yung-jen Hsu, National Taiwan University, Taiwan
Lun-Wei Ku, Academia Sincia, Taiwan
Cheng-Te Li, National Cheng Kung University, Taiwan

Organizers:

Jane Yung-jen Hsu, National Taiwan University, Taiwan
Lun-Wei Ku, Academia Sinica, Taiwan
Cheng-Te Li, National Cheng-Kung University, Taiwan

Program Committee:

Zeljko Agic, University of Copenhagen
Nikolaos Aletras, Amazon UK
Tim Althoff, Stanford University
Hadi Amiri, University of Maryland
Ion Androutsopoulos, Athens University of Economics and Business
Alexandra Balahur, European Commission Joint Research Centre
Roberto Basili, University of Rome Tor Vergata
Fabrício Benevenuto, Federal University of Minas Gerais
Kalina Bontcheva, University of Sheffield
Taylor Cassidy, US Army Research Laboratory
Berlin Chen, National Taiwan Normal University
Hsin-Hsi Chen, National Taiwan University
John Chen, Interactions LLC
Hai Leong Chieu, DSO National Laboratories
Monojit Choudhury, Microsoft Research, India
Lei Cui, Microsoft Research
Aron Culotta, Illinois Institute of Technology
Pradipto Das, Rakuten Institute of Technology
Leon Derczynski, The University of Sheffield
Marco Dinarelli, Lattice-CNRS
Koji Eguchi, Kobe University
Michael Elhadad, Ben-Gurion University of the Negev
Hugo Jair Escalante, INAOE
Wei Gao, Qatar Computing Research Institute
Spandana Gella, University of Edinburgh
Alastair Gill, King's College London
Weiwei Guo, Yahoo! Labs
Scott Hale, University of Oxford
William Hamilton, Stanford University
Bo Han, IBM Research
Catherine Havasi, Luminoso, MIT
Yulan He, Aston University
Michael Heilman, Civis Anlytics
Graeme Hirst, University of Toronto
John Henderson, MITRE

Tuan-Anh Hoang, Singapore Management University
Wen-Lian Hsu, Academia Sinica
Ruihong Huang, Texas A&M University
Ting-Hao Huang, Carnegie Mellon University
Iustina Ilisei, Cognizant Technology Solutions Corp.
Yangfeng Ji, Georgia Tech
Jing Jiang, Singapore Management University
Anders Johannsen, University of Copenhagen
David Jurgens, Stanford University
Nobuhiro Kaji, Yahoo! Japan Corp.
Pallika Kanani, Oracle Labs
Emre Kiciman, Microsoft Research
Dongwoo Kim, ANU
Suin Kim, Korea Advanced Institute of Science and Technology
Roman Klinger, Univeristy of Stuttgart
Lingpeng Kong, Carnegie Mellon University
June-Jei Kuo, National Chung Hsing University
Tsung-Ting Kuo, University of California, San Diego
Patrik Lambert, Universitat Pompeu Fabra
Man Lan, East China Normal University
Kyumin Lee, Utah State University
Sungjin Lee, Yahoo! Labs
Haibo Li, Nuance Communications
Shou-De Lin, National Taiwan University
Yu-Ru Lin, University of Pittsburgh
Chuan-Jie Lin, National Taiwan Ocean University
Kang Liu, Chinese Academy of Sciences
Zhiyuan Liu, Tsinghua University
Bin Lu, Google Inc.
Zhunchen Luo, China Defense Science and Technology Information Center
Bruno Martins, University of Lisbon
Diana Maynard, University of Sheffield
Karo Moilanen, University of Oxford
Manuel Montes-y-Gómez, National Institute of Astrophysics, Optics and Electronics
Edward Newell, McGill University
Dong Nguyen, University of Twente
Scott Nowson, Xerox Research Centre Europe
Miles Osborne, Bloomberg
George Paliouras, NCSR, Demokritos
Harris Papageorgiou, ATHENA RC
Michael Paul, University of Colorado Boulder
Barbara Plank, University of Copenhagen
Stephan Raaijmakers, TNO, The Netherlands
Sravana Reddy, Wellesley College
Saurav Sahay, Intel Labs
Hassan Saif, The Open University

Yohei Seki, University of Tsukuba
Mário J. Silva, Universidade de Lisboa
Yanchuan Sim, Carnegie Mellon University
Jan Snajder, University of Zagreb
Veselin Stoyanov, Facebook Inc.
Carlo Strapparava, FBK-irst
Keh-Yih Su, Academia Sinica
Hiroya Takamura, Tokyo Institute of Technology
Xavier Tannier, Université Paris-Sud, Université Paris-Saclay, LIMSI, CNRS
Ming-Feng Tsai, National Chengchi University
Paola Velardi, University of Roma La Sapienza
Marc Verhagen, Brandeis University
Svitlana Volkova, PNNL
Xiaojun Wan, Peking University
Hsin-Min Wang, Academia Sinica
Jenq-Haur Wang, National Taipei University of Technology
William Yang Wang, Carnegie Mellon University
Ingmar Weber, Qatar Computing Research Institute
Albert Weichselbraun, University of Applied Sciences Chur
Robert West, Stanford University
Janyce Wiebe, University of Pittsburgh
Ruifeng Xu, Harbin Institute of Technology
Yi Yang, Georgia Tech
Yi-Hsuan Yang, Academia Sinica
Bei Yu, Syracuse University
Liang-Chih Yu, Yuan Ze University
Nicholas Jing Yuan, Microsoft Research
Zhe Zhang, IBM Watson
Hua-Ping Zhang, Beijing Institute of Technology
Xin Zhao, Renmin University of China
Deyu Zhou, Southeast University
Jun Zhu, Tsinghua University

Invited Speaker:

Cristian Danescu-Niculescu-Mizil, Cornell University

Table of Contents

Identifying and Categorizing Disaster-Related Tweets
Kevin Stowe, Michael J. Paul, Martha Palmer, Leysia Palen and Kenneth Anderson 1

Identifying Eyewitness News-worthy Events on Twitter
Erika Doggett and Alejandro Cantarero 7

Why Do They Leave: Modeling Participation in Online Depression Forums
Farig Sadeque, Ted Pedersen, Thamar Solorio, Prasha Shrestha, Nicolas Rey-Villamizar and Steven Bethard 14

Twitter at the Grammys: A Social Media Corpus for Entity Linking and Disambiguation
Mark Dredze, Nicholas Andrews and Jay DeYoung 20

Steps Toward Automatic Understanding of the Function of Affective Language in Support Groups
Amit Navindgi, Caroline Brun, Cécile Boulard Masson and Scott Nowson 26

Detecting Social Roles in Twitter
Sunghwan Mac Kim, Stephen Wan and Cecile Paris 34

Identifying Sensible Participants in Online Discussions
Siddharth Jain 41

emoji2vec: Learning Emoji Representations from their Description
Ben Eisner, Tim Rocktäschel, Isabelle Augenstein, Matko Bosnjak and Sebastian Riedel 48

Learning Latent Local Conversation Modes for Predicting Comment Endorsement in Online Discussions
Hao Fang, Hao Cheng and Mari Ostendorf 55

Witness Identification in Twitter
Rui Fang, Armineh Nourbakhsh, XIAOMO LIU, Sameena Shah and Quanzhi Li 65

How Do I Look? Publicity Mining From Distributed Keyword Representation of Socially Infused News Articles
Yu-Lun Hsieh, Yung-Chun Chang, Chun-Han Chu and Wen-Lian Hsu 74

Hierarchical Character-Word Models for Language Identification
Aaron Jaech, George Mulcaire, Shobhit Hathi, Mari Ostendorf and Noah A. Smith 84

Human versus Machine Attention in Document Classification: A Dataset with Crowdsourced Annotations
Nikolaos Pappas and Andrei Popescu-Belis 94

This page intentionally left blank.

Workshop Program

Tuesday, November 1, 2016

08:50–09:00   Opening

09:00–10:00   Keynote Speech

09:00–10:00   *Social Cues in Conversational Dynamics*
Cristian Danescu-Niculescu-Mizil

10:00–10:30   Short Paper Session I

10:00–10:15   *Identifying and Categorizing Disaster-Related Tweets*
Kevin Stowe, Michael J. Paul, Martha Palmer, Leysia Palen and Kenneth Anderson

10:15–10:30   *Identifying Eyewitness News-worthy Events on Twitter*
Erika Doggett and Alejandro Cantarero

10:30–11:00   *Coffee Break*

11:00–12:15   Short Paper Session II

11:00–11:15   *Why Do They Leave: Modeling Participation in Online Depression Forums*
Farig Sadeque, Ted Pedersen, Thamar Solorio, Prasha Shrestha, Nicolas Rey-Villamizar and Steven Bethard

11:15–11:30   *Twitter at the Grammys: A Social Media Corpus for Entity Linking and Disambiguation*
Mark Dredze, Nicholas Andrews and Jay DeYoung

11:30–11:45   *Steps Toward Automatic Understanding of the Function of Affective Language in Support Groups*
Amit Navindgi, Caroline Brun, Cécile Boulard Masson and Scott Nowson

11:45–12:00   *Detecting Social Roles in Twitter*
Sunghwan Mac Kim, Stephen Wan and Cecile Paris

12:00–12:15   *Identifying Sensible Participants in Online Discussions*
Siddharth Jain

12:30–14:00   *Lunch*

14:00–15:30   **Long Paper Session I**

14:00–14:30   *emoji2vec: Learning Emoji Representations from their Description*
Ben Eisner, Tim Rocktäschel, Isabelle Augenstein, Matko Bosnjak and Sebastian Riedel

14:30–15:00   *Learning Latent Local Conversation Modes for Predicting Comment Endorsement in Online Discussions*
Hao Fang, Hao Cheng and Mari Ostendorf

15:00–15:30   *Witness Identification in Twitter*
Rui Fang, Armineh Nourbakhsh, XIAOMO LIU, Sameena Shah and Quanzhi Li

15:30–16:00   *Coffee Break / Poster Session and Discussion*

16:00–17:30   **Long Paper Session II**

16:00–16:30   *How Do I Look? Publicity Mining From Distributed Keyword Representation of Socially Infused News Articles*
Yu-Lun Hsieh, Yung-Chun Chang, Chun-Han Chu and Wen-Lian Hsu

16:30–17:00   *Hierarchical Character-Word Models for Language Identification*
Aaron Jaech, George Mulcaire, Shobhit Hathi, Mari Ostendorf and Noah A. Smith

17:00–17:30   *Human versus Machine Attention in Document Classification: A Dataset with Crowdsourced Annotations*
Nikolaos Pappas and Andrei Popescu-Belis

17:30–17:40   Award and Closing

Identifying and Categorizing Disaster-Related Tweets

Kevin Stowe, Michael Paul, Martha Palmer, Leysia Palen, Ken Anderson
University of Colorado, Boulder, CO 80309
`[kest1439, mpaul, mpalmer, palen, kena]@colorado.edu`

Abstract

This paper presents a system for classifying disaster-related tweets. The focus is on Twitter data generated before, during, and after Hurricane Sandy, which impacted New York in the fall of 2012. We propose an annotation schema for identifying relevant tweets as well as the more fine-grained categories they represent, and develop feature-rich classifiers for relevance and fine-grained categorization.

1 Introduction

Social media provides a powerful lens for identifying people's behavior, decision-making, and information sources before, during, and after wide-scope events, such as natural disasters (Becker et al., 2010; Imran et al., 2014). This information is important for identiying what information is propagated through which channels, and what actions and decisions people pursue. However, so much information is generated from social media services like Twitter that filtering of noise becomes necessary.

Focusing on the 2012 Hurricane Sandy event, this paper presents classification methods for (i) filtering tweets relevant to the disaster, and (ii) categorizing relevant tweets into fine-grained categories such as preparation and evacuation. This type of automatic tweet categorization can be useful both during and after disaster events. During events, tweets can help crisis managers, first responders, and others take effective action. After the event, analysts can use social media information to understand people's behavior during the event. This type of understanding is of critical importance for improving risk communication and protective decision-making leading up to and during disasters, and thus for reducing harm (Demuth et al., 2012).

Our experiments show that such tweets can be classified accurately, and that combining a variety of linguistic and contextual features can substantially improve classifier performance.

2 Related Work

2.1 Analyzing Disasters with Social Media

A number of researchers have used social media as a data source to understand various disasters (Yin et al., 2012; Kogan et al., 2015), with applications such as situational awareness (Vieweg et al., 2010; Bennett et al., 2013) and understanding public sentiment (Doan et al., 2012). For a survey of social media analysis for disasters, see Imran et al. (2014).

Closely related to this work is that of Verma et al. (2011), who constructed classifiers to identify tweets that demonstrate situational awareness in four datasets (Red River floods of 2009 and 2010, the Haiti earthquake of 2010, and Oklahoma fires of 2009). Situational awareness is important for those analyzing social media data, but it does not encompass the entirety of people's reactions. A primary goal of our work is to capture tweets that relate to a hazard event, regardless of situational awareness.

2.2 Tweet Classification

Identifying relevant information in social media is challenging due to the low signal-to-noise ratio. A number of researchers have used NLP to address this challenge. There is significant work in the medi-

1

Proceedings of The Fourth International Workshop on Natural Language Processing for Social Media, pages 1–6,
Austin, TX, November 1, 2016. ©2016 Association for Computational Linguistics

cal domain related to identifying health crises and events in social media data. Multiple studies have been done to analyze flu-related tweets (Culotta, 2010; Aramaki et al., 2011). Most closely related to our work (but in a different domain) is the flu classification system of Lamb et al. (2013), which first classifies tweets for relevance and then applies finer-grained classifiers.

Similar systems have been developed to categorize tweets in more general domains, for example by identifying tweets related to news, events, and opinions (Sankaranarayanan et al., 2009; Sriram et al., 2010). Similar classifiers have been developed for sentiment analysis (Pang and Lee, 2008) to identify and categorize sentiment-expressing tweets (Go et al., 2009; Kouloumpis et al., 2011).

3 Data

3.1 Collection

In late October 2012, Hurricane Sandy generated a massive, disperse reaction in social media channels, with many users expressing their thoughts and actions taken before, during, and after the storm. We performed a keyword collection for this event capturing all tweets using the following keywords from October 23, 2012 to April 5, 2013:

DSNY, cleanup, debris, frankenstorm, garbage, hurricane, hurricanesandy, lbi, occupysandy, perfectstorm, sandy, sandycam, stormporn, superstorm

22.2M unique tweets were collected from 8M unique Twitter users. We then identified 100K users with a geo-located tweet in the time leading up to the landfall of the hurricane, and gathered all tweets generated by those users creating a dataset of 205M tweets produced by 92.2K users. We randomly selected 100 users from approximately 8,000 users who: (i) tweeted at least 50 times during the data collection period, and (ii) posted at least 3 geo-tagged tweets from within the mandatory evacuation zones in New York City. It's critical to filter the dataset to focus on users that were at high risk, and this first pass allowed us to lower the percentage of users that were not in the area and thus not affected by the event. Our dataset includes *all* tweets from these users, not just tweets containing the keywords. Seven users were removed for having predominately non-English tweets. The final dataset contained 7,490 tweets from 93 users, covering a 17 day time period starting one week before landfall (October 23rd to November 10th). Most tweets were irrelevant: Halloween, as well as the upcoming presidential election, yielded a large number of tweets not related to the storm, despite the collection bias toward Twitter users from affected areas.

3.2 Annotation Schema

Tweets were annotated with a fine-grained, multi-label schema developed in an iterative process with domain experts, social scientists, and linguists who are members of our larger project team. The schema was designed to annotate tweets that reflect the attitudes, information sources, and protective decision-making behavior of those tweeting. This schema is not exhaustive—anything deemed relevant that did not fall into an annotation category was marked as **Other**—but it is much richer than previous work. Tweets that were not labeled with any category were considered irrelevant (and as such, considered negative examples for relevance classification). Two additional categories, reporting on family members and referring to previous hurricane events, were seen as important to the event, but were very rare in the data (34 of 7,490 total tweets). The categories identified and annotated are as follows: Tweets could be labeled with any of the following:

Sentiment Tweets that express emotions or personal reactions towards the event, such as humor, excitement, frustration, worry, condolences, etc.

Action Tweets that describe physical actions taken to prepare for the event, such as powering phones, acquiring generators or alternative power sources, and buying other supplies.

Preparation Tweets that describe making plans in preparation for the storm, including those involving altering plans.

Reporting Tweets that report first-hand information available to the tweeter, including reporting on the weather and the environment around them, as well as the observed social situations.

Information Tweets that share or seek information from others (including public officials). This category is distinct from Reporting in that it only includes information received or request from outside sources, and not information perceived first-hand.

Movement Tweets that mention evacuation or sheltering behavior, including mentions of leaving, staying in place, or returning from another location. Tweets about movement are rare, but especially important in determining a user's response to the event.

3.3 Annotation Results

Two annotators were trained by domain experts using 726 tweets collected for ten Twitter users. Annotation involved a two-step process: first, tweets were labeled for relevance, and then relevant tweets were labeled with the fine-grained categories described above. The annotators were instructed to use the linguistic information, including context of previous and following tweets, as well as the information present in links and images, to determine the appropriate category. A third annotator provided a deciding vote to resolve disagreements.

Table 1 shows the label proportions and annotator agreement for the different tasks. Because each tweet could belong to multiple categories, κ scores were calculated based on agreement per category: if a tweet was marked by both annotators as a particular category, it was marked as agreement for that category. Agreement was only moderate for relevance ($\kappa = .569$). Many tweets did not contain enough information to easily distinguish them, for example: *"tryin to cure this cabin fever!"* and *"Thanks to my kids for cleaning up the yard"* (edited to preserve privacy). Without context, it is difficult to determine whether these tweeters were dealing with hurricane-related issues.

Agreement was higher for fine-grained tagging ($\kappa = .814$). The hardest categories were the rarest (Preparation and Movement), with most confusions between Preparation, Reporting, and Sentiment.[1]

4 Classification

We trained binary classifiers for each of the categories in Table 1, using independent classifiers for each of the fine-grained categories (for which a tweet may have none, or multiple).

---

[1]Dataset available at https://github.com/kevincstowe/chime-annotation

Category	Count	% tweets	Agreement
Relevance			
Relevance	1757	23.5%	48.6% (κ=.569)
Fine-Grained Annotations			
Reporting	1369	77.9%	80.2% (κ=.833)
Sentiment	786	44.7%	71.8% (κ=.798)
Information	600	34.1%	89.8% (κ=.934)
Action	295	16.8%	72.5% (κ=.827)
Preparation	188	10.7%	41.1% (κ=.565)
Movement	53	3.0%	43.3% (κ=.600)

Table 1: The number and percentage of tweets for each label, along with annotator agreement.

4.1 Model Selection

Our baseline features are the counts of unigrams in tweets, after preprocessing to remove capitalization, punctuation and stopwords. We initially experimented with different classification models and feature selection methods using unigrams for relevance classification. We then used the best-performing approach for the rest of our experiments. 10% of the data was held out as a development set to use for these initial experiments, including parameter optimization (e.g., SVM regularization).

We assessed three classification models that have been successful in similar work (Verma et al., 2011; Go et al., 2009): support vector machines (SVMs), maximum entropy (MaxEnt) models, and Naive Bayes. We experimented with both the full feature set of unigrams, as well as a truncated set using standard feature selection techniques: removing rare words (frequency below 3) and selecting the n words with the highest pointwise mutual information between the word counts and document labels.

Each option was evaluated on the development data. Feature selection was substantially better than using all unigrams, with the SVM yielding the best F1 performance. For the remaining experiments, SVM with feature selection was used.

4.2 Features

In addition to unigrams, bigram counts were added (using feature selection described above), as well as:

- The **time** of the tweet is particularly relevant to the classification, as tweets during and after the event are more likely to be relevant than those before. The day/hour of the tweet is represented

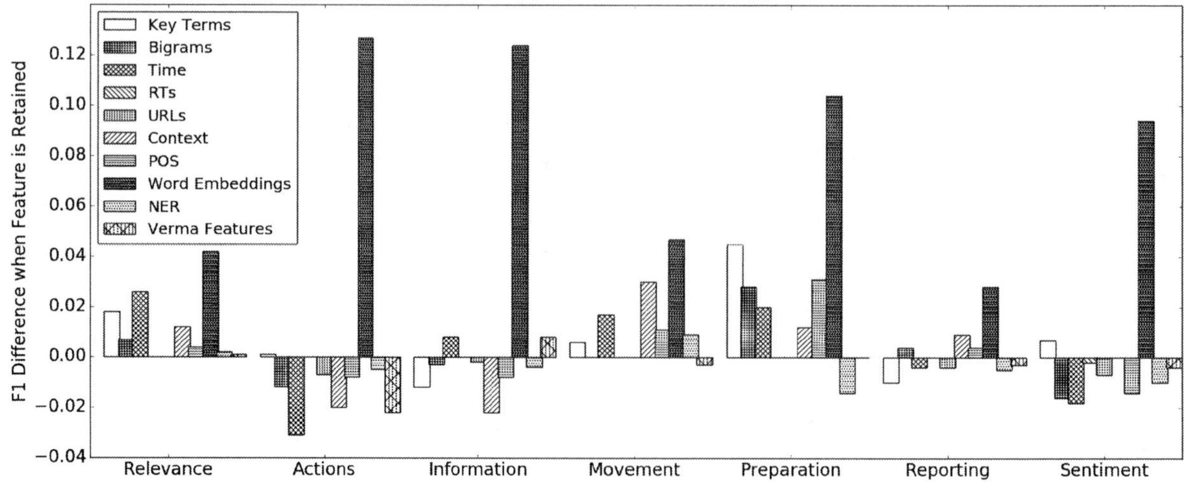

Figure 1: Negated difference in F1 for each feature removed from the full set (positive indicates improvement).

as a one-hot feature vector.

- We indicate whether a tweet is a **retweet** (RT), which is indicative of information-sharing rather than first-hand experience.

- Each **URL** found within a tweet was stripped to its base domain and added as a lexical feature.

- The annotators noted that **context** was important in classification. The unigrams from the previous tweet and previous two tweets were considered as features.

- We included n-grams augmented with their **part-of-speech** tags, as well as **named entities**, using the Twitter-based tagger of Ritter et al. (2011).

- **Word embeddings** have been used extensively in recent NLP work, with promising results (Goldberg, 2015). A Word2Vec model (Mikolov et al., 2013) was trained on the 22.2M tweets collected from the Hurricane Sandy dataset, using the Gensim package (Řehůřek and Sojka, 2010), using the C-BOW algorithm with negative sampling (n=5), a window of 5, and with 200 dimensions per word. For each tweet, the mean embedding of all words was used to create 200 features.

- The work of Verma et al. (2011) found that formal, objective, and impersonal tweets were useful indicators of situational awareness, and as such developed classifiers to tag tweets with four different categories: formal vs informal, subjective vs objective, personal vs impersonal, and sit-

	Baseline			All Features			Best Features		
	F1	P	R	F1	P	R	F1	P	R
Relevance	.66	.80	.56	.71	.81	.64	**.72**	.79	.66
Actions	.26	.44	.19	.39	.46	.35	**.41**	.42	.40
Information	.33	.57	.24	.48	.57	.41	**.49**	.50	.49
Movement	.04	.04	.04	.07	.10	.07	**.08**	.10	.07
Preparation	.30	.44	.23	.36	.41	.32	**.36**	.38	.35
Reporting	.52	.76	.40	.73	.71	.75	**.75**	.71	.80
Sentiment	.37	.64	.26	**.53**	.58	.49	.52	.52	.52

Table 2: Results for relevance and fine-grained classification.

uational awareness vs not. We used these four **Verma** classifiers to tag our Hurricane Sandy dataset and included these tags as features.

4.3 Classification Results

Classification performance was measured using five-fold cross-validation. We conducted an ablation study (Figure 1), removing individual features to determine which contributed to performance. Table 2 shows the cross-validation results using the baseline feature set (selected unigrams only), all features, and the best feature set (features which had a significant effect in the ablation study). In all categories except for Movement, the best features improved over the baseline with $p < .05$.

4.4 Performance Analysis

Time, context, and word embedding features help relevance classification. Timing information is helpful for distinguishing certain categories (e.g., Preparation happens before the storm while Movement can happen before or after). Context was also helpful, consistent with annotator observations. A larger context window would be theoretically more useful, as we noted distant tweets influenced annotation choices, but with this relatively small dataset increasing the context window also prohibitively increased sparsity of the feature.

Retweets and URLs were not generally useful, likely because the information was already captured by the lexical features. Part-of-speech tags yielded minimal improvements, perhaps because the lexical features critical to the task are unambiguous (e.g., "hurricane" is always a noun), nor did the addition of features from Verma et al. (2011), perhaps because these classifiers had only moderate performance to begin with and were being extended to a new domain.

Fine-grained classification was much harder. Lexical features (bigrams and key terms) were useful for most categories, with other features providing minor benefits. Word embeddings greatly improved performance across all categories, while most features had mixed results. This is consistent with our expectations of latent semantics : tweets within the same category tend to contain similar lexical items, and word embeddings allow this similarity to be captured despite the limited size of the dataset.

The categories that were most confused were Information and Reporting, and the categories with the worst performance were Movement, Actions, and Preparation. Movement simply lacks data, with only 53 labeled instances. Actions and Preparation contain wide varieties of tweets, and thus patterns to distinguish them are sparse. More training data would help fine-grained classification, particularly for Actions, Preparation, and Movement.

Classification for Reporting performs much better than others. This is likely because these tweets tend to fall into regular patterns: they often use weather and environment-related lexical items like "wind" and "trees", and frequently contain links to images. They also are relatively frequent, making their patterns easier to identify.

4.5 Performance in Other Domains

To see how well our methods work on other datasets, we compared our model to the situational awareness classification in the Verma et al. (2011) datasets de-

	Verma Acc	Ext. Acc	Verma F1	Ext. F1
SA	.845	**.856**	.423	**.551**

Table 3: Verma Comparison

scribed above. We replicated the original Verma et al. (2011) model with similar results, and then adjusted the model to incorporate features that performed positively from our experiments to create an 'extended' model. This entailed adding the mean word embeddings for each tweet as well as adjusting the unigram model to incorporate only key terms by PMI. They report only accuracy, which our system improves marginally, while making this modifications greatly improved F1, as shown in table 3.

5   Conclusion

Compared to the most closely related work of Verma et al. (2011), our proposed classifiers are both more general (identifying all relevant tweets, not just situational awareness) and richer (with fine-grained categorizations). Our experimental results show that it is possible to identify relevant tweets with high precision while maintaining fairly high recall. Fine-grained classification proved much more difficult, and additional work will be necessary to define appropriate features and models to detect more specific categories of language use. Data sparsity also causes difficulty, as many classes lack the positive examples necessary for the machine to reliably classify them, and we continue to work on further annotation to alleviate this issue.

Our primary research aims are to leverage both relevance classification and fine-grained classification to assist crisis managers and first responders. The preliminary results are show that relevant information can be extracted automatically via batch processing after events, and we aim to continue exploring possibilities to extend this approach to real-time processing. To make this research more applicable, we aim to produce a real-time processing system that can provide accurate classification during an event rather than after, and the apply current results to other events and domains.

References

Eiji Aramaki, Sachiko Maskawa, and Mizuki Morita. 2011. Twitter catches the flu: Detecting influenza epidemics using Twitter. In *Conference on Empirical Methods in Natural Language Processing (EMNLP)*, pages 1568–1576.

Hila Becker, Mor Naaman, and Luis Gravano. 2010. Learning similarity metrics for event identification in social media. In *ACM International Conference on Web Search and Data Mining (WSDM)*, pages 291–300.

K J Bennett, J M Olsen, S Harris, S Mekaru, A A Livinski, and J S Brownstein. 2013. The perfect storm of information: combining traditional and non-traditional data sources for public health situational awareness during hurricane response. *PLoS Curr*, 5.

Aron Culotta. 2010. Towards detecting influenza epidemics by analyzing twitter messages. In *Proceedings of the First Workshop on Social Media Analytics*, SOMA '10, pages 115–122, New York, NY, USA. ACM.

Julie L. Demuth, Rebecca E. Morss, Betty Hearn Morrow, and Jeffrey K. Lazo. 2012. Creation and communication of hurricane risk information. *Bulletin of the American Meteorological Society*, 93(8):1133–1145.

Son Doan, Bao Khanh Ho Vo, and Nigel Collier. 2012. An analysis of Twitter messages in the 2011 Tohoku earthquake. In *Lecture Notes of the Institute for Computer Sciences, Social-Informatics and Telecommunications Engineering*, volume 91 LNICST, pages 58–66.

Alec Go, Richa Bhayani, and Lei Huang. 2009. Twitter sentiment classification using distant supervision. *CS224N Project Report, Stanford*, 1:12.

Yoav Goldberg. 2015. A primer on neural network models for natural language processing. *CoRR*, abs/1510.00726.

Muhammad Imran, Carlos Castillo, Fernando Diaz, and Sarah Vieweg. 2014. Processing social media messages in mass emergency: A survey. *arXiv preprint arXiv:1407.7071*.

Marina Kogan, Leysia Palen, and Kenneth M Anderson. 2015. Think local, retweet global: Retweeting by the geographically-vulnerable during Hurricane Sandy. In *ACM Conference on Computer Supported Cooperative Work & Social Computing (CSCW)*.

Efthymios Kouloumpis, Theresa Wilson, and Johanna Moore. 2011. Twitter sentiment analysis: The good the bad and the omg! *ICWSM*, 11:538–541.

Alex Lamb, Michael J Paul, and Mark Dredze. 2013. Separating fact from fear: Tracking flu infections on twitter. In *HLT-NAACL*, pages 789–795.

Tomas Mikolov, Ilya Sutskever, Kai Chen, Greg S Corrado, and Jeff Dean. 2013. Distributed representations of words and phrases and their compositionality. In C. J. C. Burges, L. Bottou, M. Welling, Z. Ghahramani, and K. Q. Weinberger, editors, *Advances in Neural Information Processing Systems 26*, pages 3111–3119. Curran Associates, Inc.

Bo Pang and Lillian Lee. 2008. Opinion mining and sentiment analysis. *Foundations and trends in information retrieval*, 2(1-2):1–135.

Radim Řehůřek and Petr Sojka. 2010. Software Framework for Topic Modelling with Large Corpora. In *Proceedings of the LREC 2010 Workshop on New Challenges for NLP Frameworks*, pages 45–50, Valletta, Malta, May. ELRA.

Alan Ritter, Sam Clark, Oren Etzioni, et al. 2011. Named entity recognition in tweets: an experimental study. In *Proceedings of the Conference on Empirical Methods in Natural Language Processing*, pages 1524–1534.

Jagan Sankaranarayanan, Hanan Samet, Benjamin E Teitler, Michael D Lieberman, and Jon Sperling. 2009. Twitterstand: news in tweets. In *Proceedings of the 17th acm sigspatial international conference on advances in geographic information systems*, pages 42–51. ACM.

Bharath Sriram, Dave Fuhry, Engin Demir, Hakan Ferhatosmanoglu, and Murat Demirbas. 2010. Short text classification in twitter to improve information filtering. In *Proceedings of the 33rd international ACM SIGIR conference on Research and development in information retrieval*, pages 841–842. ACM.

Sudha Verma, Sarah Vieweg, William J Corvey, Leysia Palen, James H Martin, Martha Palmer, Aaron Schram, and Kenneth Mark Anderson. 2011. Natural language processing to the rescue? extracting" situational awareness" tweets during mass emergency. In *ICWSM*.

Sarah Vieweg, Amanda L. Hughes, Kate Starbird, and Leysia Palen. 2010. Microblogging during two natural hazards events: what Twitter may contribute to situational awareness. In *CHI*.

Jie Yin, Andrew Lampert, Mark Cameron, Bella Robinson, and Robert Power. 2012. Using social media to enhance emergency situation awareness. *IEEE Intelligent Systems*, 27(6):52–59.

Identifying Eyewitness News-Worthy Events on Twitter

Erika Varis Doggett
Timeline Labs
Santa Monica, CA
`erika.varis@timelinelabs.com` *

Alejandro Cantarero
Timeline Labs
Santa Monica, CA
`alejandro@timelinelabs.com` †

Abstract

In this paper we present a filter for identifying posts from eyewitnesses to various event types on Twitter, including shootings, police activity, and protests. The filter combines sociolinguistic markers and targeted language content with straightforward keywords and regular expressions to yield good accuracy in the returned tweets. Once a set of eyewitness posts in a given semantic context has been produced by the filter, eyewitness events can subsequently be identified by enriching the data with additional geolocation information and then applying a spatio-temporal clustering. By applying these steps we can extract a complete picture of the event as it occurs in real-time, sourced entirely from social media.

1   Introduction

Current information has always been of paramount interest to a variety of professionals, notably reporters and journalists, but also to crime and disaster response teams (Diakopoulos et al., 2012; Vieweg et al., 2010). With the explosion of the internet and social media, more information is available–and at a faster rate–on current events than ever before. A large proportion of non-professional people are now in the position of news reporters, spreading information through their social networks in many cases faster than traditional news media (Beaumont, 2008; Beaumont, 2009; Ritholtz, 2013; Thielman,

2013; Petrović et al., 2013), whether by sharing and re-sharing the first news message of an event, or through immediate personal eyewitness accounts. This average eyewitness represents a valuable and untapped information source for news professionals and others. But given the wide variability of texts and topics included in social media, the question remains: how to sift the wheat from the chaff?

When your information source is an average user, distinction of eyewitness posts from noise and off-topic data is difficult. Everyday social media users may be situated on the scene, but they do not always frame their posts in the most informative or consistent language. Their intended audience is a personal network of friends for whom a lot of contextual information is already available, allowing their utterances to be highly informative for that network, but still ambiguous for strangers, or automated programs.

1.1   Related work

Previous studies have attempted to programmatically identify eyewitnesses with limited success. Imran (2013) achieved only a .57 precision accuracy for their machine learning eyewitness classifier. Diakopoulos et al. (2012) reported a high accuracy for a static eyewitness classifier at .89, but it is unclear exactly how it was constructed, losing replicability and verifiability. In addition, their classifier only analyzed static datasets, whereas the speed of current events reporting on social media calls for a tool for online use.

In this paper we present a linguistic method for identifying eyewitness social media messages from

---

* Current affiliation: The   Walt   Disney   Studios
`Erika.Varis.Doggett@disney.com`

† Current   affiliation: tronc,   Inc.
`acantarero@tronc.com`

Proceedings of The Fourth International Workshop on Natural Language Processing for Social Media, pages 7–13,
Austin, TX, November 1, 2016. ©2016 Association for Computational Linguistics

a microblogging service such as Twitter, in a real-time streaming environment. Our system identifies messages on different eyewitness topics, including shootings, police activity, and protests, and can easily be extended to further areas, such as celebrity sightings and weather disasters. We further identify events corresponding to groups of related messages by enriching the data with geographical location and then running a spatio-temporal clustering algorithm.

Our work provides the novel contributions of a system that functions in a real-time streaming environment, combines information such as semantic and spatio-temporal clustering, and utilizes simple and fast computational tools over classifiers that require large training data and long setup time. In §2 we outline our process for finding eyewitness posts and events. Section 3 presents results from this system, and we provide some concluding remarks in §4.

2 Method

An eyewitness post on a social network is a text document giving a first person account from a witness to the event. As such, we looked to build filtering rules based on language related to an event, excluding posts from official agencies (e.g. police, fire departments), news outlets, and after-the-fact or remote commentary. In this section, we describe how filters can be constructed that are capable of doing this in real-time on Twitter.

2.1 Datasets

We collected Twitter data from several real events to find a set of eyewitness tweets to inform the creation of linguistic filters. Such a dataset can be collected from the Twitter API (or any suitable 3rd party vendor) by doing broad searches in a narrow time window right after an event has happened. To build a rule set for shootings, for example, we pulled data from multiple mass shootings, including shootings in 2013-2014 at LAX in Los Angeles; Isla Vista, CA; and the Las Vegas Wal-mart and Cici's Pizza. In these cases, searches around the local place-names at the time of the shootings produced a very broad set of documents, which were then manually checked for true eyewitness texts, resulting in an informative set of eyewitness tweets. By examining these eyewitness tweets, we discovered several

consistent language patterns particular to eyewitness language.

2.2 Language patterns

One of the challenges of social media language is that users exhibit a wide range of phrasing to indicate an event has occurred. It is because of our world knowledge that we are able, as human language speakers, to understand that the person is discussing a newsworthy event (Doyle and Frank, 2015).

With that in mind, we propose building filters that consist of three parts. The first is a semantic context. Examples here might be criminal shootings, unusual police activity, or civil unrest. This semantic context may be built using heuristic rules, or it may also be derived from a machine learning approach. The second part is the existence of salient linguistic features that indicate an eyewitness speaker. Finally, we look at similar linguistic features that indicate the user is not an eyewitness, useful for blocking non-eyewitness posts.

2.2.1 Eyewitness features

First person. First person pronouns are often dropped on social media, but when present this is a strong indicator that the event being described was witnessed first-hand.

Immediate temporal markers. Words such as "just", "now", "rn"[1] indicate the event happened immediately prior to the tweet or is ongoing.

Locative markers. Language may be used to define a place in relation to the speaker, such as "home", "work", "school", or "here".

Exclamative or emotive punctuation. Eyewitnesses to an exciting or emotional event express their level of excitement in their messages. Common ways this may be achieved are through punctuation (exclamation and question marks), emoticons, emoji, or typing in all capital letters. These are relatively common features used in social media NLP (Thelwall et al., 2010; Agarwal et al., 2011; Neviarouskaya et al., 2007).

Lexical exclamations and expletives. A normal person is likely to use colorful language when witnessing an event. Phrases such as "smh"[2], "wtf", and expletives are often part of their posts.

---

[1] Twitter short-hand for "right now".

[2] "Shake my head"

2.2.2 Non-eyewitness features

Non-eyewitness features are crucial as a post may match the semantic context and have at least one of the linguistic eyewitness markers above, but still not be an eyewitness account of an event. The main markers we found for non-eyewitness language fall into a handful of categories, described below.

Jokes, memes, and incongruous emotion or sentiment. The expected reaction to a violent crime or disaster may include shock, sadness, anxiety, confusion, and fear, among others (Shalev, 2002; Armsworth and Holaday, 1993; North et al., 1994; Norris, 2007)[3]. As such, it is reasonable to remove posts with positive sentiment and emotion from eyewitness documents related to a traumatic incident (e.g. shootings).

Wrong part of speech, mood, or tense. The verb "shoot" in the first person is unlikely to be used in a criminal shooting context on a social network. The conditional mood, for example in phrases such as "what if, would've, wouldn't", indicates a hypothetical situation rather than a real event. Similarly, future tense does not indicate someone is witnessing or has witnessed an event.

Popular culture references. Flagging and removing posts with song lyrics or references to music, bands, video games, movies, or television shows can greatly improve results as it is not uncommon for eyewitness features to be referencing a fictional event the user saw in one of these mediums.

Temporal markers. Language such as "last night, last week, weeks ago, months ago" and similar phrases suggest an event happened an extended period of time in the past, and is not a current eyewitness.

2.3 Finding eyewitness events

Identifying an event from a set of eyewitness posts can be done using a simple clustering approach. Most common clustering methods on text data focus on semantic similarity. However, the eyewitness filters we created already enforced a level of semantic similarity for their resulting documents, so such clustering would not be effective for our use case.

Multiple separate events of a newsworthy nature are unlikely to be occurring simultaneously in the same location at the same time, or such instances will be considered part of a single large event. Therefore, we propose using a spatio-temporal clustering algorithm to identify potential events. By forcing the spatial proximity to be small (limited to approximately a neighborhood in size) and the temporal locality to be similarly tight, say less than 30 minutes, we can effectively group documents related to events. A good summary of such methods is provided in Kisilevich et al. (2010).

2.4 Method summary

In this section, we describe a complete process for finding eyewitness posts and events.

We start by enriching each document in the feed with geolocation information of the Twitter user, for use in the clustering step to identify events. Geolocation information is central to our approach to finding events, but less than 5% of tweets have location data available. There are many approaches that can be used to enrich social media posts with a prediction of a user's location. Good summaries are available in Ajao et al. (2015) and Jurgens et al. (2015). We implemented the method described in Apreleva and Cantarero (2015) and were able to add user location information to about 85% of users in our datasets with an 8 km median error. This is accurate enough to place users in their city or neighborhood and enables us to find more posts related to the same event.

After enriching the data, we apply the semantic context topic filters, then the eyewitness linguistic features, and then remove documents matching the non-eyewitness features. This produces a set of eyewitness documents. Specific examples of how to construct these filter rules for criminal shootings, police activity, and protests are available on github[4]. Further event types could be easily constructed by combining a relevant semantic context with the eyewitness linguistic features presented here.

---

[3]While it is possible to have a psycho- or sociopathic witness who would not react with typical trauma emotions (Fowles, 1980; Ekman, 1985; Herpetz et al., 2001; Patrick, 1994), we judged this situation to be sufficiently rare to be discounted. In addition, while "gallows humor" occurs among first responders, it is not generally widely spread outside their cohort (Moran, 2002), or is indicative of after-the-fact third party commentary (Phillips, 2015; Davies, 2003).

[4]https://github.com/erikavaris/topics

This set of eyewitness documents can then be run through a spatio-temporal clustering approach to find events. In our examples, the set of eyewitness documents never had more than around 100-200 documents in a 24-hour period. Since this set is so small, we were able to use a simple approach to clustering. We start by computing the complete distance matrix for all points in the dataset using the greater circle distance measure. The greater circle distance is the shortest distance between two points on a sphere, a good approximation to distances on the surface of the Earth. We can then cluster points using an algorithm such as DBSCAN (Ester et al., 1996). DBSCAN clusters together points based on density and will mark as outliers points in low-density regions. It is commonly available in many scientific computing and machine learning packages in multiple programming languages, and hence a good choice for our work.

For each cluster we then look at the max distance between points in the cluster and check that it is less than a distance τ_d. In our experiments we set the threshold to be about 10 km. If the cluster is within this threshold, we then sort the posts in the cluster by time, and apply a windowing function over the sorted list. If there are more than τ_s documents in the windowed set, we label this set as an event. We used $\tau_s = 1$ for our experiments and time windowing functions, t_w, in sizes between 20 and 40 minutes.

3 Experiments

Using the method described in the previous section, we built filter rules for criminal shootings, unusual police activity, and protests. We ran each filter rule over the Twitter Firehose (unsampled data) on a 24/7 basis. We then sampled random days from each filter, pulling data back for 24 hours, and applied the spatio-temporal algorithm to identify potential events.

Since the resulting sets of documents are relatively small, we measured the accuracy of our method by hand. Generally a method of this type might report on the precision and recall of the solution, but it is not possible to truly measure the recall without reading all messages on Twitter in the time period to make sure posts were not missed. In our case, we simply conducted a search of news articles after the fact to see if any major events were not picked up by the filter rules on the days that were sampled. For the days that we sampled, there were no major news events that failed to show up in our filters.

We optimized for precision than recall in this study as the goal is to surface potential events occurring on Twitter that may be newsworthy. It is more useful to correctly identify a set of documents as interesting with high accuracy than it is to have found every newsworthy event on the network but with many false positives.

Labeling the accuracy (precision) of a method surrounding semantic topic goals is subjective, so we had multiple people classify the resulting sets as eyewitness, non-eyewitness, and off-topic, and then averaged the results. We used the label "non-eye" on posts that were referencing real events, but were clearly second- or third-hand commentary and not clearly embedded in the local community. Most often these posts represented a later stage of news dissemination where the author heard about the event from afar and decided to comment on it.

While the authors of these tweets were not true eyewitnesses to these events, they are potentially interesting from a news commentary perspective, and were accurate to the event topic. Thus, we may consider the general event semantic accuracy as the combined values of "eyewitness" and "non-eye" tweets.

3.1 Results

3.2 Eyewitness posts

Accuracy results for different sets of eyewitness posts on different dates are shown in Table 1.

What day data was pulled had an impact on the accuracy measurement. Table 1 illustrates this difference particularly in the shooting results. For 02/02/2015, there was more Twitter traffic pertaining to shootings than there was on 06/15/2015, which likely influenced the higher eyewitness accuracy of 72% vs. 46%. We have generally observed on Twitter that when major events are occurring the conversation becomes more focused and on topic, and when nothing major is happening results are lower volume and more noisy.

Table 1: Accuracy results for different eyewitness filters. Data were pulled for a 24 hour period on the random dates shown. Count is the total number of documents in each set.

Topic	Date	Count	Eyewitness	Non-Eye	Off-Topic	Semantic Accuracy
Shooting	2/4/15	126	72%	21%	7%	93%
Shooting	6/15/15	41	46%	20%	34%	66%
Police	3/24/15	100	73%	14%	13%	87%
Police	6/17/15	293	71%	11%	18%	82%
Protests	5/23/15	196	56%	31%	13%	87%
Protests	6/23/15	89	52%	25%	24%	77%
Averages			62%	20%	18%	82%

In these data pulls, the combined eyewitness and non-eyewitness general semantic accuracy was 93% and 66%, respectively. We note that on average the accuracy of our filters is 82% across the days and filters measured.

3.2.1 Events

The approach outlined in 2.3 successfully surfaced on-topic events from the sets of eyewitness tweets. We found its effectiveness to be low on individual filter rules due to the low volume of tweets. We were able to find more relevant clusters by combining the criminal eyewitness topic streams – shootings, police activity, and protests – that corresponded to events we could later find in the news media.

In running these experiments, we found that it was important to add an additional parameter to the cluster that ensured there were tweets from different users. It was common to find multiple tweets that would cluster from the same user that was sharing updates on a developing situation. Both of these behaviors are of potential interest and the algorithm may be adjusted to weight the importance of multiple updates versus different user accounts.

4   Conclusion

This paper presents a novel combinatory method of identifying eyewitness accounts of breaking news events on Twitter, including simple yet extensive linguistic filters together with grouping bursts of information localized in time and space. Using primarily linguistic filters based on sociolinguistic behavior of users on Twitter, a variety of event types are explored, with easily implemented extensions to further event types.

The filters are particularly appealing in a business application; with minimal training we were able to teach users of our platform to construct new rules to find eyewitness events in different topical areas. These users had no knowledge of programming, linguistics, statistics, or machine learning. We found this to be a compelling way to build real-time streams of relevant data when resources would not allow placing a computational linguist, data scientist, or similarly highly trained individual on these tasks.

The system offers a straightforward technique for eyewitness filtering compared with Diakopoulos et al. (2012), easily implemented in a streaming environment, requiring no large training datasets such as with machine learning, and achieving higher accuracies than comparable machine learning approaches (Imran et al., 2013). Together with spatio-temporal clustering to identify eyewitness tweets that are spatially and temporally proximate, our eyewitness filter presents a valuable tool for surfacing breaking news on social media.

For future research, a machine learning layer could be added with broader linguistic filters, and may help achieve higher recall while maintaining the high accuracy achieved with our narrow linguistic keywords.

References

Apoorv Agarwal, Boyi Xie, Ilia Vovsha, Owen Rambow, and Rebecca Passonneau. 2011. Sentiment analysis of twitter data. In *Proceedings of the Workshop on Language in Social Media*, LSM 2011, Portland, Oregon, June. Association for Computational Linguistics.

Oluwaseun Ajao, Jun Hong, and Weiru Liu. 2015. A survey of location inference techniques on twitter. *Journal of Information Science*, 41(6):855–864.

Sofia Apreleva and Alejandro Cantarero. 2015. Predicting the location of users on twitter from low density graphs. In *Big Data (Big Data), 2015 IEEE International Conference on*, pages 976–983, Oct.

Mary W. Armsworth and Margot Holaday. 1993. The effects of psychological trauma on children and adolescents. *Journal of counseling and Development : JCD*, 72(1), September.

Claudine Beaumont. 2008. Mumbai attacks: Twitter and flickr used to break news. *The Daily Telegraph*, November.

Claudine Beaumont. 2009. New york plane crash: Twitter breaks the news, again. *The Daily Telegraph*, January.

Christie Davies. 2003. Jokes that follow mass-mediated disasters in a global electronic age. In Peter Narváez, editor, *Of Corpse: Death and Humor in Folklore and Popular Culture*. Utah State University Press, Logan, Utah.

Nicholas Diakopoulos, Munmun De Choudhury, and Mor Naaman. 2012. Finding and assessing social media information sources in the context of journalism. In *Proceedings of the SIGCHI Conference on Human Factors in Computing Systems*, CHI '12, pages 2451–2460, New York, NY, USA. ACM.

Gabriel Doyle and Michael C. Frank. 2015. Shared common ground influences information density in microblog texts. In *Human Language Technologies: The 2015 Annual Conference of the North American Chapter of the ACL*, Denver, Colorado, June. Association for Computational Linguistics.

Paul Ekman. 1985. *Telling lies: Clues to deceit in the marketplace, marriage, and politics*. New York: Norton.

Martin Ester, Hans-Peter Kriegel, Jörg Sander, and Xiaowei Xu. 1996. A density-based algorithm for discovering clusters in large spatial databases with noise. In *Kdd*, pages 226–231. AAAI Press.

Don C. Fowles. 1980. The three arousal model: Implications of gray's two-factor learning theory for heart rate, electrodermal activity, and psychopathy. *Psychophysiology*, 17(2):87–104.

Sabine C. Herpetz, Ulrike Werth, Gerald Lukas, Mutaz Qunaibi, Annette Schuerkens, Hanns-Juergen Kunert, Roland Freese, Martin Flesch, Ruediger Mueller-Isberner, Michael Osterheider, and Henning Sass. 2001. Emotion in criminal offenders with psychopathy and borderline personality disorder. *Arch Gen Psychiatry*, 58(8).

Muhammad Imran, Shady Elbassuoni, Carlos Castillo, Fernando Diaz, and Patrick Meier. 2013. Extracting information nuggets from disaster-related messages in social media. In T. Comes, F. Fiedrich, S. Fortier, J. Geldermann, and L. Yang, editors, *Proceedings from the 10th International ISCRAM Conference*, Baden-Baden, Germany, May.

David Jurgens, Tyler Finethy, James McCorriston, Yi Tian Xu, and Derek Ruths. 2015. Geolocation prediction in twitter using social networks: a critical analysis and review of current practice. In *Proceedings of the 9th International AAAI Conference on Weblogs and Social Media (ICWSM)*.

Slava Kisilevich, Florian Mansmann, Mirco Nanni, and Salvatore Rinzivillo, 2010. *Data Mining and Knowledge Discovery Handbook*, chapter Spatio-temporal clustering, pages 855–874. Springer US, Boston, MA.

Carmen C. Moran. 2002. Humor as a moderator of compassion fatigue. In Charles R. Figley, editor, *Treating Compassion Fatigue*, Psychological Stress Series. Routledge, June.

Alena Neviarouskaya, Helmut Prendinger, and Mitsuru Ishizuka. 2007. Textual affect sensing for sociable and expressive online communication. *ASCII*, 4738.

Fran H. Norris. 2007. Impact of mass shootings on survivors, families, and communities. *PTSD Research Quarterly*, 18(1).

Carol S. North, Elizabeth M. Smith, and Edward L. Spitznagel. 1994. Posttraumatic stress disorder in survivors of a mass shooting. *American Journal of Psychiatry*, 151(1), January.

Christopher J. Patrick. 1994. Emotion and psychopathy: Startling new insights. *Psychophysiology*, 31.

Saša Petrović, Miles Osborne, Richard McCreadie, Craig Macdonald, Iadh Ounis, and Luke Shrimpton. 2013. Can twitter replace newswire for breaking news? In *International AAAI Conference on Web and Social Media*, ICWSM, Boston, MA, July. Association for the Advancement of Artificial Intelligence (AAAI).

Whitney Phillips. 2015. *This is Why We Can't Have Nice Things: Mapping the Relationship Between Online Trolling and Mainstream Culture*. MIT Press, February.

Barry Ritholtz. 2013. Twitter is becoming the first and quickest source of investment news. *The Washington Post*, April.

Arieh Y. Shalev. 2002. Treating survivors in the acute aftermath of traumatic events. In Rachel Yehuda, editor, *Treating Trauma Survivors with PTSD*. American Psychiatric Publishing, Inc., Washington, D.C.

Mike Thelwall, Kevan Buckley, Georgios Paltoglou, and Di Cai. 2010. Sentiment strength detection in short informal text. *Journal for the American Society for Information Science and Technology*, 61(12).

Sam Thielman. 2013. Twitter breaks news of the boston marathon explosions. *AdWeek*, April.

Sarah Vieweg, Amanda L. Hughes, Kate Starbird, and Leysia Palen. 2010. Microblogging during two natural hazards events: What twitter may contribute to situational awareness. In *Proceedings of the SIGCHI Conference on Human Factors in Computing Systems*, CHI '10, pages 1079–1088, New York, NY, USA. ACM.

Why Do They Leave: Modeling Participation in Online Depression Forums

Farig Sadeque
School of Information
University of Arizona
Tucson, AZ 85721
farig@email.arizona.edu

Ted Pedersen
Dept. of Computer Science
University of Minnesota, Duluth
Duluth, MN 55812-3036
tpederse@d.umn.edu

Thamar Solorio
Dept. of Computer Science
University of Houston
Houston, TX 77204-3010
solorio@cs.uh.edu

Prasha Shrestha
Dept. of Computer Science
University of Houston
Houston, TX 77204-3010
pshrestha3@uh.edu

Nicolas Rey-Villamizar
Dept. of Computer Science
University of Houston
Houston, TX 77204-3010
nrey@uh.edu

Steven Bethard
School of Information
University of Arizona
Tucson, AZ 85721
bethard@email.arizona.edu

Abstract

Depression is a major threat to public health, accounting for almost 12% of all disabilities and claiming the life of 1 out of 5 patients suffering from it. Since depression is often signaled by decreasing social interaction, we explored how analysis of online health forums may help identify such episodes. We collected posts and replies from users of several forums on `healthboards.com` and analyzed changes in their use of language and activity levels over time. We found that users in the Depression forum use fewer social words, and have some revealing phrases associated with their last posts (e.g., *cut myself*). Our models based on these findings achieved 94 F_1 for detecting users who will withdraw from a Depression forum by the end of a 1-year observation period.

1 Introduction

According to the World Health Organization, 30.8% of all years lived with disability (YLDs) are due to mental and neurological conditions (WHO, 2001). Among these conditions, depression alone accounts for a staggering 11.9% of all the disability. The Global Burden of Diseases, Injuries, and Risk Factors Study estimated that depression is responsible for 4.4% of the Disability-Adjusted Life Years (DALYs) lost, and if the demographic and epidemiological transition trends continue, by the year 2020 depression will be the second leading cause of DALYs lost, behind only ischaemic heart disease (WHO, 2003).

Although depression carries a significant amount of the total burden of all the diseases, this is not its most tragic outcome. Depression claims the lives of 15-20% of all its patients through suicide (Goodwin and Jamison, 1990), one of the most common yet avoidable outcomes of this disorder. Early detection of depression has been a topic of interest among researchers for some time now (Halfin, 2007), but the cost of detection or diagnosis is extremely high, as 30% of world governments who provide primary health care services do not have this type of program (Detels, 2009), and these diagnoses are done based on patients' self-reported experiences and surveys.

Social media offers an additional avenue to search for solutions to this problem. Posts, comments, or replies on different social media sites, e.g., Facebook or Twitter, in conjunction with natural language processing techniques, can capture behavioral attributes that assist in detecting depression among the users (De Choudhury et al., 2013). One property of depression that has not been well explored in social media is its temporal aspect: it may be episodic, recurrent, or chronic, with a recurrence rate of 35% within 2 years. Thus it is critical, when using social media to look at depression, to study how behavioral patterns change over a detailed timeline of the user. For example, decreased social interaction, increased negativity, and decreased energy may all be signals of depression.

In this work, we make the following contributions:

1. We collect a large dataset of user interactions over time from online health forums about depression and other related conditions.
2. We identify phrases (e.g. *cut myself*, *depression medication*) that are highly associated with the last post or reply of a user in a depression forum.
3. We show that users in depression forums have a substantially lower use of social words than

Proceedings of The Fourth International Workshop on Natural Language Processing for Social Media, pages 14–19,
Austin, TX, November 1, 2016. ©2016 Association for Computational Linguistics

users of related forums.

4. We show that user demographics, activity levels, and timeline information can accurately predict which users will withdraw from a forum.

While these contributions obviously do not represent a solution to depression, we believe they form a significant first step towards understanding how the study of social media timelines can contribute.

There are several other works that have analyzed participation continuation problems in different online social paradigms using different approaches, i.e. friendship relationship among users (Ngonmang et al., 2012), psycholinguistic word usage (Mahmud et al., 2014), linguistic change (Danescu-Niculescu-Mizil et al., 2013), activity timelines (Sinha et al., 2014), and combinations of the above (Sadeque et al., 2015). Also there are numerous works that contributes to the mental health research (De Choudhury et al., 2016; De Choudhury, 2015; Gkotsis et al., 2016; Colombo et al., 2016; Desmet and Hoste, 2013) We believe ours is the first work to integrate language and timeline analysis for studying decreasing social interaction in depression forums.

2   Data

Our data is collected from HealthBoards[1], one of the oldest and largest support group based online social networks with hundreds of support groups dedicated to people suffering from physical or mental ailments. Users in these forums can either initiate a thread, or reply to a thread initiated by others.

We focused on the forums Depression, Relationship Health, and Brain/Nervous System Disorders. While depression remains our main focus, the other two forums represent related conditions and serve as control groups to which we can compare the Depression forum. Relationship Health includes social factors that interact heavily with mental health. Brain/Nervous System Disorder considers a more physical perspective, including the neuropsychiatric disorders Arachnoiditis, Alzheimer's Disease and Dementia, Amyotrophic Lateral Sclerosis (ALS), Aneurysm, Bell's Palsy, Brain and Head Injury, Brain and Nervous System Disorders, Brain Tumors, Cerebral Palsy and Dizziness/Vertigo.

	Depression	Relationship	Brain/Nervous
Posts	19535	17810	13244
Replies	105427	199430	74974
Users	15340	12352	14072
Reply/Post	5.4 (0.1)	11.2 (0.1)	5.6 (0.1)
Post/User	1.3 (0.03)	1.4 (0.03)	0.9 (0.03)
Reply/User	6.9 (0.4)	16.1 (1.3)	5.3 (0.7)
Gender: male	20.77%	22.15%	22.99%
Gender: female	54.07%	57.52%	59.16%
Gender: unspecified	25.16%	20.33%	17.85%

Table 1: Summary of the data collected from Health-Boards. Numbers in parentheses are standard errors.

We crawled all of the posts (thread initiations) and replies to existing threads for these support groups from the earliest available post until the end of April 2016. The posts and replies were downloaded as HTML files, one per thread, where each thread contains an initial post and zero or more replies. The HTML files were parsed and filtered for scripts and navigation elements to collect the actors, contents and general information about the thread. We stored this collected information using the JSON-based Activity Stream 2.0 specification from the World Wide Web Consortium (W3C, 2015). All collected contents were part-of-speech tagged using the Stanford part-of-speech tagger (Manning et al., 2014) and all words were tagged with their respective psycholinguistic categories by matching them against the Linguistic Inquiry and Word Count (LIWC)[2] lexicon.

Table 1 gives descriptive statistics of the dataset. All three forums are roughly similar in number of users. However, users in the Depression forum are less engaged than users in Relationship Health, having a lower average number of replies per post and a lower average number of replies per user. While the Depression forum is similar to the Brain/Nervous System Disorder forum in terms of posts and replies per user, there are more users in the Depression forums that choose not to specify their gender.

2.1   Language Analysis

We hypothesized that the final post of a user might include linguistic cues of their decreasing social interaction. For this experiment, we considered users who were inactive for at least the one year preceding the day of data collection. We gathered the contents of their posts, and used pointwise mutual information (PMI) between unigrams (and bigrams) and last posts

---

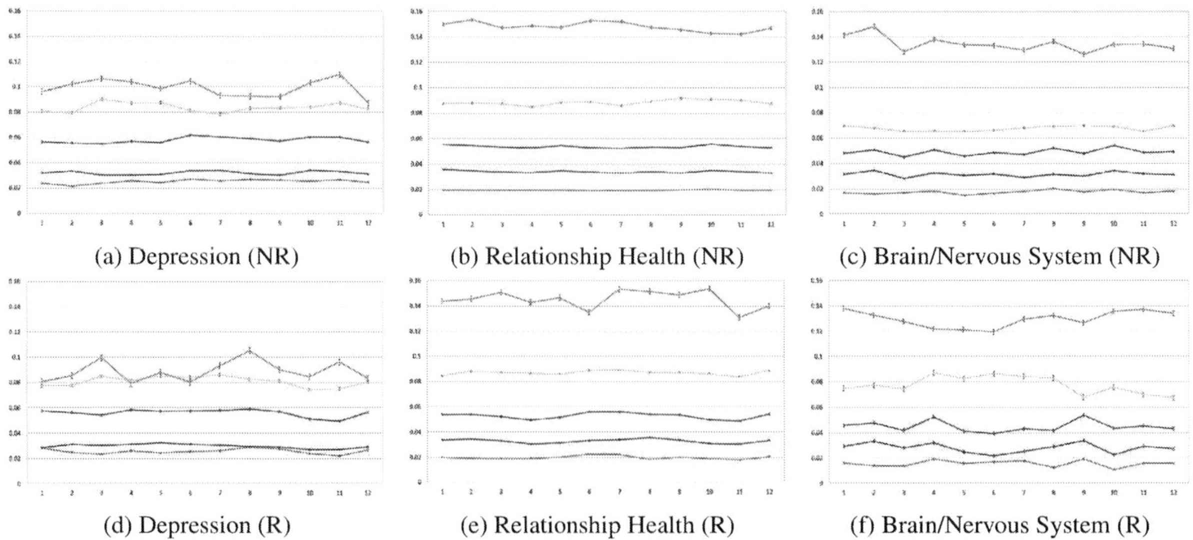

(a) Depression (NR)   (b) Relationship Health (NR)   (c) Brain/Nervous System (NR)

(d) Depression (R)   (e) Relationship Health (R)   (f) Brain/Nervous System (R)

Figure 1: The final 12 months of word use by category: Social (top; green), Cognition (2nd from top; yellow), Affect (middle; blue), Positive Emotion (crimson; 2nd from bottom), and Negative Emotion (orange; bottom).

Depression		Relationship		Brain/Nervous	
Bigrams	PMI	Bigrams	PMI	Bigrams	PMI
I+Feel	0.54	i+no	0.77	got+Bells	0.76
of+Pristiq	0.53	this+disorder	0.74	centre+of	0.73
My+fiance	0.52	a+narcissist	0.70	neural+canal	0.72
My+partner	0.50	wife+said	0.67	prominence+of	0.72
depression+med.	0.48	He+constantly	0.66	ears+from	0.68
in+middle	0.47	dad+does	0.65	bulge+with	0.68
'm+suffering	0.47	confessed+that	0.65	mild+posterior	0.67
slept+with	0.46	Just+recently	0.64	small+intestine	0.67
cut+myself	0.46	my+fiance	0.63	your+biggest	0.67
Any+help	0.46	she+continued	0.63	are+increasing	0.67

Table 2: Top 10 bigrams from each forum based on their PMI with last posts. For space, we abbreviated *medication* as *med.*

to identify words (and bigrams) that occurred in last posts more often than would be expected by chance. We excluded unigrams occurring less than 50 times and bigrams occurring less than 10 times.

Table 2 lists the top 10 bigrams most associated with last posts in each forum. These n-grams suggest differences in reasons for leaving different types of forums. Depression has some especially revealing phrases: people appear to withdraw from the forum after starting treatment (*of Pristiq, depression medication*), but also after apparent calls for help (*'m suffering, cut myself, Any help*).

We next hypothesized that there may be observable changes over time in the language of users who are disengaging from the community. We identified the five LIWC psycholinguistic classes that were most associated with last posts across the forums (using PMI as above): Social, Cognition, Affect, Positive Emotion, and Negative Emotion. We selected the most active users that (1) posted in at least two different years, and (2) made at least 100 posts or replies. We then divided these users into two cohorts. The first cohort included the top 100 users who were inactive for at least one year preceding the day of data collection, which we call the non-returning (NR) cohort. The second cohort included the top 100 users with high activity but not marked as inactive yet, which we call the returning (R) cohort.

We then considered the 12 months ending at the user's last post or reply, and graphed the frequency that words from the five psycholinguistic classes were used. Figure 1 shows the use of words from different psycholinguistic classes over time. For most word classes, usage is fairly constant over time and similar across the forums. However, use of social words in the Depression forum is about 40% lower than in Relationship Health or Brain/Nervous System Disorder. This reduced use of social words may indicate less social interaction and less energy, consistent with signs of recurring depressive episodes. Interestingly, both the returning (R) cohort and the non-returning (NR) cohort exhibit this behavior.

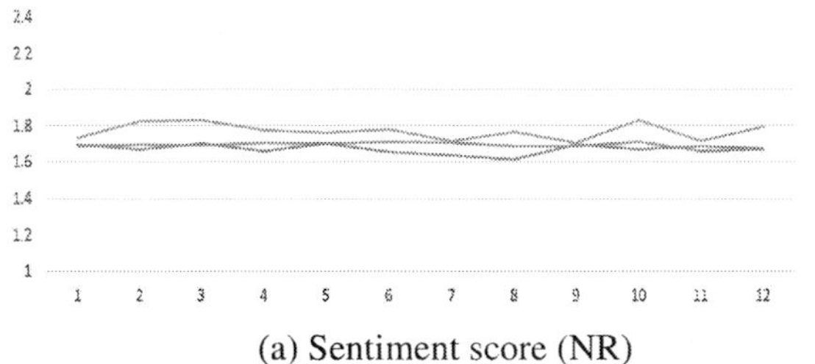

(a) Sentiment score (NR)

Figure 2: Sentiment score of activities over the final 12 months for three forums for Depression forums (blue), Relationship Health forums (orange), and Brain/Nervous System Disorder forums (grey).

2.2 Sentiment Analysis

We hypothesized that sentiment scores of users' later activities might provide some insight into their decreasing social interaction. We encountered many posts with negative sentiment after which the user stopped participating in the forum, for example:

> ... I was really frightened of what was happening to me, my Mum took me straight back to the doctors, to a different one, they were useless, they put me straight on zoloft, I took the zoloft for about 3 days when everything got worse, I couldn't eat, I kept throwing up, I was having constant panic attacks I just wanted to sleep but lived in fear when I was alone... [3]

To investigate, we took the same users from the language analysis and calculated sentiment for all of their posts and replies using the Stanford CoreNLP (Manning et al., 2014) sentiment analyzer (Socher et al., 2013). The analyzer scores each sentence from 0 to 4, with 0 being extremely negative and 4 being extremely positive. We take as the score for an activity (post or reply) the average of the sentence-level scores for all sentences in that activity.

We graphed the average activity sentiment scores for each forum by averaging the scores over the last 12 months of each user. Figure 2 shows that there was little change in sentiment scores over time, and the lines closely follow the average score for respective forums (Depression: 1.68, Relationship Health: 1.70, Brain/Nervous System Disroder: 1.78). (The figure

	Depression		Relationship		Brain/Nervous	
	Return	Non-return	Return	Non-return	Return	Non-return
AvgInit	114.3	192.5	139.3	420.1	236.3	332.8
AvgMax	218.7	453.3	215.8	492.8	225.2	445.0
AvgMed	1.5	8.8	1.1	15.9	2.7	3.0

Table 3: Average initial (AvgInit), maximum (AvgMax), and median (AvgMed) idle time (in days) for users in the forums.

shows non-returning users; returning users were similar.) This finding refutes our hypothesis regarding sentiment scores of later activities being useful for predicting continued participation.

2.3 Idle Time Analysis

We hypothesized that a user's idle time predict whether they remain socially engaged in the forum. We define idle time as the time between two sequential activities (posting or replying). For each forum, we identified all users who posted in at least two different years, and selected 50 random users who were active within the one year preceding the day of data collection, and 50 random users who were not. We then calculated the initial idle time (from account creation to first activity), maximum idle time, and median idle time. Table 3 shows average initial, maximum, and median idle times across the forums. In general, non-returning users wait longer before their first activity, and have larger maximum and median idle times. Depression forum users have smaller initial idle times than Relationship Health or Brain/Nervous System Disorder users, both for returning and non-returning users.

3 Prediction Task

Having observed linguistic and timeline features that suggest when a user is withdrawing from a Depression forum, we began to construct a predictive model for identifying users that are entering such episodes. This task is similar to the *continued participation* prediction task introduced by Sadeque et al. (2015). Formally, we consider the model

$$
m_{\Delta t}(u) = \begin{cases} 1 & \text{if } \exists a \in activities(u) : \\ & \quad start(u) + \Delta t < time(a) < \\ & \quad\quad start(u) + \Delta t + maxtime(u) \\ 0 & \text{otherwise} \end{cases}
$$

17

Obs	BL	D	A	T	DAT	DATP	DATU	DATB	DATG	DATS
1	78.6	78.7	66.8	81.9	83.3	82.9	78.4	81.2	79.3	83.4
6	87.3	82.9	75.5	90.2	91.1	90.7	90.9	91.1	91.1	91.2
12	92.5	84.1	78.8	93.7	94.0	94.0	94.1	94.0	94.0	94.1

Table 4: F-1 scores predicting which users will stop participating in the Depression forum, for different observation periods (Obs; in months) and different feature sets. BL: Classifier that predicts all inactive.

where Δt is the observation period, u is a user, $start(u)$ is the time at which the user u created an account, $activities(u)$ is the set of all activities of user u, $time(a)$ is the time of the activity a, and

$$maxtime(u) = \max_{a \in activities(u)} time(a)$$

Intuitively, m should predict 0 iff Δt time has elapsed since the user created their account and the user will be inactive in the forum for longer than ever before.

We considered the following classes of features:

D User profile demographics: gender and whether a location and/or an avatar image was provided.

A Activity information: number of thread initiations, number of replies posted, number of replies received from others, number of self-replies.

T Timeline information: initial, final, maximum and median idle times.

U/B/G Bag of unigrams/bigrams/1-skip-2-grams from the last post of the observation period.

P Counts of words for each LIWC psycholinguistic class in the last post of the observation period.

S Sentiment score of the last post of the observation period

We trained an L2 regularized logistic regression from LibLinear (Fan et al., 2008) using the data collected from the Depression forum. Throwaway accounts (Leavitt, 2015), defined as accounts with activity levels below the median (2 posts or replies), were excluded from training and testing, though their replies to other users were included for feature extraction. After removing such accounts, 8398 user accounts remained, of which we used 6000 for training our model, and 2398 for testing.

Table 4 shows the performance of this model on different observation periods (1 month, 6 months, 12 months) and different combinations of the feature classes. It also shows the performance of a baseline model (BL) that predicts that all users will be inac-

tive, the most common classification. We measure performance in terms of F_1 (the harmonic mean of precision and recall) on identifying users who withdraw from the forum by the end of the observation period. The most predictive features are the timeline (T) features, resulting in F_1 of 93.7 for a 12 month observation period. Though demographic (D) and activity (A) features underperform the baseline alone, adding them to the timeline features (DAT column) yields a 6% error reduction: 94.0 F_1. The improvement is larger for 1 and 6 month observation periods: 8% and 10% error reductions, respectively.

Adding the language-based features (the DATP, DATU, DATB, DATG, DATS columns) does not increase performance. This is despite our findings in section 2.1 that some phrases were associated with final posts in the forum, but consistent with our findings in Section 2.2 that sentiment analysis was not a strong predictor. This failure of linguistic features may be due to the relatively modest associations; for example, *cut myself* had a PMI of 0.46, and is thus only 38% more likely to show up in a last post than expected by chance. It may also be due to the simplicity of our linguistic features. Consider *Im getting to that rock bottom phase again and im scared*. By PMI, *rock bottom* is not highly associated with last posts, since people often talk about recovering from *rock bottom*. Only present tense *rock bottom* is concerning, but none of our features capture this kind of temporal phenomenon.

4 Conclusion

Our analysis of user language and activities in depression-oriented health forums showed that certain phrases and a decline in the use of social words are associated with decreased social interaction in these forums. Our predictive models, based on this analysis, accurately identify users who are withdrawing from the forum, and we found that while demographic, activity, and timeline features were predictive, simple linguistic features did not provide additional benefits. We believe that better understanding of the attributes that contribute to the lack of social engagement in online social media can provide valuable insights for predicting medical issues like depressive episodes, and we hope that our current work helps to form a foundation for such future research.

References

Gualtiero B. Colombo, Pete Burnap, Andrei Hodorog, and Jonathan Scourfield. 2016. Analysing the connectivity and communication of suicidal users on twitter. *Computer Communications*, 73, Part B:291 – 300. Online Social Networks.

Cristian Danescu-Niculescu-Mizil, Robert West, Dan Jurafsky, Jure Leskovec, and Christopher Potts. 2013. No country for old members: User lifecycle and linguistic change in online communities. In *Proceedings of the 22Nd International Conference on World Wide Web*, WWW '13, pages 307–318, Republic and Canton of Geneva, Switzerland. International World Wide Web Conferences Steering Committee.

Munmun De Choudhury, Michael Gamon, Scott Counts, and Eric Horvitz. 2013. Predicting depression via social media. In *ICWSM*, page 2.

Munmun De Choudhury, Emre Kiciman, Mark Dredze, Glen Coppersmith, and Mrinal Kumar. 2016. Discovering shifts to suicidal ideation from mental health content in social media. In *Proceedings of the 2016 CHI Conference on Human Factors in Computing Systems*, pages 2098–2110. ACM.

Munmun De Choudhury. 2015. Social media for mental illness risk assessment, prevention and support. In *Proceedings of the 1st ACM Workshop on Social Media World Sensors*, pages 1–1. ACM.

Bart Desmet and VéRonique Hoste. 2013. Emotion detection in suicide notes. *Expert Syst. Appl.*, 40(16):6351–6358, November.

Roger Detels. 2009. *The Scope and Concerns of Public Health*. Oxford University Press Inc., New York.

Rong-En Fan, Kai-Wei Chang, Cho-Jui Hsieh, Xiang-Rui Wang, and Chih-Jen Lin. 2008. Liblinear: A library for large linear classification. *The Journal of Machine Learning Research*, 9:1871–1874.

George Gkotsis, Anika Oellrich, Tim JP Hubbard, Richard JB Dobson, Maria Liakata, Sumithra Velupillai, and Rina Dutta. 2016. The language of mental health problems in social media. In *Third Computational Linguistics and Clinical Psychology Workshop (NAACL)*, pages 63–73. Association for Computational Linguistics.

Frederick K. Goodwin and Kay Redfield Jamison. 1990. *Manic-Depressive Illness: Bipolar Disorder and Recurring Depression*. Oxford University Press Inc., New York.

Aron Halfin. 2007. Depression: the benefits of early and appropriate treatment. *The American journal of managed care*, 13(4 Suppl):S927, November.

Alex Leavitt. 2015. "this is a throwaway account": Temporary technical identities and perceptions of anonymity in a massive online community. In *Proceedings of the 18th ACM Conference on Computer Supported Cooperative Work & Social Computing*, CSCW '15, pages 317–327, New York, NY, USA. ACM.

Jalal Mahmud, Jilin Chen, and Jeffrey Nichols. 2014. Why are you more engaged? predicting social engagement from word use. *CoRR*, abs/1402.6690.

Christopher Manning, Mihai Surdeanu, John Bauer, Jenny Finkel, Steven Bethard, and David McClosky. 2014. The stanford corenlp natural language processing toolkit. In *Proceedings of 52nd Annual Meeting of the Association for Computational Linguistics: System Demonstrations*, pages 55–60, Baltimore, Maryland, June. Association for Computational Linguistics.

Blaise Ngonmang, Emmanuel Viennet, and Maurice Tchuente. 2012. Churn prediction in a real online social network using local community analysis. In *Proceedings of the 2012 International Conference on Advances in Social Networks Analysis and Mining (ASONAM 2012)*, ASONAM '12, pages 282–288, Washington, DC, USA. IEEE Computer Society.

Farig Sadeque, Thamar Solorio, Ted Pedersen, Prasha Shrestha, and Steven Bethard. 2015. Predicting continued participation in online health forums. In *SIXTH INTERNATIONAL WORKSHOP ON HEALTH TEXT MINING AND INFORMATION ANALYSIS (LOUHI)*, page 12.

Tanmay Sinha, Nan Li, Patrick Jermann, and Pierre Dillenbourg. 2014. Capturing attrition intensifying structural traits from didactic interaction sequences of mooc learners. In *Proceedings of the 2014 Empirical Methods in Natural Language Processing Workshop on Modeling Large Scale Social Interaction in Massively Open Online Courses*.

Richard Socher, Alex Perelygin, Jean Y Wu, Jason Chuang, Christopher D Manning, Andrew Y Ng, and Christopher Potts Potts. 2013. Recursive deep models for semantic compositionality over a sentiment treebank. In *EMNLP*.

W3C. 2015. Activity streams 2.0: Working Draft 15 December 2015. http://www.w3.org/TR/2015/WD-activitystreams-core-20151215/.

World Health Organization WHO. 2001. The world health report 2001 mental health: New understanding, new hope. http://www.who.int/whr/2001/en/whr01_en.pdf?ua=1. Last Accessed: 2016-05-29.

World Health Organization WHO. 2003. Global burden of disease (GBD) 2000: version 3 estimates. http://www.who.int/entity/healthinfo/gbdwhoregionyld2000v3.xls?ua=1. Last Accessed: 2016-05-28.

Twitter at the Grammys:
A Social Media Corpus for Entity Linking and Disambiguation

Mark Dredze, Nicholas Andrews, Jay DeYoung
Human Language Technology Center of Excellence
Johns Hopkins University
810 Wyman Park Drive
Baltimore, MD 20211 USA
`{mdredze,noa}@cs.jhu.edu`

Abstract

Work on cross document coreference resolution (CDCR) has primarily focused on news articles, with little to no work for social media. Yet social media may be particularly challenging since short messages provide little context, and informal names are pervasive. We introduce a new Twitter corpus that contains entity annotations for entity clusters that supports CDCR. Our corpus draws from Twitter data surrounding the 2013 Grammy music awards ceremony, providing a large set of annotated tweets focusing on a single event. To establish a baseline we evaluate two CDCR systems and consider the performance impact of each system component. Furthermore, we augment one system to include temporal information, which can be helpful when documents (such as tweets) arrive in a specific order. Finally, we include annotations linking the entities to a knowledge base to support entity linking. Our corpus is available: `https://bitbucket.org/mdredze/tgx`

1 Entity Disambiguation

Who is who and what is what? Answering such questions is usually the first step towards deeper semantic analysis of documents, e.g., extracting relations and roles between entities and events. Entity disambiguation identifies real world entities from textual references. Entity linking – or more generally Wikification (Ratinov et al., 2011) – disambiguates reference in the context of a knowledge base, such as Wikipedia (Cucerzan, 2007; McNamee and Dang, 2009; Dredze et al., 2010; Zhang

et al., 2010; Han and Sun, 2011). Entity linking systems use the name mention and a context model to identify possible candidates and disambiguate similar entries. The context model includes a variety of information from the context, such as the surrounding text or facts extracted from the document. Though early work on the task goes back to Cucerzan (2007), the name entity linking was first introduced as part of TAC KBP 2009 (McNamee and Dang, 2009).

Without a knowledge base, cross-document coreference resolution (CDCR) clusters mentions to form entities (Bagga and Baldwin, 1998b). Since 2011, CDCR has been included as a task in TAC-KBP (Ji et al., 2011) and has attracted renewed interest (Baron and Freedman, 2008b; Rao et al., 2010; Lee et al., 2012; Green et al., 2012; Andrews et al., 2014). Though traditionally a task restricted to small collections of formal documents (Bagga and Baldwin, 1998b; Baron and Freedman, 2008a), recent work has scaled up CDCR to large heterogenous corpora, e.g. the Web (Wick et al., 2012; Singh et al., 2011; Singh et al., 2012).

While both tasks have traditionally considered formal texts, recent work has begun to consider informal genres, which pose a number of interesting challenges, such as increased spelling variation and (especially for Twitter) reduced context for disambiguation. Yet entity disambiguation, which links mentions across documents, is especially important for social media, where understanding an event often requires reading multiple short messages, as opposed to news articles, which have extensive background information. For example, there have now

20

Proceedings of The Fourth International Workshop on Natural Language Processing for Social Media, pages 20–25,
Austin, TX, November 1, 2016. ©2016 Association for Computational Linguistics

been several papers to consider named entity recognition in social media, a key first step in an entity disambiguation pipeline (Finin et al., 2010; Liu et al., 2011; Ritter et al., 2011; Fromreide et al., 2014; Li et al., 2012; Liu et al., 2012; Cherry and Guo, 2015; Peng and Dredze, 2015). Additionally, some have explored entity linking in Twitter (Liu et al., 2013; Meij et al., 2012; Guo et al., 2013), and have created datasets to support evaluation. However, to date no study has evaluated CDCR on social media data,[1] and there is no annotated corpus to support such an effort.

In this paper we present a new dataset that supports CDCR in Twitter: the TGX corpus (Twitter Grammy X-doc), a collection of Tweets collected around the 2013 Grammy music awards ceremony. The corpus includes tweets containing references to people, and references are annotated both for entity linking and CDCR. To explore this task for social media data and consider the challenges, opportunities and the performance of state of the art CDCR methods, we evaluate two state-of-the-art CDCR systems. Additionally, we modify one of these systems to incorporate temporal information associated with the corpus. Our results include improved performance for this task, and an analysis of challenges associated with CDCR in social media.

2 Corpus Construction

A number of datasets have been developed to evaluate CDCR, and since the introduction of the TAC-KBP track in 2009, some now include links to a KB (e.g. Wikipedia). See Singh et al. (2012) for a detailed list of datasets. For Twitter, there have been several recent entity linking datasets, all of which number in the hundreds of tweets (Meij et al., 2012; Liu et al., 2013; Guo et al., 2013). None are annotated to support CDCR.

Our goal is the creation of a Twitter corpus to support CDCR, which will be an order of magnitude larger than corresponding Twitter corpora for entity linking. We created a corpus around the 2013 Grammy Music Awards ceremony. The popular ceremony lasted several hours generating many

tweets. It included many famous people that are in Wikipedia, making it suitable for entity linking and aiding CDCR annotation. Additionally, Media personalities often have popular nicknames, creating an opportunity for name variation analysis.

Using the Twitter streaming API[2], we collected tweets during the event on Feb 10, 2013 between 8pm and 11:30pm Eastern time (01:00am and 04:30 GMT). We used Carmen geolocation[3] (Dredze et al., 2013) to identify tweets that originated in the United States or Canada and removed tweets that were not identified as English according to the Twitter metadata. We then selected tweets containing "grammy" (case insensitive, and including "#grammy"), reducing 564,892 tweets to 50,429 tweets. Tweets were processed for POS and NER using Twitter NLP Tools [4] (Ritter et al., 2011). Tweets that did not include a person mention were removed. Using an automated NER system may miss some tweets, especially those with high variation in person names, but it provided a fast and effective way to identify tweets to include in our data set. For simplicity, we randomly selected a single person reference per tweet.[5] The final set contained 15,736 tweets.

We randomly selected 5,000 tweets for annotation, a reasonably sized subset for which we could ensure consistent annotation. Each tweet was examined by two annotators who grouped the mentions into clusters (CDCR) and identified the corresponding Wikipedia page for the entity if it existed (entity linking). As part of the annotation, annotators fixed incorrectly identified mention strings. Similar to Guo et al. (2013), ambiguous mentions were removed, but unlike their annotations, we kept all persons including those not in Wikipedia. Mentions that were comprised of usernames were excluded.

The final corpus contains 4,577 annotated tweets, 10,736 unlabeled tweets, and 273 entities, of which 248 appear in Wikipedia. The corpus is divided into five folds by entity (about 55 entities per fold),

---

[1]Andrews et al. (2014) include CDCR results on an early version of our dataset but did not provide any dataset details or analysis. Additionally, their results averaged over many folds, whereas we will include results on the official dev/test splits.

[2]https://dev.twitter.com/streaming/reference/get/statuses/sample

[3]https://github.com/mdredze/carmen

[4]https://github.com/aritter/twitter_nlp

[5]In general, **within** document coreference is run before CDCR, and the cross-document task is to cluster within-document coreference chains. In our case, there were very few mentions to the same person within the same tweet, so we did not attempt to make within-document coreference decisions.

Mentions per entity: mean	16.77
Mentions per entity: median	1
Number of entities	273
Number of mentions (total tweets)	15,313
Number of unique mention strings	1,737
Number of singleton entities	166
Number of labeled tweets	4,577
Number of unlabeled tweets	10,736
Words/tweet (excluding name): mean	10.34
Words/tweet (excluding name): median	9

Table 1: Statistics describing the TGX corpus.

where splits were obtained by first sorting the entities by number of mentions, then doing systematic sampling of the entities on the sorted list. The first split is reserved for train/dev purposes and the remaining splits are reserved for testing. This allows for a held out evaluation instead of relying on cross-validation, which ensures that future work can conduct system development without the use of the evaluation set. Some summary statistics appear in Table 1 and examples of entities in Table 2. The full corpus, including annotations (entity linking and CDCR), POS and NER tags are available at `https://bitbucket.org/mdredze/tgx`.[6]

3 Models

We consider two recent models that represent state-of-the-art performance on CDCR. While TGX has entity linking annotations, we focus on CDCR since Twitter entity linking has been previously explored.

Green et al. (2012) (GREEN) developed a pipeline system for cross document entity disambiguation. First, entities with dissimilar mention strings are identified via "cannot-link" constraints. Then, subject to these constraints, entities are disambiguated based on context via a hierarchical clustering step. Neither of the two steps requires explicit supervision, but instead relies on the careful tuning of hyperparameters. In our experiments, we use a grid search to find the hyperparameters that yield the highest score on the development split, and then use those same hyperparameters for testing with no further tuning. We compare the performance of the full pipeline (FULL), as well as a variation which does no disambiguation (NO-CONTEXT).

Andrews et al. (2014) (PHYLO) developed a generative model for clustering entities across documents based on name and context similarity.[7] Their work extended a phylogenetic name model (Andrews et al., 2012) that learns groups of name variations through string transducers by composing a phylogeny of name variation based on unlabeled data. As above, we present versions of the model with both context and name matching (FULL) as well as without context (NO-CONTEXT). Parameters are tuned on dev data as with GREEN.

A unique property of TGX is its temporal ordering, where documents are timestamped and time impacts entity priors. Figure 4 shows the number of mentions for the top 10 entities over time. The curves are highly peaked, suggesting that there is a small window in time in which the entity is popular, though there are occurrences over the whole event.

We modify PHYLO to include consider temporal information. The model is a generative account of the process by which authors choose particular name spellings, either by copying some existing spelling (possibly introducing variation) or coming up with new names from scratch. This process is modeled in two parts: (1) a name model which assigns probabilities to different spelling variations, and a (2) parent model which assigns probabilities to different parent-child relationships. The parent-child relations give ancestral lineages which form a phylogenetic tree; the connected components of this tree give a partition of names into entity clusters.

Andrews et al. proposed a log-linear model for the parent model to incorporate topic features in order to disambiguate between entities with similar names. By incorporating different features in this log-linear model we give the model more flexibility in explaining the choice of parent. To incorporate temporal information, we introduce features that look at the proximity of pairs of named-entities in time. There are several options for incorporating temporal features; we use a simple overlapping sliding window approach. We use a width of 10 minutes with 5 minute overlaps; every tweet is in two windows except for the first and last 5 minutes. The indicator of a shared bucket fires if a parent and child appear in the same bucket. Unsupervised training can learn

---

[6] Permitted by the Twitter terms of service: `https://dev.twitter.com/overview/terms/agreement-and-policy`

[7] Code available: `https://bitbucket.org/noandrews/phyloinf`

Entity Name	# Mentions	Example Mentions
Taylor Swift	742	taylor,t-swizzle,swift,tswift,taylor freaken swiift,tay,t swift,taylor alison swift
Adelle	370	adel,adelle,adele
Miranda Lambert	266	miranda lambert,lambert,amanda miranda,miranda lamberts,miranda
Carrie Underwood	264	carrie,underwood,carrie underwear,kerry underwoods
Elton John	227	elton j,sir elton,elton,elton john
Johnny Depp	204	johnny deep,johnny,johnny d,johnny jack sparrow,johhny depp,john depp
Ed Sheeran	189	ed sharon,sherran,ed shee-ran,ed sheerannn,ed sheeren,ed sheeeeeeran,ed sheerin
Miguel	182	miguel
Wiz Khalifa	141	khalifa,wizard,wiz kalifa,wiz kahalifa,wiz
Marcus Mumford	140	marcus,marcus mumford,mark mumford,munford

Table 2: The 10 largest entities. 90% of the labeled tweets refer to the 38 most common entities.

Model		Dev. B^3	Test B^3
	EXACT	67.8	69.9
GREEN	NO-CONTEXT	78.0	77.2
	FULL	88.5	79.7
PHYLO	NO-CONTEXT	96.9	72.3
	FULL	97.4	72.1
	FULL+TIME	97.7	72.3

Table 3: CDCR performance (larger B^3 is better).

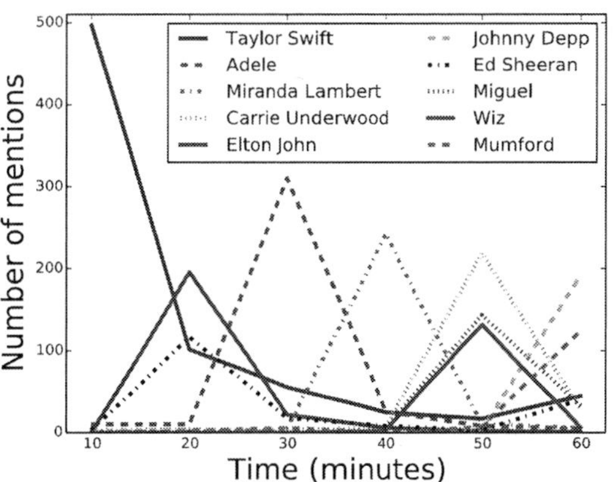

Figure 1: The number of (labeled) mentions for the 10 most common entities shown in 10 minute bins. The entities clearly spike at given points in the dataset. For example, Taylor Swift is most popular in the first few minutes of the data because she performed the opening number.

positive weights for these features by observing that mentions with similar names and contexts, which makes them likely to paired in the phylogeny, are also likely to appear in the same time buckets. We refer to this model as FULL+TIME.

Finally, we compare to an exact mention match baseline (EXACT), which clusters all mentions with identical string mentions.

4 Experiments

Following Green et al. (2012) and other CDCR papers, we report results in terms of B^3 (Bagga and Baldwin, 1998a) in Table 3. First, we note that the performance of EXACT is relatively high. This is attributable to popular artists that use a single alias as a stage name, such as Adele or Beyonce. The result is that these artists are not susceptible to name variation, except for common misspellings. Only 3.6% of the mentions are singletons, so they are unlikely to significantly help this method.

Next, both CDCR models in all configurations improve over the EXACT baseline. While all versions of PHYLO improve over GREEN on development data, the PHYLO models overfit and do worse on test. These results differ from Andrews et al. (2014), which may be due to our hyper-parameter

selection method. Additionally, for both models, adding context improves over clustering based on names alone, but test data suffers for PHYLO. Judging by the resulting clusters, context primarily aided in identifying two references to the same entity that had a low name similarity score.

Analysis An analysis of the mistakes made by the CDCR systems point to several sources of error. While some entities had little name variation (e.g., Adelle and Miguel) aside from spelling errors, others had significant diversity. Table 2 shows the 10 most referenced entities, including number of mentions and variations. People like Taylor Swift have numerous name variations, which include references to nicknames and full names. This name variation accounted for many of the errors in our output. For instance, the system produced a large high-precision cluster consisting of "Taylor Swift" mentions, and another cluster consisting of the following three mentions: T-Swizzle, TSwift, T-Swift. Similarly, LLCoJ, Llcoolj, LLCOOLJ and LLCoolJ, were incorrectly placed in their own cluster separate from another high-precision cluster consisting of primarily "LL Cool J" mentions. These errors highlight challenges of dealing with informal communications.

Similarly, we found several errors due to superficial name similarity. For instance, the system placed Jessica Biel and Melissa in the same cluster. The system also produced a low-precision cluster LL and Allison Williams, where LL refers to "LL Cool J."

While abbreviations are common sources of errors in newswire for organizations and countries, we saw this for people: Neil Patrick Harris vs. NPH. We also saw more typical variations due to forms of address, e.g., Taylor vs. Taylor Swift, and Mayer vs. John Mayer. We did not see many errors where two entities were confused with each other due to context. Instead, low recall clusters were of the type described above.

Finally, there are several properties of the data unique to social media that could help improve results. First, since our simple time features were helpful, but more sophisticated temporal models could further improve the results. Second, Twitter specific properties, such as hashtags and links, could be integrated into a modified generative model. Third, conversations could provide a larger context for resolution, or aid in identifying name variations for a mention. We plan to consider these directions.

References

Nicholas Andrews, Jason Eisner, and Mark Dredze. 2012. Name phylogeny: A generative model of string variation. In *Empirical Methods in Natural Language Processing (EMNLP)*.

Nicholas Andrews, Jason Eisner, and Mark Dredze. 2014. Robust entity clustering via phylogenetic inference. In *Association for Computational Linguistics (ACL)*.

A. Bagga and B. Baldwin. 1998a. Algorithms for scoring coreference chains. In *LREC*.

A. Bagga and B. Baldwin. 1998b. Entity-based cross-document coreferencing using the vector space model. In *COLING-ACL*.

A. Baron and M. Freedman. 2008a. Who is Who and What is What: Experiments in cross-document coreference. In *EMNLP*.

Alex Baron and Marjorie Freedman. 2008b. Who is Who and What is What: Experiments in cross-document coreference. In *Empirical Methods in Natural Language Processing (EMNLP)*.

Colin Cherry and Hongyu Guo. 2015. The unreasonable effectiveness of word representations for twitter named entity recognition. In *North America Chapter of Association for Computational Linguistics (NAACL)*. Association for Computational Linguistics.

Silviu Cucerzan. 2007. Large-scale named entity disambiguation based on wikipedia data. In *Empirical Methods in Natural Language Processing (EMNLP)*, pages 708–716.

Mark Dredze, Paul McNamee, Delip Rao, Adam Gerber, and Tim Finin. 2010. Entity disambiguation for knowledge base population. In *Conference on Computational Linguistics (Coling)*.

Mark Dredze, Michael J Paul, Shane Bergsma, and Hieu Tran. 2013. Carmen: A twitter geolocation system with applications to public health. In *AAAI Workshop on Expanding the Boundaries of Health Informatics Using AI (HIAI)*.

Tim Finin, William Murnane, Anand Karandikar, Nicholas Keller, Justin Martineau, and Mark Dredze. 2010. Annotating named entities in twitter data with crowdsourcing. In *NAACL Workshop on Creating Speech and Language Data With Mechanical Turk*.

Hege Fromreide, Dirk Hovy, and Anders Søgaard. 2014. Crowdsourcing and annotating NER for Twitter# drift. In *LREC*.

Spence Green, Nicholas Andrews, Matthew R Gormley, Mark Dredze, and Christopher D Manning. 2012. Entity clustering across languages. In *Proceedings of the 2012 Conference of the North American Chapter of the Association for Computational Linguistics: Human Language Technologies*, pages 60–69. Association for Computational Linguistics.

Stephen Guo, Ming-Wei Chang, and Emre Kıcıman. 2013. To link or not to link? a study on end-to-end tweet entity linking. In *Proceedings of NAACL-HLT*, pages 1020–1030.

Xianpei Han and Le Sun. 2011. A generative entity-mention model for linking entities with knowledge base. In *Proceedings of the 49th Annual Meeting of the Association for Computational Linguistics: Human Language Technologies - Volume 1*, HLT '11, pages 945–954, Stroudsburg, PA, USA. Association for Computational Linguistics.

Heng Ji, Ralph Grishman, and Hoa Trang Dang. 2011. Overview of the tac2011 knowledge base population track. In *Text Analysis Conference (TAC)*.

Heeyoung Lee, Marta Recasens, Angel Chang, Mihai Surdeanu, and Dan Jurafsky. 2012. Joint entity and event coreference resolution across documents. In *Proceedings of the 2012 Joint Conference on Empirical Methods in Natural Language Processing and Computational Natural Language Learning*, pages 489–500. Association for Computational Linguistics.

Chenliang Li, Jianshu Weng, Qi He, Yuxia Yao, Anwitaman Datta, Aixin Sun, and Bu-Sung Lee. 2012. Twiner: Named entity recognition in targeted twitter stream. In *SIGIR Conference on Research and Development in Information Retrieval*, SIGIR '12, pages 721–730, New York, NY, USA. ACM.

Xiaohua Liu, Shaodian Zhang, Furu Wei, and Ming Zhou. 2011. Recognizing named entities in tweets. In *Association for Computational Linguistics (ACL)*, pages 359–367. Association for Computational Linguistics.

Xiaohua Liu, Ming Zhou, Furu Wei, Zhongyang Fu, and Xiangyang Zhou. 2012. Joint inference of named entity recognition and normalization for tweets. In *Association for Computational Linguistics (ACL)*, ACL '12, pages 526–535, Stroudsburg, PA, USA. Association for Computational Linguistics.

Xiaohua Liu, Yitong Li, Haocheng Wu, Ming Zhou, Furu Wei, and Yi Lu. 2013. Entity linking for tweets. In *Association for Computational Linguistics (ACL)*.

Paul McNamee and Hoa Dang. 2009. Overview of the TAC 2009 knowledge base population track. In *Text Analysis Conference (TAC)*.

Edgar Meij, Wouter Weerkamp, and Maarten de Rijke. 2012. Adding semantics to microblog posts. In *Proceedings of the fifth ACM international conference on Web search and data mining*, pages 563–572. ACM.

Nanyun Peng and Mark Dredze. 2015. Named entity recognition for chinese social media with jointly trained embeddings. In *Empirical Methods in Natural Language Processing (EMNLP)*.

Delip Rao, Paul McNamee, and Mark Dredze. 2010. Streaming cross document entity coreference resolution. In *Proceedings of the 23rd International Conference on Computational Linguistics: Posters*, pages 1050–1058. Association for Computational Linguistics.

Lev Ratinov, Dan Roth, Doug Downey, and Mike Anderson. 2011. Local and global algorithms for disambiguation to wikipedia. In *Proceedings of the 49th Annual Meeting of the Association for Computational Linguistics: Human Language Technologies-Volume 1*, pages 1375–1384. Association for Computational Linguistics.

Alan Ritter, Sam Clark, Oren Etzioni, et al. 2011. Named entity recognition in tweets: an experimental study. In *Proceedings of the Conference on Empirical Methods in Natural Language Processing*, pages 1524–1534. Association for Computational Linguistics.

Sameer Singh, Amarnag Subramanya, Fernando Pereira, and Andrew McCallum. 2011. Large-scale cross-document coreference using distributed inference and hierarchical models. In *Proceedings of the 49th Annual Meeting of the Association for Computational Linguistics: Human Language Technologies-Volume 1*, pages 793–803. Association for Computational Linguistics.

Sameer Singh, Amarnag Subramanya, Fernando Pereira, and Andrew McCallum. 2012. Wikilinks: A large-scale cross-document coreference corpus labeled via links to wikipedia. Technical report, Technical report, University of Massachusetts.

Michael Wick, Sameer Singh, and Andrew McCallum. 2012. A discriminative hierarchical model for fast coreference at large scale. In *Proceedings of the 50th Annual Meeting of the Association for Computational Linguistics: Long Papers-Volume 1*, pages 379–388. Association for Computational Linguistics.

Wei Zhang, Jian Su, Chew Lim Tan, and Wen Ting Wang. 2010. Entity linking leveraging: automatically generated annotation. In *Proceedings of the 23rd International Conference on Computational Linguistics*, COLING '10, pages 1290–1298, Stroudsburg, PA, USA. Association for Computational Linguistics.

Steps Toward Automatic Understanding of the Function of Affective Language in Support Groups

Amit Navindgi[*]   **Caroline Brun, Cécile Boulard Masson**   **Scott Nowson**[*]
Veritas Technologies   Xerox Research Centre Europe   Accenture Centre for Innovation
Mountain View, CA   Meylan, France   Dublin, Ireland
`navindgi@usc.edu`   `{caroline.brun,`   `scott.nowson@accenture.com`
`cecile.boulard}`
`@xrce.xerox.com`

Abstract

Understanding expression of emotions in support forums has great value and NLP methods are key to automating this. Many approaches use subjective categories which are more fine-grained than a straightforward polarity-based spectrum. However, the definition of such categories is non-trivial, and we argue for a need to incorporate communicative elements even beyond subjectivity. To support our position, we report experiments on a sentiment-labelled corpus of posts from a medical support forum. We argue that a more fine-grained approach to text analysis important, and also simultaneously recognising the social function behind affective expressions enables a more accurate and valuable level of understanding.

1 Introduction

There are a wealth of opinions on the internet. Social media has lowered the accessibility bar to an even larger audience who are now able to share their voice. However, more than just opinions on external matters, people are able to share their emotions and feelings, talking openly about very personal matters. Online presence has been shown to increase the chance of sharing personal information and emotions compared to face-to-face interactions (Hancock et al., 2007).

Medical support forums are one platform on which users generate emotion-rich content, exchange factual information about elements such as treatments or hospitals, and provide emotional support to others (Bringay et al., 2014). This sharing through open discussion is known to be considerably beneficial (Pennebaker et al., 2001).

Understanding affective language in the healthcare domain is an effective application of natural language technologies. Sentiment mining on platforms such as Twitter, for example, is a quick method to gauge public opinion of government policies (Speriosu et al., 2011). However, the level of affective expressions in a support forum setting is considerably more complex than a traditional positive-negative polarity spectrum.

More than just a more-fined grained labelling scheme, we also need a deeper understanding on the language being used. Much sentiment analysis research has focused on classifying the overall sentiment of documents onto a positive-negative spectrum (Hu and Liu, 2004). Recently, research work targeting finer grained analysis has emerged, such as aspect-based sentiment analysis (Liu, 2012; Pontiki et al., 2014), or semantic role labelling of emotions (Mohammad et al., 2014). This relatively new trend in social media analytics enables the detection of not simply binary sentiment, but more nuanced sentiments and mixed feelings. Such affective expressions often serve a social purpose (Rothman and Magee, 2016).

With this in mind, we explore a dataset drawn from a health-related support forum, labelled for a variety of expressed sentiments. Here, we do not necessarily seek state-of-the-art performance, but use this task to argue for two key positions:

- that sub-document level analysis is required to

---

[*]Work carried out while all authors at Xerox Research Centre Europe.

Proceedings of The Fourth International Workshop on Natural Language Processing for Social Media, pages 26–33,
Austin, TX, November 1, 2016. ©2016 Association for Computational Linguistics

best understand affective expressions

- that to fully understand expressions of emotion in support forums, a fine-grained annotation scheme is required which takes into account the social function of such expressions.

This paper begins by reviewing work related to our propositions above. In Section 3 we describe the data which we have used, paying particular attention to the annotation scheme. We then report on our experiments, which were defined in order to support the hypotheses above. Following this, in Section 5 we discuss the implication of this work.

2   Related Work

As reported earlier, polarity-based studies in the healthcare domain have considerable value. One work squarely in the public policy domain sought to classify tweets related to the recent health care reform in the US into positive and negative (Speriosu et al., 2011). Ali et al. (2013) experimented with data from multiple forums for people with hearing-loss. They use the subjectivity lexicon of Wilson et al. (2005) and count-based syntactic features (e.g. number of adjectives, adverbs, etc.). This approach outperformed a baseline bag-of-words model, highlighting the importance of subjective lexica for text analysis in health domain. Ofek et al. (2013) use a dynamic sentiment lexicon to improve sentiment analysis in an online community for cancer survivors.

Sokolova and Bobicev (2013) took the lexicon approach further: they defined a more fine-grained annotation scheme (see Section 3) and labelled data from an IVF-related forum. Their category-specific set of lexicons performed better, at 6-class classification, than a generic subjectivity lexicon. In selecting their data, Sokolova and Bobicev (2013) – as Ali et al. (2013) and others have done – tapped into the domain of on-line support communities. Eastin and LaRose (2005) showed that people who seek support on-line – be it emotional or informational support – typically find it.

Informational support is based on sharing knowledge and experiences. Emotional support – framed as empathic communication – has four motivations: understanding, emotions, similarities and concerns (Pfeil and Zaphiris, 2007). In addition to direct support, another dimension of such online groups is self-disclosure (Prost, 2012). Barak and Gluck-Ofri (2007) identify self-disclosure as specific to open support groups (e.g. "Emotional Support for Adolescents") as opposed to, for example, subject-specific discussion forums (e.g. "Vegetarianism and Naturalism" or "Harry Potter The Book"). Self-disclosure serves three social functions (Tichon and Shapiro, 2003): requesting implicit support by showing confusion and worries; providing support by sharing details of a personal experience and sharing information to further develop social relationships.

3   Data

3.1   Data Source

The data used here[1] is that of Bobicev and Sokolova (2015), an extension of the data described in Sokolova and Bobicev (2013). Data was collected from discussion threads on a sub-forum of an *In Vitro Fertilization (IVF)* medical forum[2] used by participants who belong to a specific age-group (over 35s). The dataset (henceforth *MedSenti*) originally contained 1321 posts across 80 different topics.

3.2   Annotation Details

There are two approaches to annotation of subjective aspects of communication: from the perspective of a reader's perception (Strapparava and Mihalcea, 2007) or that of the author (Balahur and Steinberger, 2009). In labelling *MedSenti* Sokolova and Bobicev (2013) opted for the reader-centric model and hence asked the annotators to analyse a post's sentiment as if they were other discussion participants. This is an important differentiation for automated classification style tasks - models are built to predict how people will understand the emotion expressed, as opposed to the emotion or sentiment an author feels they are conveying. The annotation scheme was evolved over multiple rounds of data exploration, and ultimately three sentiment categories were defined:

1. **confusion**, (henceforth CONF) which includes aspects such as "worry, concern, doubt, im-

---

[1] Kindly provided to us by the authors.
[2] http://ivf.ca/forums

patience, uncertainty, sadness, angriness, embarrassment, hopelessness, dissatisfaction, and dislike"

2. **encouragement**, (ENCO) includes "cheering, support, hope, happiness, enthusiasm, excitement, optimism"

3. **gratitude**, (GRAT) which represents thankfulness and appreciation

This set of labels captures important dimensions identified in the sociology literature. CONF here, for example, maps to expressions of confusion (Tichon and Shapiro, 2003) and those of concern (Pfeil and Zaphiris, 2007).

CONF is essentially a negative category while ENCO is positive. GRAT would therefore be a subset of positive expressions. In contrast, however, it was clear that certain expressions which might be considered negative on a word level – such as those of compassion, sorrow, and pity – were used with a positive, supportive intention. They were therefore included in the ENCO category, and were often posted with other phrases which would in isolation fall under this label.

In addition to the subjective categories, Sokolova and Bobicev (2013) identified two types of objective posts: those with strictly *factual* information (FACT), and those which combined factual information and short emotional expression (typically of the ENCO type) which were labelled as *endorsement* (ENDO). Each of the 1321 individual posts was labelled with one of the above five classes by two annotators.[3]

3.3 Data and Label Preprocessing

We select document labels as per Bobicev and Sokolova (2015): when two labels match, reduce to a single label; when the labels disagree the post is marked with a sixth label *ambiguous* (AMBI), which was not used in any experiment here. Posts with previous post quotation are annotated with ("QOTEHERE"), and quoting posts which contained no additional content were removed. This leaves 1137 posts in our *MedSenti* corpus, with the category distribution as per Table 1.

---

[3]Fleiss kappa = 0.73 (Bobicev and Sokolova, 2015).

Class	# Posts	%age	# Sents	%age
CONF	115	10.1	1087	13.5%
ENCO	309	27.2	1456	18.0%
ENDO	161	14.2	1538	19.1%
GRAT	122	10.7	733	9.1%
FACT	430	37.8	3257	40.4%
TOTAL	**1137**		**8071**	

Table 1: Class distribution of posts and sentences

4 Experiments

To support our positions for understanding affective expressions in support forums, and highlight some of the challenges with current approaches, we report a series of experiments.

4.1 Broad methodology

We use a robust dependency syntactic parser (Ait-Mokhtar et al., 2001) to extract a wide range of textual features, from n-grams to more sophisticated linguistic attributes. Our experiments are framed as multi-class classification tasks using liblinear (Fan et al., 2008) and used 5-fold stratified cross-validation. We do not use, here, a domain-tuned lexicon. We re-implemented the Health Affect Lexicon (Sokolova and Bobicev, 2013) and it performed as well as previously reported. However, such lexicons do not generalise well, and label-based tuning is very task specific. We use the current set of categories to make more general points about work in support-related domains.

4.2 Document Level analysis

Here, we consider each post as a single unit of text with a single label.

4.2.1 5-class classification

We utilised combinations of different linguistic feature sets, ranging from basic n-grams, through semantic dependency features. Here, we list the best performing combination: word uni-, bi-, and tri-grams; binary markers for questions, conjunctions and uppercase characters; and a broad-coverage polarity lexicon. Results can be seen in Table 2

Our best overall score (macro averaged $F1 = 0.449$) is significantly above the majority class baseline ($F = 0.110$). This compares favorably with the six-class performance of semantic features of the original data analysis ($F1 = 0.397$, Sokolova and

	P	*R*	*F*
CONF	0.363	0.357	0.360
ENCO	0.555	0.854	0.673
ENDO	0.147	0.062	0.087
GRAT	0.583	0.492	0.533
FACT	0.573	0.502	0.535
MacroAvg	0.444	0.453	0.449

Table 2: Precision, Recall and F1 for the best feature set on 5-class document-level classification

Bobicev, 2013). However, more important – and not previously reported – is the per-category performance which gives more insight into the data. Essentially, we see that ENCO, GRAT and FACT perform relatively well while CONF and in particular ENDO are considerably poor.

To further explore this result we analyzed the error matrix (Navindgi et al., 2016). Looking at ENDO we see that incredibly only 6% has been correctly classified, while 86% is classified as either FACT or ENCO. This is theoretically understandable since the ENDO category is defined as containing aspects of both the other two categories directly. The reverse mis-classification is considerably less common, as is mis-classification as GRAT. CONF is also mis-classified as FACT a majority, with 43%. One-vs-All analysis allows further insight (Navindgi et al., 2016). It is clear that this challenge is not a trivial one - there are distinct patterns of errors when classifying at the document level. In order to investigate this further, we move to sentence-level classification.

4.3 Sentence Level analysis

In sentence-level analysis, we tokenise each post into its constituent sentences. The 1137 *MedSenti* posts become 8071 sentences, *MedSenti-sent*. As manual annotation at sentence level would be too costly, we used automated methods to label the corpus with the five categories of sentiment.

4.3.1 Naïve Labelling

The most trivial approach to label sentences is for each sentence to inherit the label of the post in which it is present. Following this method, we obtain the distribution as reported in Table 1

We run the 5-class classification scenario on *MedSenti-sent* using the same conditions and the previous best feature set; the results are shown in

Table 3. Overall, the performance is worse than the post-level counterpart, with the exception of a small improvement to ENDO. FACT is the best performing individual category, though now with greater recall than precision.

	P	*R*	*F*
CONF	0.235	0.157	0.188
ENCO	0.343	0.360	0.351
ENDO	0.174	0.088	0.117
GRAT	0.264	0.225	0.243
FACT	0.443	0.598	0.509
MacroAvg	0.291	0.286	0.289

Table 3: Precision, Recall and F1 for Sentence-level classification

We also explore the model performance with the error matrix (Navindgi et al., 2016). Our main observation is that the drop in performance of the four subjective categories is largely due to mis-classification of sentences as FACT. Sentences in this category are the majority in *MedSenti-sent*. However, the proportional differences with *MedSenti* do not seem to be not enough to explain the significant changes.

A more likely explanation is simply that the errors arise because – at the very least – there can be FACT-like sentences in any post. At the time of creation, annotators were asked to label "the most dominant sentiment in the whole post" (Sokolova and Bobicev, 2013, p. 636). For example, post 141143 contains the sentence:

> Also, a nurse told me her cousin, 44, got pregnant (ivf)- the cousin lives in the USA.

The post itself is labelled ENCO. Strictly speaking, this sentence reports a fact, although it is easy to see how its purpose is to encourage others.

4.3.2 Subjectivity-informed labelling

One approach to re-labelling of data is to take advantage of coarser levels of annotation: that of subjectivity. Is it possible to at least distinguish which sentences are objective, and could be labelled as FACT? We have developed a subjectivity model[4] built for the SemEval 2016 Aspect Based Sentiment Analysis track (Pontiki et al., 2016), which

---

[4] brun-perez-roux:2016:SemEval

was among the top performing models for polarity detection. We ran this model on all sentences of the corpus in order to assess their subjectivity. Any sentence with a subjectivity likelihood of < 0.7 we consider to be *objective*; we also removed any *subjective* sentences which were previously FACT. This *MedSenti-sent-subj* set consists of 4147 sentences. We use the same experimental settings as previously, with results presented in Table 4.

	P	R	F
CONF	0.315	0.169	0.220
ENCO	0.390	0.457	0.421
ENDO	0.289	0.126	0.176
GRAT	0.284	0.294	0.289
FACT	0.543	0.745	0.628
MacroAvg	0.364	0.358	0.361

Table 4: Precision, Recall and F1 for Sentence-level classification of subjectivity-adjusted corpus

Performance is marginally better with this approach (against a majority macro averaged baseline of $F1 = 0.107$). Importantly, in analysing the error matrix[5] the proportion of data mis-classified has dropped considerably (from 51% to 37%). However, a related consequence is that the error-rate between the *subjective* categories has increased.

5 Discussion

Despite the disappointing results in our sentence level experiments, we maintain that this level of analysis, as a step toward aspect-based understanding, is important to explore further. One reason for poor performance with both the *MedSenti-sent* and *MedSenti-sent-subj* is the approach to annotation at the sentence level. Naturally manual annotation of 8K sentences is considerably expensive and time consuming. However, there are clear examples in the data set of distinct labels being required. Consider the following example, (with manually annotated, illustrative labels):

post_id_226470 author1 "author2 said [...] <ENCO> Thanks,I think we were afraid of rushing into such a big decision but now I feel it is most important not to have regrets. </ENCO> <FACT>

---

[5] Not presented here for space concerns.

The yale biopsy is a biopsy of the lining of my uterus and it is a new test conducted by Yale University. Here is a link you can read: URL This test is optional and I have to pay for it on my own... no coverage.</FACT>"

The first statement of this post is clearly intended to encourage the person to whom the author was responding. The second set of sentences is conveying deliberately factual information about their situation. In the *MedSenti* set this post is labelled as ENDO- the combination of ENCO and FACT. However, the FACT component of the post is a response to a question in an even earlier post than the quoted message. It could be argued therefore that these sentiment do not relate in the way for which the ENDO label was created. To consider post-level labels, then, we would argue is too coarse grained.

To explore the possible confusion introduced by the ENDO category, particularly after removing the objective sentences in *MedSenti-sent-subj*, we conducted experiments with this category. In this three-class experiment (ENCO, CONF, and GRAT), performance was again reasonable against baseline ($F1 = 0.510$ over $F1 = 0.213$), but the error rate was still high, particularly for GRAT. Regardless of the linguistic feature sets, the models do not appear to be capturing the differences between the subjective categories. This seems contradictory to the original authors' intention of building "a set of sentiments that [...] makes feasible the use of machine learning methods for automate sentiment detection." (Sokolova and Bobicev, 2013, p. 636). This is interesting because, from a human reader perspective (see Section 3), the annotation scheme makes intuitive sense. That the expressions of "negative" emotions such as sympathy be considered in the "positive" category of ENCO aligns with the social purpose behind such expressions (Pfeil and Zaphiris, 2007). Without explicitly calling attention to it, Sokolova and Bobicev (2013) encoded social purpose into their annotation scheme. As with previous effort in the space, the scheme they have defined is very much tuned to the emotional support domain.

In an attempt to understand potential reasons for errors, we created a visualisation of the annotation scheme in terms of scheme category label, higher level polarity, and sentiment target, which can be seen in Figure 1. As per the definitions of the cat-

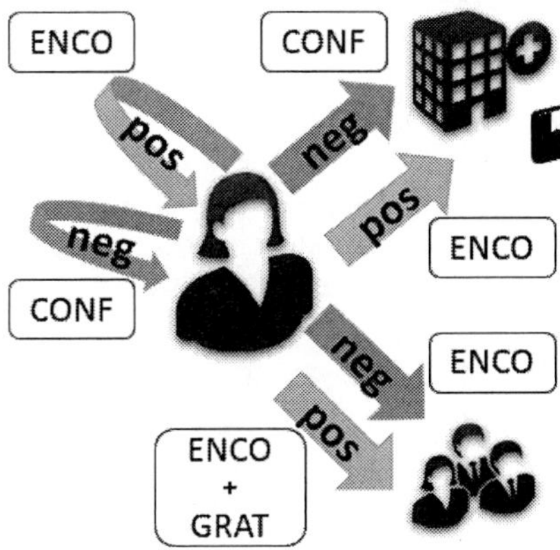

Figure 1: Visualisation of polarity to category mapping given affect target – one of either self, fellow forum participant, or external entity

egories, emotions expressed towards external entities, or oneself are clearly either positive-ENCO or negative-CONF. However, the pattern is different in interpersonal expression between forum contributors. In the medical support environment "negative" expressions, as previously discussed serve a positive and supportive purpose. Also, the category of GRAT– a positive expression – is always in this situation directed to another participant. This makes the interpersonal expression loadings both overloaded both in terms of classification and polarity. These relationships, in many ways, make machine modelling therein overly noisy.

Of course, it is fair to say that one direction of work in such a social domain that we did not explore is context. The original authors report subsequently on incorporating context into their experiments: both in terms of the position within a discussion of a post (Bobicev and Sokolova, 2015) and the posting history of an author (Sokolova and Bobicev, 2015). In this work we have eschewed context, though acknowledge that it is significantly important: in the ENCO-FACT sample above, for example, context may enable a better understanding that the ENCO sentence is in response to another ENCO statement, while the FACT is a response to a direct question. In this sense, there is a clear motivation to understand document-level relationships at the sentence level.

Another direction which could be explored is an alternative annotation scheme. Prost (2012) suggests an annotation scheme used to identify the sharing of both practice-based and emotional support among participants of online forums for teachers. This annotation scheme is a combination of schemes developed for social support forums with those created for practice-based forums. Identifed categories and sub-categories are described in Table 5.

Category	Subcategory
Self disclosure	professional experience
	personal experience
	emotional expression
	support request
Knowledge sharing	from personal experience
	Concrete info or documents
Opinion/evaluation	*na*
Giving advice	*na*
Giving emotional support	*na*
Requesting clarification	*na*
Community building	reference to community
	humour
	broad appreciation
	direct thanks
Personal attacks	*na*

Table 5: Categories and subcategories from support annotation scheme of Prost (2012)

Most of the categories are relevant for both types of forums, support and practice-based. Prost annotated texts at the sub-sentence level, with these 15 categories. In order to produce the volumes of data that would be necessary for machine-learning based approaches to understanding support forum, this is impractical. There is clearly a balance to be struck between utility and practicality. However, Prost's scheme illustrates that in sociological circles, it is important to consider the social context of subjective expressions: there are two categories equivalent to GRAT here, one which is more directed, and the other which concerns a bigger picture expression of the value of community.

6   Conclusion

In this work we have argued two positions. Despite seemingly poor results at sentence-level, we are convinced that the examples we have provided demonstrate that document-level analysis is insufficient to accurately capture expressions of sentiment in emotional support forums. We have also shown that there are important social dimensions to this type of domain which should also be taken into account. It is clear that there is considerable value to be gained from automated understanding of this increasing body of data; we in the Social NLP community need to consider some more refined approaches in order to maximise both the value itself and its fidelity.

References

Salah Ait-Mokhtar, Jean-Pierre Chanod, and Claude Roux. 2001. A multi-input dependency parser. In *Proceedings of the Seventh International Workshop on Parsing Technologies*.

Tanveer Ali, David Schramm, Marina Sokolova, and Diana Inkpen. 2013. Can i hear you? sentiment analysis on medical forums. In *Proceedings of the sixth international joint conference on natural language processing, Asian Federation of Natural Language Processing, Nagoya, Japan, October 2013*, pages 667–673.

Alexandra Balahur and Ralf Steinberger. 2009. Rethinking sentiment analysis in the news: from theory to practice and back. In *Proceedings of the 1st Workshop on Opinion Mining and Sentiment Analysis, 2009*.

Azy Barak and Orit Gluck-Ofri. 2007. Degree and reciprocity of self-disclosure in online forums. *Cyberpsychology & Behavior*, 10(3):407–417.

Victoria Bobicev and Marina Sokolova. 2015. No sentiment is an island - sentiment classification on medical forums. In Nathalie Japkowicz and Stan Matwin, editors, *Discovery Science - 18th International Conference, DS 2015, Banff, AB, Canada, October 4-6, 2015, Proceedings*, volume 9356 of *Lecture Notes in Computer Science*, pages 25–32. Springer.

Sandra Bringay, Eric Kergosien, Pierre Pompidor, and Pascal Poncelet, 2014. *Identifying the Targets of the Emotions Expressed in Health Forums*, pages 85–97. Springer Berlin Heidelberg, Berlin, Heidelberg.

Matthew S. Eastin and Robert LaRose. 2005. Alt.support: modeling social support online. *Computers in Human Behaviour*, 21(6):977–992.

Rong-En Fan, Kai-Wei Chang, Cho-Jui Hsieh, Xiang-Rui Wang, and Chih-Jen Lin. 2008. LIBLINEAR: A library for large linear classification. *Journal of Machine Learning Research*, 9:1871–1874.

Jeffrey T. Hancock, Catalina Toma, and Nicole Ellison. 2007. The truth about lying in online dating profiles. In *Proceedings of the SIGCHI Conference on Human Factors in Computing Systems*, CHI '07, pages 449–452, New York, NY, USA. ACM.

Minqing Hu and Bing Liu. 2004. Mining and summarizing customer reviews. In *KDD*, pages 168–177.

Bing Liu. 2012. *Sentiment Analysis and Opinion Mining*. Synthesis Lectures on Human Language Technologies. Morgan & Claypool Publishers.

Saif Mohammad, Xiaodan Zhu, and Joel Martin, 2014. *Proceedings of the 5th Workshop on Computational Approaches to Subjectivity, Sentiment and Social Media Analysis*, chapter Semantic Role Labeling of Emotions in Tweets, pages 32–41. Association for Computational Linguistics.

Amit Navindgi, Caroline Brun, Cécile Boulard Masson, and Scott Nowson. 2016. Toward automatic understanding of the function of affective language in support groups. *Computation and Language, arXiv preprint, http://arxiv.org/abs/1610.01910*.

Nir Ofek, Cornelia Caragea, Lior Rokach, and Greta E Greer. 2013. Improving sentiment analysis in an online cancer survivor community using dynamic sentiment lexicon. In *Social Intelligence and Technology (SOCIETY), 2013 International Conference on*, pages 109 – 113.

James W. Pennebaker, Emmanuelle Zech, and Bernard Rim, 2001. *Disclosing and sharing emotion: Psychological, social, and health consequences*, pages 517–539. American Psychological Association.

Ulrike Pfeil and Panayiotis Zaphiris. 2007. Patterns of empathy in online communication. In *Proceedings of the SIGCHI Conference on Human Factors in Computing Systems (CHI07)*, pages 919–928, San Jose, CA, USA.

Maria Pontiki, Dimitrios Galanis, John Pavlopoulos, Harris Papageorgiou, Ion Androutsopoulos, and Suresh Manandhar. 2014. Semeval-2014 task 4: Aspect based sentiment analysis. In *International Workshop on Semantic Evaluation (SemEval)*.

Maria Pontiki, Dimitris Galanis, Haris Papageorgiou, Ion Androutsopoulos, Suresh Manandhar, Mohammad AL-Smadi, Mahmoud Al-Ayyoub, Yanyan Zhao, Bing Qin, Orphee De Clercq, Veronique Hoste, Marianna Apidianaki, Xavier Tannier, Natalia Loukachevitch, Evgeniy Kotelnikov, Núria Bel, Salud María Jiménez-Zafra, and Gülşen Eryiğit. 2016. Semeval-2016 task 5: Aspect based sentiment analysis. In *Proceedings of the 10th International Workshop on Semantic Evaluation (SemEval-2016)*, pages 19–30, San Diego, California, June. Association for Computational Linguistics.

Magali Prost. 2012. *changes entre professionnels de l'ducation sur les forums de discussion: entre soutien psychologique et acquisition de connaissances sur la pratique*. Ph.D. thesis, Telecom ParisTech, Paris, France.

Naomi B. Rothman and Joe C. Magee. 2016. Affective expressions in groups and inferences about members' relational well-being: The effects of socially engaging and disengaging emotions. *Cognition & Emotion, Special Issue on Emotions in Groups*, 30(1):150–166.

Marina Sokolova and Victoria Bobicev. 2013. What sentiments can be found in medical forums? In Galia Angelova, Kalina Bontcheva, and Ruslan Mitkov, editors, *Recent Advances in Natural Language Processing, RANLP 2013, 9-11 September, 2013, Hissar, Bulgaria*, pages 633–639. RANLP 2013 Organising Committee / ACL.

Marina Sokolova and Victoria Bobicev. 2015. Learning relationship between authors' activity and sentiments: A case study of online medical forums. In Galia Angelova, Kalina Bontcheva, and Ruslan Mitkov, editors, *Recent Advances in Natural Language Processing, RANLP 2015, 7-9 September, 2015, Hissar, Bulgaria*, pages 604–610. RANLP 2015 Organising Committee / ACL.

Michael Speriosu, Nikita Sudan, Sid Upadhyay, and Jason Baldridge. 2011. Twitter polarity classification with label propagation over lexical links and the follower graph. In *Proceedings of the First workshop on Unsupervised Learning in NLP*, EMNLP '11, pages 53–63.

Carlo Strapparava and Rada Mihalcea. 2007. Semeval-2007 task 14: Affective text. In *Proceedings of the 2008 ACM symposium on Applied computing, 2008*.

Jennifer G. Tichon and Margaret Shapiro. 2003. The process of sharing social support in cyberspace. *Cyberpsychology & Behavior*, 6(2):161–170.

Theresa Wilson, Janyce Wiebe, and Paul Hoffmann. 2005. Recognizing contextual polarity in phrase-level sentiment analysis. In *Proc. of HLT-EMNLP-2005*.

Detecting Social Roles in Twitter

Sunghwan Mac Kim, Stephen Wan and **Cécile Paris**
Data61, CSIRO, Sydney, Australia
{Mac.Kim, Stephen.Wan, Cecile.Paris}@csiro.au

Abstract

For social media analysts or social scientists interested in better understanding an audience or demographic cohort, being able to group social media content by demographic characteristics is a useful mechanism to organise data. Social roles are one particular demographic characteristic, which includes work, recreational, community and familial roles. In our work, we look at the task of detecting social roles from English Twitter profiles. We create a new annotated dataset for this task. The dataset includes approximately 1,000 Twitter profiles annotated with social roles. We also describe a machine learning approach for detecting social roles from Twitter profiles, which can act as a strong baseline for this dataset. Finally, we release a set of word clusters obtained in an unsupervised manner from Twitter profiles. These clusters may be useful for other natural language processing tasks in social media.

1 Introduction

Social media platforms such as Twitter have become an important communication medium in society. As such, social scientists and media analysts are increasingly turning to social media as a cheap and large-volume source of real-time data, supplementing "traditional" data sources such as interviews and questionnaires. For these fields, being able to examine demographic factors can be a key part of analyses. However, demographic characteristics are not always available on social media data. Consequently, there has been a growing body of work in-

Figure 1: An example of a Twitter profile.

vestigating methods to estimate a variety of demographic characteristics from social media data, such as gender and age on Twitter and Facebook (Mislove et al., 2011; Sap et al., 2014) and YouTube (Filippova, 2012). In this work we focus on estimating social roles, an under-explored area.

In social psychology literature, Augoustinos et al. (2014) provide an overview of schemata for social roles, which includes achieved roles based on the choices of the individual (e.g., writer or artist) and ascribed roles based on the inherent traits of an individual (e.g., teenager or schoolchild). Social roles can represent a variety of categories including gender roles, family roles, occupations, and hobbyist roles. Beller et al. (2014) have explored a set of social roles (e.g., occupation-related and family-related social roles) extracted from the tweets. They used a pragmatic definition for social roles: namely, the word following the simple self-identification pattern "I am a/an ". In contrast, our manually annotated dataset covers a wide range of social roles without using this fixed pattern, since it is not necessarily mentioned before the social roles.

On Twitter, users often list their social roles in their profiles. Figure 1, for example, shows the Twitter profile of a well-known Australian chef, Manu Feildel (@manufeildel). His profile provides infor-

Proceedings of The Fourth International Workshop on Natural Language Processing for Social Media, pages 34–40,
Austin, TX, November 1, 2016. ©2016 Association for Computational Linguistics

mation about his social roles beyond simply listing occupations. We can see that he has both a profession, *Chef*, as well as a community role, *Judge* on My Kitchen Rules (MKR), which is an Australian cooking show.

The ability to break down social media insights based on social roles is potentially a powerful tool for social media analysts and social scientists alike. For social media analysts, it provides the opportunity to identify whether they reach their target audience and to understand how subsets of their target audience (segmented by social role) react to various issues. For example, a marketing analyst may want to know what online discussions are due to parents versus other social roles.

Our aim in this paper is to provide a rich collection of English Twitter profiles for the social role identification task. The dataset includes a approximately 1,000 Twitter profiles, randomly selected, which we annotated with social roles. Additionally, we release unsupervised Twitter word clusters that will be useful for other natural language processing (NLP) tasks in social media.[1] Finally, we investigate social role tagging as a machine learning problem. A machine learning framework is described for detecting social roles in Twitter profiles.

Our contributions are threefold:

- We introduce a new annotated dataset for identifying social roles in Twitter.
- We release a set of Twitter word clusters with respect to social roles.
- We propose a machine learning model as a strong baseline for the task of identifying social roles from Twitter profiles.

2 Crowdsourcing Annotated Data

Twitter user profiles often list a range of interests that they associate with, and these can vary from occupations to hobbies (Beller et al., 2014; Sloan et al., 2015). The aim of our annotation task was to manually identify social role-related words in English Twitter profile descriptions. A social role is defined as a single word that could be extracted from the description. These can include terms such as *engineer*,

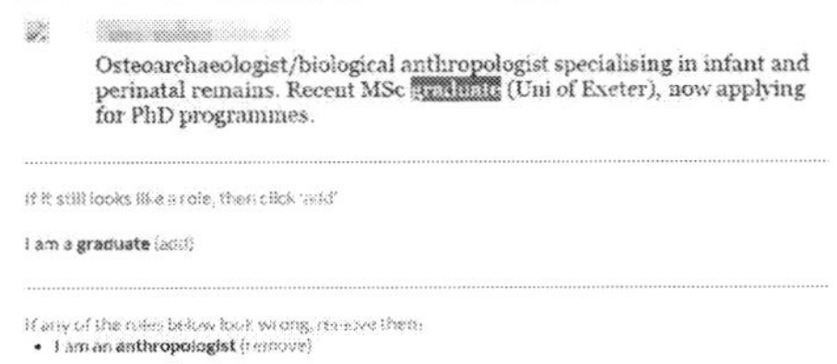

Figure 2: The Crowdflower annotation interface.

mother, and *fan*. For instance, we obtain *Musician* and *Youtuber* as social roles from "Australian Musician and Youtuber who loves purple!".[2]

To study social roles in Twitter profiles, we compiled a dataset of approximately 1,000 randomly selected English Twitter profiles which were annotated with social roles. These samples were drawn from a large number of Twitter profiles crawled by a social network-based method (Dennett et al., 2016). Such a dataset provides a useful collection of profiles for researchers to study social media and to build machine learning models.

Annotations were acquired using the crowdsourcing platform Crowdflower.[3], which we now outline.

2.1 Crowdflower Annotation Guidelines

We asked Crowdflower annotators to identify social roles in the Twitter profiles presented to them, using the following definition: "Social roles are words or phrases that could be pulled out from the profile and inserted into the sentence *I am a/an …*". Note that the profile does not necessarily need to contain the phrase "I am a/an" before the social role, as described in Section 1.

The annotation interface is presented in Figure 2. The annotator is asked to select spans of text. Once a span of text is selected, the interface copies this text into a temporary list of candidate roles. The annotator can confirm that the span of text should be kept as a role (by clicking the 'add' link which moves the text span to a second list representing the "final candidates"). It is also possible to remove a candidate role from the list of final candidates (by clicking 'remove'). Profiles were allowed to have more than one social role.

Annotators were asked to keep candidate roles as short as possible as in the following instruction: *if*

---

[1] Our dataset and word clusters are publicly available at `https://data.csiro.au`.

[2] This is a real example.

[3] crowdflower.com

Number of annotated profiles	983
Average description length	13.02 words
Longest description length	74 words
Shortest description length	1 word
Number of unique roles	488

Table 1: Descriptive statistics for the annotated data.

the Twitter profile contains "Bieber fan", just mark the word "fan".[4] Finally, we instructed annotators to only mark roles that refer to the owner of the Twitter profile. For example, annotators were asked not to mark *wife* as a role in: *I love my wife*. Our Crowdflower task was configured to present five annotation jobs in one web page. After each set of five jobs, the annotator could proceed to the next page.

2.2 Crowdflower Parameters

To acquire annotations as quickly as possible, we used the *highest speed* setting in Crowdflower and did not place additional constraints on the annotator selection, such as language, quality and geographic region. The task took approximately 1 week. We offered 15 cents AUD per page. To control annotation quality, we utilised the Crowdflower facility to include test cases called *test validators*, using 50 test cases to evaluate the annotators. We required a minimum accuracy of 70% on test validators.

2.3 Summary of Annotation Process

At the completion of the annotation procedure, Crowdflower reported the following summary statistics that provide insights on the quality of the annotations. The majority of the judgements were sourced from annotators deemed to be *trusted* (i.e., reliable annotators) (4750/4936). Crowdflower reported an inter-annotator agreement of 91.59%. Table 1 presents some descriptive statistics for our annotated dataset. We observe that our Twitter profile dataset contains 488 unique roles.

In Table 2, we present the top 10 ranked social roles. As can be seen, our extracted social roles include terms such as *student* and *fan*, highlighting that social roles in Twitter profiles include a diverse range of personal attributes. In Table 3, we see that more than half (56.2%) of the descriptions do not contain any role, and approximately 22.7% contain

---

[4]While this decision could give us a coarse-grain granularity of social roles, it was an application-specific requirement from a visualisation point of view to minimise roles.

Social role	Frequency
student	25
fan	24
girl	16
writer	14
teacher	13
geek	12
author	11
artist	10
directioner	9
designer	8

Table 2: Top 10 ranked social roles in Twitter profiles.

Number of roles	Frequency (%)
0	552 (56.2)
1	213 (22.7)
2	101 (10.3)
3	45 (4.6)
4	31 (3.2)
5	23 (2.3)
6	8 (0.8)
7	2 (0.2)
8	6 (0.6)
9	2 (0.2)

Table 3: Frequencies of number of roles that are used to annotate one Twitter profile in our dataset.

one role. The remaining descriptions (21.1%) contain more than one social role.

3 Word Clusters

We can easily access a large-scale unlabelled dataset using the Twitter API, supplementing our dataset, to apply unsupervised machine learning methods to help in social role tagging. Previous work showed that word clusters derived from an unlabelled dataset can improve the performance of many NLP applications (Koo et al., 2008; Turian et al., 2010; Spitkovsky et al., 2011; Kong et al., 2014). This finding motivates us to use a similar approach to improve tagging performance for Twitter profiles.

Two clustering techniques are employed to generate the cluster features: Brown clustering (Brown et al., 1992) and K-means clustering (MacQueen, 1967). The Brown clustering algorithm induces a hierarchy of words from an unannotated corpus, and it allows us to directly map words to clusters. Word embeddings induced from a neural network are often useful representations of the meaning of words, encoded as distributional vectors. Unlike Brown clustering, word embeddings do not have any form of clusters by default. K-means clustering is thus used on the resulting word vectors. Each word is mapped to the unique cluster ID to which it was assigned, and these cluster identifiers were used as features.

Bit string	Words related to social role
010110111100	**writer**, nwriter, scribbler, writter, glutton
01011010111110	**teacher**, tutor, preacher, homeschooler, nbct, hod, dutchman, nqt, tchr
0101101111110	**musician**, philologist, orchestrator, memoirist, dramatist, violist, crooner, flautist, filmaker, humourist, dramaturg, harpist, flutist, trumpeter, improvisor, trombonist, musicologist, organist, puppeteer, laureate, poetess, hypnotist, audiobook, comedienne, saxophonist, cellist, scriptwriter, narrator, muso, essayist, improviser, satirist, thespian, ghostwriter, arranger, humorist, violinist, magician, lyricist, playwright, pianist, screenwriter, novelist, performer, philosopher, composer, comedian, filmmaker, poet

Table 4: Examples of Brown clusters with respect to social roles: *writer*, *teacher* and *musician*.

Cluster	Words related to social role
937	**writer**, freelance, interviewer, documentarian, erstwhile, dramaturg, biographer, reviewer, bookseller, essayist, unpublished, critic, author, aspiring, filmmaker, dramatist, playwright, laureate, humorist, screenwriter, storyteller, ghostwriter, copywriter, scriptwriter, proofreader, copyeditor, poet, memoirist, satirist, podcaster, novelist, screenplay, poetess
642	**teacher**, learner, superintendent, pyp, lifelong, flipped, preparatory, cue, yearbook, preschool, intermediate, nwp, school, primary, grades, prek, distinguished, prep, dojo, isd, hpe, ib, esl, substitute, librarian, nbct, efl, headteacher, mfl, hod, elem, principal, sped, graders, nqt, eal, tchr, secondary, tdsb, kindergarten, edd, instructional, elementary, keystone, grade, exemplary, classroom, pdhpe
384	**musician**, songwriter, singer, troubadour, arranger, composer, drummer, session, orchestrator, saxophonist, keyboardist, percussionist, guitarist, soloist, instrumentalist, jingle, trombonist, vocal, backing, virtuoso, bassist, vocalist, pianist, frontman

Table 5: Examples of word2vec clusters with respect to social roles: *writer*, *teacher* and *musician*.

We used 6 million Twitter profiles that were automatically collected by crawling a social network starting from a seed set of Twitter accounts (Dennett et al., 2016) to derive the Brown clusters and word embeddings for this domain. For both methods, the text of each profile description was normalised to be in lowercase and tokenised using whitespace and punctuation as delimiters.

To obtain the Brown clusters, we use a publicly available toolkit, *wcluster*[5] to generate 1,000 clusters with the minimum occurrence of 40, yielding 47,167 word types. The clusters are hierarchically structured as a binary tree. Each word belongs to one cluster, and the path from the word to the root of the tree can be represented as a bit string. These can be truncated to refer to clusters higher up in the tree.

To obtain word embeddings, we used the skip-gram model as implemented in *word2vec*[6], a neural network toolkit introduced by (Mikolov et al., 2013), to generate a 300-dimension word vector based on a 10-word context window size. We then used K-means clustering on the resulting 47,167 word vectors (k=1,000). Each word was mapped to the unique cluster ID to which it was assigned.

Tables 4 and 5 show some examples of Brown clusters and word2vec clusters respectively, for three social roles: *writer*, *teacher* and *musician*. We note that similar types of social roles are grouped into the same clusters in both methods. For instance, *orchestrator* and *saxophonist* are in the same cluster containing *musician*. Both clusters are able to capture the similarities of abbreviations of importance to social roles, for example, *tchr* → *teacher*, *nbct* → *National Board Certified Teachers*, *hpe* → *Health and Physical Education*.

4 Identifying Social Roles

4.1 Social Role Tagger

This section describes a tagger we developed for the task of identifying social roles given Twitter profiles. Here, we treat social role tagging as a sequence labelling task. We use the MALLET toolkit (McCallum, 2002) implementation of Conditional Random Fields (CRFs) (Lafferty et al., 2001) to automatically identify social roles in Twitter profiles as our machine learning framework. More specifically, we employ a first-order linear chain CRF, in which the preceding word (and its features) is incorporated as context in the labelling task. In this task, each word is tagged with one of two labels: social roles are tagged with R (for "role"), whereas the other words are tagged by O (for "other").

The social role tagger uses two categories of features: (i) basic lexical features and (ii) word cluster features. The first category captures lexical cues that may be indicative of a social role. These features include morphological, syntactic, orthographic and regular expression-based features (McCallum and Li, 2003; Finkel et al., 2008). The second captures semantic similarities, as illustrated in Tables 4 and 5 (Section 3). To use Brown clusters in CRFs, we use eight bit string representations of different lengths to create features representing the ancestor clusters of the word. For word2vec clusters, the cluster identifiers are used as features in CRFs. If a word is

[5]https://github.com/percyliang/brown-cluster

[6]https://code.google.com/p/word2vec/

Model	Feature	Precision	Recall	F1
KWS		0.659	0.759	0.690
CRFs	Basic	0.830	0.648	0.725
	+ Brown	0.859	0.708	0.774
	+ W2V	0.837	0.660	0.736
	+ (Brown+W2V)	0.863	0.712	**0.779**

Table 6: 10-fold cross-validation macro-average results on the annotated dataset. (Brown: Brown cluster features, W2V: Word2vec cluster features).

not associated with any clustering, its corresponding cluster features are set to null in the feature vector for that word.

4.2 Evaluation

We evaluate our tagger on the annotated Twitter dataset using precision, recall and F1-score. We use 10-fold cross-validation and report macro-averages. Significance tests are performed using the Wilcoxon signed-rank test (Wilcoxon, 1945). We compare the CRF-based tagger against a keyword spotting (KWS) method. This baseline uses social roles labelled in the training data to provide keywords to spot for in the test profiles without considering local context. On average, over the 10-fold cross-validation, 54% of the social roles in the test set are seen in the training set. This indicates that the KWS baseline has potential out-of-vocabulary (OOV) problems for unseen social roles.

To reduce overfitting in the CRF, we employ a zero mean Gaussian prior regulariser with one standard deviation. To find the optimal feature weights, we use the limited-memory BFGS (L-BFGS) (Liu and Nocedal, 1989) algorithm, minimising the regularised negative log-likelihood. All CRFs are trained using 500 iterations of L-BFGS with the Gaussian prior variance of 1 and no frequency cutoff for features, inducing approximately 97,300 features. We follow standard approaches in using the forward-backward algorithm for exact inference in CRFs.

Table 6 shows the evaluation results of 10-fold cross-validation for the KWS method and the CRF tagger. With respect to the different feature sets, we find that the combination of the word cluster features obtained by the two methods outperform the basic features in terms of F1 (77.9 vs. 72.5 respectively), in general providing a statistically significant improvement of approximately 5% ($p < 0.01$).

The improvement obtained with word cluster fea-

tures lends support to the intuition that capturing similarity in vocabulary within the feature space helps with tagging accuracy. Word cluster models provide a means to compare words based on semantic similarity, helping with cases where lexical items in the test set are not found in the training set (e.g., linguist, evangelist, teamster). In addition, the cluster features allow CRFs to detect informal and abbreviated words as social roles. Our tagger identifies both *teacher* and *tchr* as social roles from the two sentences: "I am a school teacher" and "I am a school tchr". This is particularly useful in social media because of the language variation in vocabulary that is typically found.

In this experiment, we show that social role tagging is possible with a reasonable level of performance (F1 77.9), significantly outperforming the KWS baseline (F1 69.0). This result indicates the need for a method that captures the context surrounding word usage. This allows language patterns to be learned from data that disambiguate word sense and prevents spurious detection of social roles from the data. This is evidenced by the lower precision and F1-score for the KWS baseline, which over-generates candidates for social roles.

5 Conclusion and Future Work

In this work, we constructed a new manually annotated English Twitter profile dataset for social role identification task. In addition, we induced Twitter word clusters from a large unannotated corpus with respect to social roles. We make these resources publicly available in the hope that they will be useful in research on social media. Finally, we developed a social role tagger using CRFs, and this can serve as a strong baseline in this task. In future work, we will look into being able to identify multi-word social roles to obtain a finer-grained categorisation (e.g., "chemical engineer" vs. "software engineer").

Acknowledgments

The authors are grateful to anonymous SocialNLP@EMNLP reviewers. We would also like to thank David Milne, who ran the data collection and annotation procedure, and Bo Yan, who collected the additional data for the clustering methods.

References

Martha Augoustinos, Iain Walker, and Ngaire Donaghue. 2014. *Social cognition: an integrated introduction.* SAGE London, third edition.

Charley Beller, Rebecca Knowles, Craig Harman, Shane Bergsma, Margaret Mitchell, and Benjamin Van Durme. 2014. I'm a belieber: Social roles via self-identification and conceptual attributes. In *Proceedings of the 52nd Annual Meeting of the Association for Computational Linguistics*, pages 181–186, Baltimore, Maryland, June. Association for Computational Linguistics.

Peter F. Brown, Peter V. deSouza, Robert L. Mercer, Vincent J. Della Pietra, and Jenifer C. Lai. 1992. Class-based n-gram models of natural language. *Computational Linguistics*, 18(4):467–479, December.

Amanda Dennett, Surya Nepal, Cecile Paris, and Bella Robinson. 2016. Tweetripple: Understanding your twitter audience and the impact of your tweets. In *Proceedings of the 2nd IEEE International Conference on Collaboration and Internet Computing*, Pittsburgh, PA, USA, November. IEEE.

Katja Filippova. 2012. User demographics and language in an implicit social network. In *Proceedings of the 2012 Joint Conference on Empirical Methods in Natural Language Processing and Computational Natural Language Learning*, pages 1478–1488, Jeju Island, Korea, July. Association for Computational Linguistics.

Jenny Rose Finkel, Alex Kleeman, and Christopher D. Manning. 2008. Efficient, feature-based, Conditional Random Field parsing. In *Proceedings of the 46th Annual Meeting of the Association for Computational Linguistics: Human Language Technologies*, pages 959–967, Columbus, Ohio, June. Association for Computational Linguistics.

Lingpeng Kong, Nathan Schneider, Swabha Swayamdipta, Archna Bhatia, Chris Dyer, and Noah A. Smith. 2014. A dependency parser for tweets. In *Proceedings of the 2014 Conference on Empirical Methods in Natural Language Processing*, pages 1001–1012, Doha, Qatar, October. Association for Computational Linguistics.

Terry Koo, Xavier Carreras, and Michael Collins. 2008. Simple semi-supervised dependency parsing. In *Proceedings of the 46th Annual Meeting of the Association for Computational Linguistics: Human Language Technologies*, pages 595–603, Columbus, Ohio, June. Association for Computational Linguistics.

John D. Lafferty, Andrew McCallum, and Fernando C. N. Pereira. 2001. Conditional Random Fields: Probabilistic models for segmenting and labeling sequence data. In *Proceedings of the Eighteenth International Conference on Machine Learning*, pages 282–289, San Francisco, CA, USA. Morgan Kaufmann Publishers Inc.

Dong C. Liu and Jorge Nocedal. 1989. On the limited memory BFGS method for large scale optimization. *Mathematical Programming*, 45(3):503–528, Dec.

J. MacQueen. 1967. Some methods for classification and analysis of multivariate observations. In *Proceedings of the Fifth Berkeley Symposium on Mathematical Statistics and Probability, Volume 1: Statistics*, pages 281–297, Berkeley, California. University of California Press.

Andrew McCallum and Wei Li. 2003. Early results for named entity recognition with conditional random fields, feature induction and web-enhanced lexicons. In *Proceedings of the 2003 Conference of the North American Chapter of the Association for Computational Linguistics: Human Language Technologies*, pages 188–191, Edmonton, Canada. Association for Computational Linguistics.

Andrew Kachites McCallum. 2002. Mallet: A machine learning for language toolkit.

Tomas Mikolov, Wen-tau Yih, and Geoffrey Zweig. 2013. Linguistic regularities in continuous space word representations. In *Proceedings of the 2013 Conference of the North American Chapter of the Association for Computational Linguistics: Human Language Technologies*, pages 746–751, Atlanta, Georgia, June. Association for Computational Linguistics.

Alan Mislove, Sune Lehmann, Yong-Yeol Ahn, Jukka-Pekka Onnela, and J. Niels Rosenquist. 2011. Understanding the demographics of twitter users. In *Proceedings of the Fifth International AAAI Conference on Weblogs and Social Media*, pages 554–557. The AAAI Press.

Maarten Sap, Gregory Park, Johannes Eichstaedt, Margaret Kern, David Stillwell, Michal Kosinski, Lyle Ungar, and Hansen Andrew Schwartz. 2014. Developing age and gender predictive lexica over social media. In *Proceedings of the 2014 Conference on Empirical Methods in Natural Language Processing*, pages 1146–1151, Doha, Qatar, October. Association for Computational Linguistics.

Luke Sloan, Jeffrey Morgan, Pete Burnap, and Matthew Williams. 2015. Who tweets? deriving the demographic characteristics of age, occupation and social class from twitter user meta-data. *PLoS ONE*, 10(3):e0115545, 03.

Valentin I. Spitkovsky, Hiyan Alshawi, Angel X. Chang, and Daniel Jurafsky. 2011. Unsupervised dependency parsing without gold part-of-speech tags. In *Proceedings of the 2011 Conference on Empirical Methods in Natural Language Processing*, pages 1281–1290, Edinburgh, Scotland, UK., July. Association for Computational Linguistics.

Joseph Turian, Lev-Arie Ratinov, and Yoshua Bengio. 2010. Word representations: A simple and general method for semi-supervised learning. In *Proceedings of the 48th Annual Meeting of the Association for Computational Linguistics*, pages 384–394, Uppsala, Sweden, July. Association for Computational Linguistics.

Frank Wilcoxon. 1945. Individual comparisons by ranking methods. *Biometrics Bulletin*, 1(6):80–83.

Identifying Sensible Participants in Online Discussions

Siddharth Jain
siddhajj@usc.edu
University of Southern California

Abstract

This paper investigates the problem of identifying participants in online discussions whose contribution can be considered sensible. Sensibleness of a participant can be indicative of the influence a participant may have on the course/outcome of the discussion, as well as other participants in terms of persuading them towards his/her stance. The proposed sensibleness model uses features based on participants' contribution and the discussion domain to achieve an F1-score of 0.89 & 0.78 for *Wikipedia: Articles for Deletion* and *4forums.com* discussions respectively.

1 Introduction

In contentious online discussions, people are very quick to classify other participants as being 'sensible' or not. What exactly this means is very hard to define. However, if one looks beyond the flippant 'anyone who agrees with me is sensible', it is possible to identify characteristics that tend to signal more thoughtful contributions. These include avoiding ad hominem attacks, making contributions that others respond favorably towards, obeying common rules of discourse, and so on. Sensibleness of a participant is quantified based on his/her contribution to the discussion, which is relevant to the discussion and reasoned in a way that is appealing to other participants.

In this paper, domain independent characteristics are identified and their stability is tested through human annotations to develop a classification system for determining sensibleness of participants in dis-

cussions on Wikipedia and 4forums.com. The proposed method leverages features obtained through argumentation mining. Domain specific characteristics are also incorporated in the analysis of the Wikipedia corpus.

2 Related Work

The pioneering work in argumentation mining is that of Moens (Moens et al., 2007), who addressed mining argumentation from legal documents. Recently, the focus has moved to mining user-generated content, such as online debates (Cabrio and Villata, 2012), discussions on regulations (Park and Cardie, 2014), and product reviews (Ghosh et al., 2014). Hasan (Hasan and Ng, 2014) use a probabilistic framework for argument recognition jointly with the related task of *stance* classification. Rosenthal (Rosenthal and McKeown, 2012) detect opinionated claims in online discussions in which author expresses a belief. They investigate the impact of features such as sentiment and committed belief on their system.

To date, almost no computational work has focused on the surface signals of "sense" in rhetoric. Danescu-Niculescu-Mizil (Danescu-Niculescu-Mizil et al., 2013) proposes a framework for identifying politeness. Although politeness seems an important aspect in identifying sensibleness, it is not mandatory. For example, the comment "I don't care how much you love the city. It cannot be on Wikipedia as it doesn't have enough coverage to satisfy Wikipedia policy." doesn't seem polite, though the author does seem sensible. Sun (Sun and Ng, 2012) propose a graph model to represent

Proceedings of The Fourth International Workshop on Natural Language Processing for Social Media, pages 41–47,
Austin, TX, November 1, 2016. ©2016 Association for Computational Linguistics

the relationship between online posts of one topic, in order to identify influential users. Tang (Tang and Yang, 2012) proposed a new approach to incorporate users' reply relationships to identify influential users of online healthcare communities. All these network based approaches determine the influence of a participant based on his/her centrality to the community/discussion and do not pay much attention to the specific content provided by the participants.

3   Corpus and Annotation

The corpus (Jain et al., 2014) for sensibleness annotation consists of 80 discussions from Wikipedia's Article for Deletion (AfD) discussion forum and 10 discussions from 4forums.com discussion forum. Sensibleness is highly dependent on the domain and nature of the discussion. Wikipedia discussions are goal-oriented: each participant tries to sway the decision of the discussion in their favor. Also, since Wikipedia pages should meet the requirements stated in their policies, one would expect the discussions to revolve around such policies. Therefore a criterion for people to be sensible in such discussions is that they appeal to authority in support of their arguments/claims. Additional criteria include not becoming emotional, avoiding tangents not relevant to the main topic, peer reviews, etc.

	Wikipedia	4forums.com
#Discussions	80	10
#participants	768	174
#Comments	1487	624
#Words	96138	51659

Table 1: Corpora stats.

In contrast, the discussions on 4forums.com are opinion-oriented, where participants primarily focus on presenting their own opinion and reasoning, but do not seriously consider that of others except to dispute it. In this domain, sensibleness analysis differs from the Wikipedia domain in several ways. First, expressing emotions may be considered sensible; second, tangential discussions that are not relevant to the main topic may be considered sensible if other participants follow.

Annotating sensibleness: Three annotators were asked to annotate the sensibleness of each participant in the discussions. The coding manual was cre-

ated after several annotation rounds using different Wikipedia discussions through a process of refinement and consensus. Here are some of the questions the annotators seek to answer to determine sensibleness of a participant:

- "Does the participant sound reasonable and knowledgeable?"
- "How many positive/negative responses does the participant have?"
- "Does the participant start or get involved in tangential discussion?"
- "How much emotion does the participant express and what is the tone of it?"
- Does the participant mention Wikipedia policies? (For Wikipedia discussions only)

Each discussion is treated separately for annotation, i.e. a participant's sensibleness value for one discussion doesn't affect his/her sensibleness value for any other discussion. The possible values for sensibleness in the annotations are +1 (= sensible), -1 (= non-sensible), and 0 (= indeterminable). The annotation agreement score is kappa=0.73 using Fleiss' kappa (Fleiss, 1971) measure.

	Wikipedia	4forums.com
#Sensible	641	139
#Non-sensible	109	31
#Indeterminable	18	4

Table 2: Sensibleness distribution in the corpora.

Annotating claims: Analyzing the argumentation structure of participants' comments is an important aspect of the sensibleness model. For this analysis, Wikipedia discussions are annotated for claims and claim-links. A *claim* is defined as any assertion made in a discussion that the author intends the reader to believe to be true, and that can be disputed. A *claim-link* is defined as the causal/conditional dependency between claims. The same annotators performed this task, achieving an agreement score of kappa=0.76 for claim delimitation and kappa=0.81 for linkage.

4   Sensibleness Model

The classification model for sensibleness is created by extracting relevant features from participant's comments. Supervised machine learning is applied to determine the sensibleness value.

4.1 Argumentation Structure

The argumentation structure of the comments is an important aspect in determining sensibleness. For example, while *"This page violates Wikipedia policies"* and *"This page violates Wikipedia policies because it has no sources"* both express an opinion, the second is deemed more sensible because it provides a reason for the opinion. In contrast, *"Violent offenders can stay off our street"* presents an opinion that does not contain any claim and doesn't contribute anything significant toward the discussion. Therefore it can be considered non-sensible. The argumentation structure analysis is divided into three parts: *claim detection*, *claim delimitation*, and *claim-link detection*.

4.1.1 Claim Detection

Each sentence is classified as either having or not having a claim using several lexical features. The features include word n-grams(1-3), POS tag n-grams(1-3), and dependency triples (Marneffe et al., 2006). The classifier also uses generalized back-off features for n=grams and dependency triples as proposed by Joshi (Joshi and Penstein-Rosé, 2009). Similarly back-off features for lexical bigrams and trigrams are used. The motivation behind these features is the diversity of the topics that prevails in the discussions, which causes data sparsity with specific word combinations, which occur very infrequently. An SVM classifier with radial basis function is used to detect the sentences that express claims.

4.1.2 Claim Delimitation

Claim delimitation is useful since a sentence may contain multiple claims. The annotated sentences are pre-processed to add B_C, I_C, and O_C tags to each word, where B_C indicates a word starting a claim, I_C indicates a word inside a claim and O_C indicates a word outside any claim. Conditional Random Field (CRF) implemented in *CRFsuite*[1] is used to tag each word automatically using features like word n-grams(1-3), POS n-grams(1-3), and a binary feature for questions.

---

[1] http://www.chokkan.org/software/crfsuite/

4.1.3 Claim-Link Detection

For claim-link detection, claim pairs are formed and determined whether they are linked. For each claim pair, features used include word and POS n-grams of the claims, word and POS unigrams for at most 5 words preceding and succeeding the claims, # of similar words between the claims, "claim distance" between the claims counting number of claims between them, and "sentence distance" between the claims counting how many sentences apart they are. An SVM classifier with radial basis function is used to detect claims that are linked.

From the argumentation structure analysis, the features extracted for the sensibleness analysis are: % of sentences made as claims, and % of claims linked to other claims.

4.2 Tangential Comments

Participants who tend to deflect from the main subject of the discussion are considered to be non-sensible. For each participant, each of his/her comments is categorized as tangential to the discussion or not. To quantify this, *itf-ipf*, a slightly modified version of *tf-idf*, is used to approximate tangentiality of any comment. For any tangential comment, the words used in the comment would be used relatively less than other words overall and would be used by relatively fewer participants. *tf* (term frequency) and *pf* (participant frequency: total number of participants who used the word in the discussion) are calculated and the *itf-ipf* value for each word w in a comment is computed as:

$$w_{itf-ipf} = \frac{1}{w_{tf}} * \log \frac{N}{w_{pf}} \qquad (1)$$

N = total number of participants in discussion.

Using the *itf-ipf* value for each word, the tangential quotient (*TQ*) for a comment (*C*) is calculated as:

$$TQ_C = \frac{\sum_{w \epsilon C} w_{itf-ipf}}{N_w} \qquad (2)$$

N_w = total number of words in comment.

The total *itf-ipf* value is divided by the total number of words to nullify the effect of the length of the comment. For Wikipedia discussions, if the value of

TQ_C for a comment is more than 1.3 standard deviations from the average tangential quotient of the discussion ($\mu+1.3\sigma$), the comment considered tangential. Similarly, for 4forums.com discussions, if the value of TQ_C for a comment is more than 1.5 standard deviations from the average tangential quotient of the discussion ($\mu+1.5\sigma$), the comment considered tangential.

% of comments as tangential comments is used as one of the features for the sensibleness model.

4.3 Peer Reviews

Peer reviews provide an external opinion on the sensibleness of a participant. They therefore play a significant part in determining sensibleness of a participant, as a system with no domain knowledge of the discussion topic cannot verify the validity of their claims. For this analysis, all sentences that contain references to other participants are identified using $NLTK$[2] toolkit's NER (Named Entity Recognition) module. Second person pronouns in replies to other participants as reference are also identified. Next, the sentences that contain the reference are analyzed using NLTK's sentiment analysis module. If the sentence has non-neutral sentiment, then the polarity of the sentence is checked. If the polarity of the sentence is positive, then it is considered a positive review towards the participant who is referenced in the sentence. Similarly, if the polarity is negative, then it is considered a negative peer review.

# of positive reviews and # negative reviews are used as features for the sensibleness analysis.

4.4 Other Features

The following intuitive features are also part of the sensibleness analysis:

- % of sentences as questions: It can be a good strategy to ask questions related to the discussion, but asking too many questions can be considered as non-sensible.
- % of comments as personal attacks: This feature is useful for identifying participants who constantly attack others rather than presenting their own arguments. A similar method to that for peer reviews is used to identify comments that are targeted towards other participants and have negative

polarity.

5 Experiments and Results

$Weka$[3] is used for all the classification tasks. The classifier for sensibleness model is trained using Wikipedia discussions over the features described in previous sections and is tested on both Wikipedia and 4forums.com discussions. For Wikipedia discussions, a domain specific feature of "Policy" is also incorporated based on the intuition that participants who mention Wikipedia policies in their comments are considered sensible. The best performing classifier for each of the argumentation structure experiment is used for the sensibleness model. The sensibleness model is compared with two baseline models ("Everyone" and "Bag of words") and several other models listed below:

- **Everyone**: Every participant is classified as sensible
- **Bag of words**: An SVM classifier with radial basis function trained on word n-grams(1-3)
- **Claims**: An SVM classifier with radial basis function trained on % of sentences containing claims
- **Claim-Links**: An SVM classifier with radial basis function trained on % of claims linked to other claims
- **Claims+Links**: An SVM classifier with radial basis function trained on % of sentences containing claims and % of claims linked to other claims
- **Tangential**: A participant is classified as sensible if he/she has less than 25% comments as tangential comments
- **Peer reviews**: A participant is classified as sensible if he/she has equal or more positive reviews than negative reviews
- **Questions**: An SVM classifier with radial basis function trained on % of sentences as questions
- **Personal attacks**: An SVM classifier with radial basis function trained on % of comments as personal attacks
- **Policy**: A participant is classified as sensible if he/she mentions Wikipedia policy in any of his/her comment. A small vocabulary is used to detect policy mentions in any comment.

McNemar's test is used to measure statistical significance. A significance difference in performance

---

for $p < 0.01$ is depicted with ▲ (gain) and ▼ (loss) and for $p < 0.05$ is depicted with △ (gain) and ▽ (loss). 10-fold cross validation is used for testing Wikipedia models. After experimenting with several classifiers, the weighted precision, recall, and F1-score for the best classifier for each model is reported. SVM with radial basis function performs the best for both "Sensibleness" and "Sensibleness+Policy" models.

Model	Precision	Recall	F1-score
Everyone	0.70	0.83	0.76
Bag of words	0.71	0.80	0.75
Claims	0.78	0.83	0.80▲
Claim-Links	0.73	0.81	0.76
Claims+Links	0.81	0.85	0.82▲
Tangential	0.79	0.84	0.79▲
Peer reviews	0.76	0.82	0.78△
Questions	0.75	0.72	0.73
Personal attacks	0.73	0.76	0.75
Policy	0.77	0.80	0.78△
Sensibleness	0.86	0.88	0.87▲
Sensibleness+ Policy	0.88	0.90	0.89▲

Table 3: Sensibleness analysis for Wikipedia. Statistical significance is measured against "Everyone" model.

Since there are no discussion policies for 4forums.com, no corresponding models are created for it. The models trained on Wikipedia discussions are used to classify sensibleness on 4forums.com. Table 7 & Table 8 show the results for sensibleness analysis for Wikipedia and 4forums.com discussions respectively.

5.1 Error analysis

Looking at the errors made by the sensibleness model for Wikipedia discussions, we find that some are due to the inability of the argumentation structure detection system to identify claims for participants with very few sentences. Any participant with no identified claims is highly likely to be classified as non-sensible by the sensibleness model and therefore if the model is unable to detect claims then it is very likely that the model will classify such instances incorrectly. Using sensibleness models

Model	Precision	Recall	F1-score
Everyone	0.64	0.80	0.71
Bag of words	0.64	0.73	0.68
Claims	0.72	0.74	0.73▲
Claim-Links	0.65	0.74	0.69
Claims+Links	0.74	0.75	0.74▲
Tangential	0.74	0.71	0.72△
Peer reviews	0.69	0.78	0.72△
Questions	0.63	0.78	0.70
Personal attacks	0.69	0.71	0.70
Sensibleness	0.77	0.79	0.78▲

Table 4: Sensibleness analysis for 4forums.com. Statistical significance is measured against "Everyone" model.

trained on Wikipedia discussions for sensibleness analysis of 4forums.com discussions fail mainly due to the difference in the argumentation structure of the two domains. Participants with lesser % claims/claim-links would be classified incorrectly on 4forums.com discussions.

6 Conclusions and Future Work

The work presented in this paper only scratches the surface of the problem of identifying sensible participants in discussions. Still, the success of the approach of counting some surface features to determine sensibleness is encouraging. The sensibleness analysis presented in this paper shows that argumentation structure and other intuitive features provide moderate accuracy for identifying sensible participants in online discussions. In future, we intend to follow up by using more subtle features identified by the annotators that are central to the model, such as identifying emotions and tones of comments. We hope this work provides an indication that it is possible to address this problem despite its difficulty and inspires other approaches.

Acknowledgments

The author thanks Prof. Eduard Hovy and Dr. Ron Artstein who provided insight and expertise that greatly assisted the research.

References

Rob Abbott, Marilyn Walker, Pranav Anand, Jean E. Fox Tree, Robeson Bowmani, and Joseph King. 2011. How can you say such things?!?: Recognizing disagreement in informal political argument. In *Proceedings of the Workshop on Languages in Social Media*, LSM '11, pages 2–11, Stroudsburg, PA, USA. Association for Computational Linguistics.

Ehud Aharoni, Anatoly Polnarov, Tamar Lavee, Daniel Hershcovich, Ran Levy, Ruty Rinott, Dan Gutfreund, and Noam Slonim. 2014. A benchmark dataset for automatic detection of claims and evidence. In *in the Context of Controversial Topics", in Proceedings of the First Workshop on Argumentation and Computation, ACL 2014*.

Sinan Aral and Dylan Walker. 2012. Identifying influential and susceptible members of social networks. *Science*, 337(6092):337–341.

Shlomo Argamon, Moshe Koppel, James W. Pennebaker, and Jonathan Schler. 2009. Automatically profiling the author of an anonymous text. *Commun. ACM*, 52(2):119–123, feb.

Eytan Bakshy, Jake M. Hofman, Winter A. Mason, and Duncan J. Watts. 2011. Everyone's an influencer: Quantifying influence on twitter. In *Proceedings of the Fourth ACM International Conference on Web Search and Data Mining*, WSDM '11, pages 65–74, New York, NY, USA. ACM.

Or Biran and Owen Rambow. 2011. Identifying justifications in written dialogs. In *Proceedings of the 2011 IEEE Fifth International Conference on Semantic Computing*, ICSC '11, pages 162–168, Washington, DC, USA. IEEE Computer Society.

Elena Cabrio and Serena Villata. 2012. Combining textual entailment and argumentation theory for supporting online debates interactions. In *Proceedings of the 50th Annual Meeting of the Association for Computational Linguistics: Short Papers - Volume 2*, ACL '12, pages 208–212, Stroudsburg, PA, USA. Association for Computational Linguistics.

Alexander Conrad, Janyce Wiebe, and Rebecca Hwa. 2012. Recognizing arguing subjectivity and argument tags. In *Proceedings of the Workshop on Extra-Propositional Aspects of Meaning in Computational Linguistics*, ExProM '12, pages 80–88, Stroudsburg, PA, USA. Association for Computational Linguistics.

Cristian Danescu-Niculescu-Mizil, Moritz Sudhof, Dan Jurafsky, Jure Leskovec, and Christopher Potts. 2013. A computational approach to politeness with application to social factors. *CoRR*, abs/1306.6078.

Rob Ennals, Beth Trushkowsky, and John Mark Agosta. 2010. Highlighting disputed claims on the web. In *Proceedings of the 19th International Conference on World Wide Web*, WWW '10, pages 341–350, New York, NY, USA. ACM.

Joseph L. Fleiss. 1971. Measuring nominal scale agreement among many raters. 76(5):378–382.

Debanjan Ghosh, Smaranda Muresan, Nina Wacholder, Mark Aakhus, and Matthew Mitsui. 2014. Analyzing argumentative discourse units in online interactions. In *Proceedings of the First Workshop on Argumentation Mining*, pages 39–48, Baltimore, Maryland, June. Association for Computational Linguistics.

Kazi Saidul Hasan and Vincent Ng. 2014. Why are you taking this stance? identifying and classifying reasons in ideological debates. In *Proceedings of the 2014 Conference on Empirical Methods in Natural Language Processing (EMNLP)*, pages 751–762, Doha, Qatar, October. Association for Computational Linguistics.

Siddharth Jain, Archna Bhatia, Angelique Rein, and Eduard Hovy. 2014. A corpus of participant roles in contentious discussions. In *Proceedings of the Ninth International Conference on Language Resources and Evaluation (LREC'14)*, Reykjavik, Iceland, may. European Language Resources Association (ELRA).

Mahesh Joshi and Carolyn Penstein-Rosé. 2009. Generalizing dependency features for opinion mining. In *Proceedings of the ACL-IJCNLP 2009 Conference Short Papers*, ACLShort '09, pages 313–316, Stroudsburg, PA, USA. Association for Computational Linguistics.

Namhee Kwon, Liang Zhou, Eduard Hovy, and Stuart W. Shulman. 2007. Identifying and classifying subjective claims. In *Proceedings of the 8th Annual International Conference on Digital Government Research: Bridging Disciplines & Domains*, dg.o '07, pages 76–81. Digital Government Society of North America.

Na Li and Denis Gillet. 2013. Identifying influential scholars in academic social media platforms. In *Proceedings of the 2013 IEEE/ACM International Conference on Advances in Social Networks Analysis and Mining*, ASONAM '13, pages 608–614, New York, NY, USA. ACM.

M. Marneffe, B. Maccartney, and C. Manning. 2006. Generating typed dependency parses from phrase structure parses. In *Proceedings of the Fifth International Conference on Language Resources and Evaluation (LREC-2006)*, Genoa, Italy, May. European Language Resources Association (ELRA).

Marie-Francine Moens, Erik Boiy, Raquel Mochales Palau, and Chris Reed. 2007. Automatic detection of arguments in legal texts. In *Proceedings of the 11th International Conference on Artificial Intelligence and Law*, ICAIL '07, pages 225–230, New York, NY, USA. ACM.

Raquel Mochales Palau and Marie-Francine Moens.
2009. Argumentation mining: The detection, classification and structure of arguments in text. In *Proceedings of the 12th International Conference on Artificial
Intelligence and Law*, ICAIL '09, pages 98–107, New
York, NY, USA. ACM.

Joonsuk Park and Claire Cardie. 2014. Identifying appropriate support for propositions in online user comments. In *Proceedings of the First Workshop on Argumentation Mining*, pages 29–38, Baltimore, Maryland,
June. Association for Computational Linguistics.

Chaïm Perelman, 1979. *The New Rhetoric: A Theory
of Practical Reasoning*, pages 1–42. Springer Netherlands, Dordrecht.

Sara Rosenthal and Kathleen McKeown. 2012. Detecting opinionated claims in online discussions. In *Sixth
IEEE International Conference on Semantic Computing, ICSC 2012, Palermo, Italy, September 19-21,
2012*, pages 30–37.

Beiming Sun and Vincent TY Ng. 2012. Identifying
influential users by their postings in social networks.
In *Proceedings of the 3rd International Workshop on
Modeling Social Media*, MSM '12, pages 1–8, New
York, NY, USA. ACM.

Xuning Tang and Christopher C. Yang. 2012. Ranking
user influence in healthcare social media. *ACM Trans.
Intell. Syst. Technol.*, 3(4):73:1–73:21.

S. Toulmin. 1958. *The Uses of Argument*. Cambridge
University Press, *2nd* edition edition.

`emoji2vec`: Learning Emoji Representations from their Description

Ben Eisner
Princeton University
beisner@princeton.edu

Tim Rocktäschel
University College London
t.rocktaschel@ucl.ac.uk

Isabelle Augenstein
University College London
i.augenstein@ucl.ac.uk

Matko Bošnjak
University College London
m.bosnjak@ucl.ac.uk

Sebastian Riedel
University College London
s.riedel@ucl.ac.uk

Abstract

Many current natural language processing applications for social media rely on representation learning and utilize pre-trained word embeddings. There currently exist several publicly-available, pre-trained sets of word embeddings, but they contain few or no emoji representations even as emoji usage in social media has increased. In this paper we release `emoji2vec`, pre-trained embeddings for all Unicode emoji which are learned from their description in the Unicode emoji standard.[1] The resulting emoji embeddings can be readily used in downstream social natural language processing applications alongside `word2vec`. We demonstrate, for the downstream task of sentiment analysis, that emoji embeddings learned from short descriptions outperforms a skip-gram model trained on a large collection of tweets, while avoiding the need for contexts in which emoji need to appear frequently in order to estimate a representation.

1 Introduction

First introduced in 1997, emoji, a standardized set of small pictorial glyphs depicting everything from smiling faces to international flags, have seen a drastic increase in usage in social media over the last decade. The Oxford Dictionary named 2015 the year of the emoji, citing an increase in usage of over 800% during the course of the year, and elected the 'Face with Tears of Joy' emoji ( ) as the Word of the Year. As of this writing, over 10% of Twitter posts and over 50% of text on Instagram contain one or more emoji (Cruse, 2015).[2] Due to their popularity and broad usage, they have been the subject of much formal and informal research in language and social communication, as well as in natural language processing (NLP).

In the context of social sciences, research has focused on emoji usage as a means of expressing emotions on mobile platforms. Interestingly, Kelly and Watts (2015) found that although essentially thought of as means of expressing emotions, emoji have been adopted as tools to express relationally useful roles in conversation. (Lebduska, 2014) showed that emoji are culturally and contextually bound, and are open to reinterpretation and misinterpretation, a result confirmed by (Miller et al., 2016). These findings have paved the way for many formal analyses of semantic characteristics of emoji.

Concurrently we observe an increased interest in natural language processing on social media data (Ritter et al., 2011; Gattani et al., 2013; Rosenthal et al., 2015). Many current NLP systems applied to social media rely on representation learning and word embeddings (Tang et al., 2014; Dong et al., 2014; Dhingra et al., 2016; Augenstein et al.,

---

[1] http://www.unicode.org/emoji/charts/full-emoji-list.html

[2] See https://twitter.com/Kyle_MacLachlan/status/765390472604971009 for an extreme example.

48

Proceedings of The Fourth International Workshop on Natural Language Processing for Social Media, pages 48–54,
Austin, TX, November 1, 2016. ©2016 Association for Computational Linguistics

2016). Such systems often rely on pre-trained word embeddings that can for instance be obtained from `word2vec` (Mikolov et al., 2013a) or `GloVe` (Pennington et al., 2014). Yet, neither resource contain a complete set of Unicode emoji representations, which suggests that many social NLP applications could be improved by the addition of robust emoji representations.

In this paper we release `emoji2vec`, embeddings for emoji Unicode symbols learned from their description in the Unicode emoji standard. We demonstrate the usefulness of emoji representations trained in this way by evaluating on a Twitter sentiment analysis task. Furthermore, we provide a qualitative analysis by investigating emoji analogy examples and visualizing the emoji embedding space.

2 Related Work

There has been little work in distributional embeddings of emoji. The first research done in this direction was an informal blog post by the Instagram Data Team in 2015 (Dimson, 2015). They generated vector embeddings for emoji similar to skip-gram-based vectors by training on the entire corpus of Instagram posts. Their research gave valuable insight into the usage of emoji on Instagram, and showed that distributed representations can help understanding emoji semantics in everyday usage. The second contribution, closest to ours, was introduced by (Barbieri et al., 2016). They trained emoji embeddings from a large Twitter dataset of over 100 million English tweets using the skip-gram method (Mikolov et al., 2013a). These pre-trained emoji representations led to increased accuracy on a similarity task, and a meaningful clustering of the emoji embedding space. While this method is able to learn robust representations for frequently-used emoji, representations of less frequent emoji are estimated rather poorly or not available at all. In fact, only around 700 emoji can be found in Barbieri et al. (2016)'s corpus, while there is support of over 1600 emoji in the Unicode standard.

Our approach differs in two important aspects. First, since we are estimating the representation of emoji directly from their description, we obtain robust representations for all supported emoji symbols — even the long tail of infrequently used ones. Sec-

❗ Man in Business Suit Levitating

Figure 1: Example description of U+1F574. We also use *business*, *man* and *suit* keywords for training.

ondly, our method works with much less data. Instead of training on millions of tweets, our representations are trained on only a few thousand descriptions. Still, we obtain higher accuracy results on a Twitter sentiment analysis task.

In addition, our work relates to the work of Hill et al. (2016) who built word representations for words and concepts based on their description in a dictionary. Similarly to their approach, we build representations for emoji based on their descriptions and keyword phrases.

Some of the limitations of our work are evident in the work of Park et al. (2013) who showed that different cultural phenomena and languages may co-opt conventional emoji sentiment. Since we train only on English-language definitions and ignore temporal definitions of emoji, our training method might not capture the full semantic characteristics of an emoji.

3 Method

Our method maps emoji symbols into the same space as the 300-dimensional Google News `word2vec` embeddings. Thus, the resulting `emoji2vec` embeddings can be used in addition to 300-dimensional `word2vec` embeddings in any application. To this end we crawl emoji, their name and their keyword phrases from the Unicode emoji list, resulting in 6088 descriptions of 1661 emoji symbols. Figure 1 shows an example for an uncommon emoji.

3.1 Model

We train emoji embeddings using a simple method. For every training example consisting of an emoji and a sequence of words $w_1, \ldots, w_N$ describing that emoji, we take the sum of the individual word vectors in the descriptive phrase as found in the Google News `word2vec` embeddings

$$v_j = \sum_{k=1}^{N} w_k$$

where w_k is the `word2vec` vector for word w_k if that vector exists (otherwise we drop the summand) and v_j is the vector representation of the description. We define a trainable vector x_i for every emoji in our training set, and model the probability of a match between the emoji representation x_i and its description representation v_j using the sigmoid of the dot product of the two representations $\sigma(x_i^T v_j)$. For training we use the logistic loss

$$\mathcal{L}(i, j, y_{ij}) = -\log(\sigma(y_{ij} x_i^T v_j - (1 - y_{ij}) x_i^T v_j))$$

where y_{ij} is 1 if description j is valid for emoji i and 0 otherwise.

3.2 Optimization

Our model is implemented in TensorFlow (Abadi et al., 2015) and optimized using stochastic gradient descent with Adam (Kingma and Ba, 2015) as optimizer. As we do not observe any negative training examples (invalid descriptions of emoji do not appear in the original training set), to increase generalization performance we randomly sample descriptions for emoji as negative instances (i.e. induce a mismatched description). One of the parameters of our model is the ratio of negative samples to positive samples; we found that having one positive example per negative example produced the best results. We perform early-stopping on a held-out development set and found 80 epochs of training to give the best results. As we are only training on emoji descriptions and our method is simple and cheap, training takes less than 3 minutes on a 2013 MacBook Pro.

4 Evaluation

We quantitatively evaluate our approach on an intrinsic (emoji-description classification) and extrinsic (Twitter sentiment analysis) task. Furthermore, we give a qualitative analysis by visualizing the learned emoji embedding space and investigating emoji analogy examples.

4.1 Emoji-Description Classification

To analyze how well our method models the distribution of correct emoji descriptions, we created a manually-labeled test set containing pairs of emoji and phrases, as well as a correspondence label. For instance, our test set includes the example: {😄,

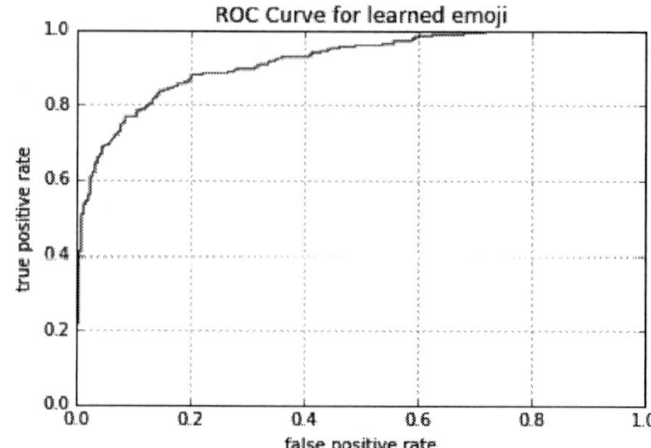

Figure 2: Receiver operating characteristic curve for learned emoji vectors evaluated against the test set.

"crying", True}, as well as the example {🐟, "fish", False}. We calculate $\sigma(x_i^T v_i)$ for each example in the test set, measuring the similarity between the emoji vector and the sum of word vectors in the phrase.

When a classifier thresholds the above prediction at 0.5 to determine a positive or negative correlation, we obtain an accuracy of 85.5% for classifying whether an emoji-description pair is valid or not. By varying the threshold used for this classifier, we obtain a receiver operating characteristic curve (Figure 4.1) with an area-under-the-curve of 0.933, which demonstrates that high quality of the learned emoji representations.

4.2 Sentiment Analysis on Tweets

As downstream task we compare the accuracy of sentiment classification of tweets for various classifiers with three different sets of pre-trained word embeddings: (1) the original Google News `word2vec` embeddings, (2) `word2vec` augmented with emoji embeddings trained by Barbieri et al. (2016), and (3) `word2vec` augmented with `emoji2vec` trained from Unicode descriptions. We use the recent dataset by Kralj Novak et al. (2015), which consists of over 67k English tweets labelled manually for positive, neutral, or negative sentiment. In both the training set and the test set, 46% of tweets are labeled neutral, 29% are labeled positive, and 25% are labeled negative. To compute the feature vectors for training, we summed the vectors corresponding to each word or emoji in the text of the Tweet. The goal of this simple sentiment analysis model is not to produce state-of-the-art results in sentiment analysis; it is simply to show that including emoji adds discriminating information to a model, which could potentially be exploited in more advanced social NLP systems.

Because the labels are rather evenly distributed, accuracy is an effective metric in determining performance on this classification task. Results are reported in Table 1. We find that augmenting `word2vec` with emoji embeddings improves overall classification accuracy on the full corpus, and substantially improves classification performance for tweets that contain emoji. It suggests that emoji embeddings could improve performance for other social NLP tasks as well. Furthermore, we find that `emoji2vec` generally outperforms the emoji embeddings trained by Barbieri et al. (2016), despite being trained on much less data using a simple model.

4.3 t-SNE Visualization

To gain further insights, we project the learned emoji embeddings into two-dimensional space using t-SNE (Maaten and Hinton, 2008). This method projects high-dimensional embeddings into a lower-dimensional space while attempting to preserve relative distances. We perform this projection of emoji representation into two-dimensional space.

From Figure 4.3 we see a number of notable semantic clusters, indicating that the vectors we trained have accurately captured some of the semantic properties of the emoji. For instance, all flag symbols are clustered in the bottom, and many smiley faces in the center. Other prominent emoji clusters include fruits, astrological signs, animals, vehicles, or families. On the other hand, symbolic representations of numbers are not properly disentangled in the embedding space, indicating limitations of our simple model. A two-dimensional projection is convenient from a visualization perspective, and certainly shows that some intuitively similar emoji are close to each other in vector space.

4.4 Analogy Task

A well-known property of `word2vec` is that embeddings trained with this method to some extent capture meaningful linear relationships between words directly in the vector space. For instance, it holds that the vector representation of 'king' minus 'man' plus 'woman' is closest to 'queen' (Mikolov et al., 2013b). Word embeddings have commonly been evaluated on such word analogy tasks (Levy and Goldberg, 2014). Unfortunately, it is difficult to build such an analogy task for emoji due to the small number and semantically distinct categories of emoji. Nevertheless, we collected a few intuitive examples in Figure 4. For every query we have retrieved the closest five emoji. Though the correct answer is sometimes not the top one, it is often contained in the top three.

Figure 4: Emoji analogy exmaples. Notice that the seemingly "correct" emoji often appears in the top three closest vectors, but not always in the top spot (furthest to the left).

5 Conclusion

Since existing pre-trained word embeddings such as Google News `word2vec` embeddings or `GloVe` fail to provide emoji embeddings, we have released `emoji2vec` — embeddings of 1661 emoji symbols. Instead of running `word2vec`'s skip-gram model on a large collection of emoji and their contexts appearing in tweets, `emoji2vec` is directly trained on Unicode descriptions of emoji. The resulting emoji embeddings can be used to augment any downstream task that currently uses `word2vec` embeddings, and might prove especially useful in social NLP tasks where emoji are used frequently (*e.g.* Twitter, Instagram, etc.). Despite the fact that our model is simpler and trained on much less data, we outperform (Barbieri et al., 2016) on the task of Twitter sentiment analysis.

As our approach directly works on Unicode descriptions, it is not restricted to emoji symbols. In the future we want to investigate the usefulness of our method for other Unicode symbol embeddings. Furthermore, we plan to improve `emoji2vec` in the future by also reading full text emoji description

Classification accuracy on entire dataset, $N = 12920$		
Word Embeddings	Random Forest	Linear SVM
Google News	57.5	58.5
Google News + (Barbieri et al., 2016)	58.2[*]	60.0[*]
Google News + `emoji2vec`	**59.5[*]**	**60.5[*]**

Classification accuracy on tweets containing emoji, $N = 2295$		
Word Embeddings	Random Forrest	Linear SVM
Google News	46.0	47.1
Google News + (Barbieri et al., 2016)	52.4[*]	57.4[*]
Google News + `emoji2vec`	**54.4[*]**	**59.2[*]**

Classification accuracy on 90% most frequent emoji, $N = 2186$		
Word Embeddings	Random Forrest	Linear SVM
Google News	47.3	45.1
Google News + (Barbieri et al., 2016)	52.8[*]	56.9[*]
Google News + `emoji2vec`	**55.0[*]**	**59.5[*]**

Classification accuracy on 10% least frequent emoji, $N = 308$		
Word Embeddings	Random Forrest	Linear SVM
Google News	44.7	43.2
Google News + (Barbieri et al., 2016)	53.9[*]	52.9[*]
Google News + `emoji2vec`	**54.5[*]**	**55.2[*]**

Table 1: Three-way classification accuracy on the Twitter sentiment analysis corpus using Random Forrests (Ho, 1995) and Linear SVM (Fan et al., 2008) classifier with different word embeddings. "*" denotes results with significance of $p < 0.05$ as calculated by McNemar's test, with the respect to classification with Google News embeddings per each classifier, and dataset

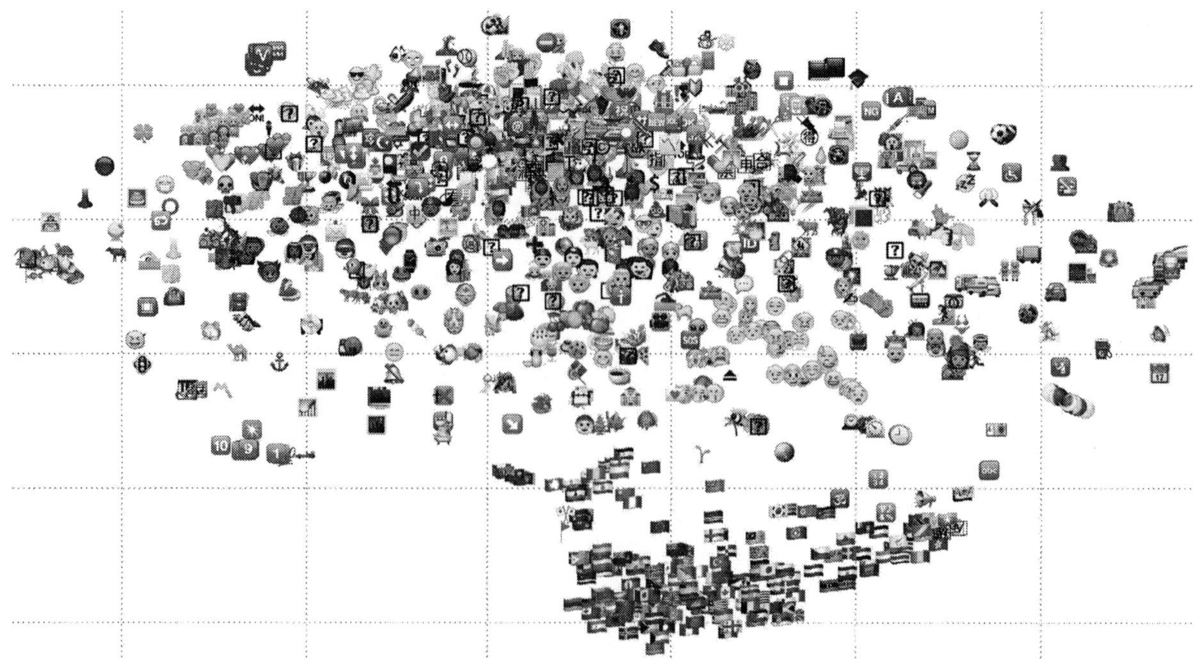

Figure 3: Emoji vector embeddings, projected down into a 2-dimensional space using the t-SNE technique. Note the clusters of similar emoji like flags (bottom), family emoji (top left), zodiac symbols (top left), animals (left), smileys (middle), etc.

from Emojipedia[3] and using a recurrent neural network instead of a bag-of-word-vectors approach for enocoding descriptions. In addition, since our approach does not capture the context-dependent definitions of emoji (such as sarcasm, or appropriation via other cultural phenomena), we would like to explore mechanisms of efficiently capturing these nuanced meanings.

Data Release and Reproducibility

Pre-trained `emoji2vec` embeddings as well as the training data and code are released at `https://github.com/uclmr/emoji2vec`. Note that the `emoji2vec` format is compatible with `word2vec` and can be loaded into gensim[4] or similar libraries.

References

Martın Abadi, Ashish Agarwal, Paul Barham, Eugene Brevdo, Zhifeng Chen, Craig Citro, Greg S Corrado, Andy Davis, Jeffrey Dean, Matthieu Devin, et al. 2015. TensorFlow: Large-Scale Machine Learning on Heterogeneous Distributed Systems. *Software available from tensorflow. org*, 1.

Isabelle Augenstein, Tim Rocktäschel, Andreas Vlachos, and Kalina Bontcheva. 2016. Stance Detection with Bidirectional Conditional Encoding. In *Proceedings of EMLNP*.

Francesco Barbieri, Francesco Ronzano, and Horacio Saggion. 2016. What does this Emoji Mean? A Vector Space Skip-Gram Model for Twitter Emojis. In *Proceedings of LREC*, May.

Joe Cruse. 2015. Emoji usage in TV conversation.

Bhuwan Dhingra, Zhong Zhou, Dylan Fitzpatrick, Michael Muehl, and William Cohen. 2016. Tweet2Vec: Character-Based Distributed Representations for Social Media. In *Proceedings of ACL*, pages 269–274.

Thomas Dimson. 2015. Machine Learning for Emoji Trends. `http://instagram-engineering.tumblr.com/post/117889701472/emojineering-part-1-machine-learning-for-emoji`. Accessed: 2016-09-05.

Li Dong, Furu Wei, Chuanqi Tan, Duyu Tang, Ming Zhou, and Ke Xu. 2014. Adaptive Recursive Neural Network for Target-dependent Twitter Sentiment Classification. In *Proceedings of ACL*, pages 49–54.

Rong-En Fan, Kai-Wei Chang, Cho-Jui Hsieh, Xiang-Rui Wang, and Chih-Jen Lin. 2008. Liblinear: A library for large linear classification. *Journal of machine learning research*, 9(Aug):1871–1874.

Abhishek Gattani, Digvijay S Lamba, Nikesh Garera, Mitul Tiwari, Xiaoyong Chai, Sanjib Das, Sri Subramaniam, Anand Rajaraman, Venky Harinarayan, and AnHai Doan. 2013. Entity Extraction, Linking, Classification, and Tagging for Social Media: A Wikipedia-Based Approach. *In Proceedings of the VLDB Endowment*, 6(11):1126–1137.

Felix Hill, Kyunghyun Cho, Anna Korhonen, and Yoshua Bengio. 2016. Learning to Understand Phrases by Embedding the Dictionary. *TACL*.

Tin Kam Ho. 1995. Random decision forests. In *Document Analysis and Recognition, 1995., Proceedings of the Third International Conference on*, volume 1, pages 278–282. IEEE.

Ryan Kelly and Leon Watts. 2015. Characterising the inventive appropriation of emoji as relationally meaningful in mediated close personal relationships. *Experiences of Technology Appropriation: Unanticipated Users, Usage, Circumstances, and Design*.

Diederik Kingma and Jimmy Ba. 2015. Adam: A Method for Stochastic Optimization. In *Proceedings of ICLR*.

Petra Kralj Novak, Jasmina Smailović, Borut Sluban, and Igor Mozetič. 2015. Sentiment of Emojis. *PLoS ONE*, 10(12):1–22, 12.

Lisa Lebduska. 2014. Emoji, Emoji, What for Art Thou? *Harlot: A Revealing Look at the Arts of Persuasion*, 1(12).

Omer Levy and Yoav Goldberg. 2014. Linguistic Regularities in Sparse and Explicit Word Representations. In *Proceedings of ConLL*, pages 171–180.

Laurens van der Maaten and Geoffrey Hinton. 2008. Visualizing data using t-sne. *Journal of Machine Learning Research*, 9(Nov):2579–2605.

Tomas Mikolov, Ilya Sutskever, Kai Chen, Greg S Corrado, and Jeff Dean. 2013a. Distributed Representations of Words and Phrases and their Compositionality. In *Proceedings of NIPS*, pages 3111–3119.

Tomas Mikolov, Wen-tau Yih, and Geoffrey Zweig. 2013b. Linguistic Regularities in Continuous Space Word Representations. In *Proceedings of NAACL-HLT*, pages 746–751.

Hannah Miller, Jacob Thebault-Spieker, Shuo Chang, Isaac Johnson, Loren Terveen, and Brent Hecht. 2016. "Blissfully happy" or "ready to fight": Varying Interpretations of Emoji. In *Proceedings of ICWSM*.

---

[3]`emojipedia.org`

[4]`https://radimrehurek.com/gensim/models/word2vec.html`

Jaram Park, Vladimir Barash, Clay Fink, and Meeyoung Cha. 2013. Emoticon style: Interpreting differences in emoticons across cultures. In *ICWSM*.

Jeffrey Pennington, Richard Socher, and Christopher Manning. 2014. Glove: Global Vectors for Word Representation. In *Proceedings of EMNLP*, pages 1532–1543, October.

Alan Ritter, Sam Clark, Mausam, and Oren Etzioni. 2011. Named Entity Recognition in Tweets: An Experimental Study. In *Proceedings of EMNLP*, pages 1524–1534.

Sara Rosenthal, Preslav Nakov, Svetlana Kiritchenko, Saif Mohammad, Alan Ritter, and Veselin Stoyanov. 2015. SemEval-2015 Task 10: Sentiment Analysis in Twitter. In *Proceedings of the SemEval*, pages 451–463.

Duyu Tang, Furu Wei, Nan Yang, Ming Zhou, Ting Liu, and Bing Qin. 2014. Learning Sentiment-Specific Word Embedding for Twitter Sentiment Classification. In *Proceedings of ACL*, pages 1555–1565.

Learning Latent Local Conversation Modes for Predicting Community Endorsement in Online Discussions

Hao Fang   Hao Cheng   Mari Ostendorf
University of Washington
{hfang,chenghao,ostendorf}@uw.edu

Abstract

Many social media platforms offer a mechanism for readers to react to comments, both positively and negatively, which in aggregate can be thought of as community endorsement. This paper addresses the problem of predicting community endorsement in online discussions, leveraging both the participant response structure and the text of the comment. The different types of features are integrated in a neural network that uses a novel architecture to learn latent modes of discussion structure that perform as well as deep neural networks but are more interpretable. In addition, the latent modes can be used to weight text features thereby improving prediction accuracy.

1   Introduction

Online discussion forums provide a platform for people with shared interests (online communities) to discuss current events and common concerns. Many forums provide a mechanism for readers to indicate positive/negative reactions to comments in the discussion, with up/down votes, "liking," or indicating whether a comment is useful. The cumulative reaction, which we will refer to as "community endorsement," can be useful to readers for prioritizing what they read or in gathering information for decision making. This paper introduces the task of automatically predicting the level of endorsement of a comment based on the response structure of the discussion and the text of the comment. To address this task, we introduce a neural network architecture that learns latent discussion structure (or, conversation) modes and adjusts the relative dependence on text vs. structural cues in classification. The neural network framework is also useful for combining text with the disparate features that characterize the submission context of a comment, i.e. relative timing in the discussion, response structure (characterized by graph features), and author indexing.

The idea of conversation modes stems from the observation that regions of a discussion can be qualitatively different: low vs. high activity, many participants vs. a few, etc. Points of high activity in the discussion (comments that elicit many responses) tend to have higher community endorsement, but some points of high activity are due to controversy. We hypothesize that these cases can be distinguished by the submission context, which we characterize with a vector of graph and timing features extracted from the local subgraph of a comment. The context vectors are modeled as a weighted combination of latent basis vectors corresponding to the different modes, where bases are learned using the weak supervision signal of community endorsement. We further hypothesize that the nature of the submission context impacts the relative importance of the actual text in a comment; hence, a mode-dependent gating mechanism is introduced to weight the contribution of text features in estimating community endorsement.

The model is assessed in experiments on Reddit discussion forum data, using karma (the difference in numbers of up and down votes) as a proxy for community endorsement, showing benefits from both the latent modes and the gating. As described further below, the prediction task differs somewhat from prior work on popularity prediction in two respects. First, the data is not constrained to control

Proceedings of The Fourth International Workshop on Natural Language Processing for Social Media, pages 55–64,
Austin, TX, November 1, 2016. ©2016 Association for Computational Linguistics

for either submission context or comment/post content, but rather the goal is to learn different context modes that impact the importance of the message. Second, the use of the full discussion thread vs. a limited time window puts a focus on participant interaction in understanding community endorsement.

2   Related Work

The cumulative response of readers to social media and online content has been studied using a variety of measurements, including: the volume of comments in response to blog posts (Yano and Smith, 2010) and news articles (Tasgkias et al., 2009; Tatar et al., 2011), the number of Twitter shares of news articles (Bandari et al., 2012), the number of reshares on Facebook (Cheng et al., 2014) and retweets on Twitter (Suh et al., 2010; Hong et al., 2011; Tan et al., 2014; Zhao et al., 2015), and the difference in the number of reader up and down votes on posts and comments in Reddit discussion forums (Lakkaraju et al., 2013; Jaech et al., 2015). An advantage of working with the Reddit data is that both positive and negative reactions are accounted for, so the total (karma in Reddit) is a reasonable proxy for community endorsement.

For all the different types of measures, a challenge in predicting the cumulative reaction is that the cases of most interest are at the tails of a Zipfian distribution. Various prediction tasks have been proposed with this in mind, including regression on a log score (Bandari et al., 2012), classification into 3-4 groups (e.g. none, low, high) (Tasgkias et al., 2009; Hong et al., 2011; Yano and Smith, 2010), a binary decision as to whether the score will double given a current score (Lakkaraju et al., 2013), and relative ranking of comments (Tan et al., 2014; Jaech et al., 2015). In our work, we take the approach of classification, but use a finer grain quantization with bins automatically determined by the score distribution.

The work on cumulative reaction has mostly considered two different scenarios: predicting responses before a comment/document has been published vs. after a limited lookahead time for extracting features based on the initial response. While the framework proposed here could handle either scenario, the experiments reported allow the classifier to use a longer future window, until most of the discussion

has played out. This provides insight into the difficulty of the task and illustrates that volume of responses alone does not reliably predict endorsement.

A few studies investigate language factors that may impact popularity through carefully controlled experiments. To tease apart the factor of content quality, Lakkaraju et al. (2013) predict resharing of duplicated image submissions, investigating both the submission context (community, time of day, resubmission statistics) and language factors. Our work differs in that content is not controlled and the submission context includes the response structure and relative timing of the comment within the discussion. Tan et al. (2014) futher control the author and temporal factors in addition to the topic of the content, by ranking pairs of tweets with almost identical content made by the same author within a limited time window. Jaech et al. (2015) control the temporal factor for ranking Reddit comments made in a time-limited window and study different language factors. Here, rather than manually controlling the submission context, we propose a model to discover latent modes of submission context (relative timing, response structure) and analyze its utility in predicting community endorsement. Furthermore, we study how the usefulness of language information in estimating the community endorsement varies depending on submission context.

3   Data and Task

Data: *Reddit* (https://www.reddit.com) is a discussion forum with thousands of subcommunities organized as *subreddits*. Users can initiate a tree-structured discussion thread by making a post in a subreddit. Comments are made either directly to the root post or to other comments within the thread, sometimes triggering sub-discussions. Each comment can receive upvotes and downvotes from registered users; the difference is shown as the *karma* score beside the comment. The graph structure of a Reddit disccussion thread is shown in Fig. 1.[1] In this paper, three popular subreddits are studied: AskMen (1,057K comments), AskWomen (814K comments), and Politics (2,180K comments).

---

[1] Visualization obtained from https://whichlight.github.io/reddit-network-vis.

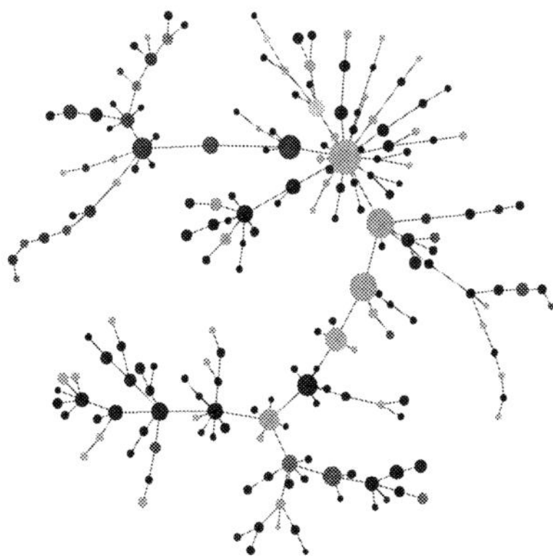

Figure 1: Visualization of a Reddit discussion thread. The orange node represents the root post; other nodes are comments (size proportional to karma), which are in black unless the user comments more than once in the thread.

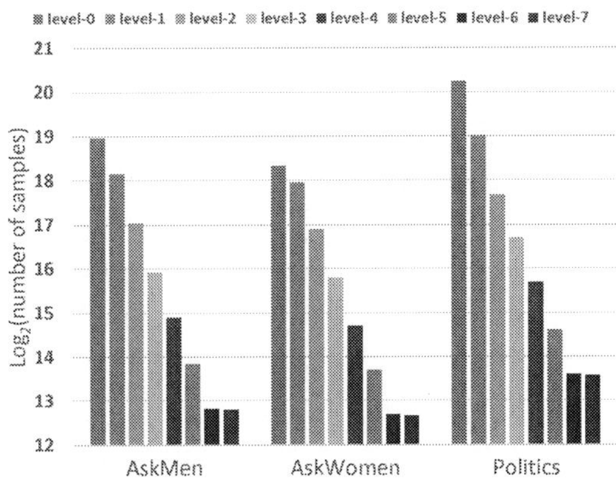

Figure 2: The data distribution for each subreddit.

Task: In many discussion forums, including the those explored here, community endorsement (i.e., karma in Reddit) has a heavy-tailed Zipfian distribution, with most comments getting minimal endorsement and high endorsement comments being rare. Since the high endorsement comments are of most interest, we do not want to treat this as a regression problem using a mean squared error (MSE) objective.[2] Instead, we quantize the karma into $J + 1$ discrete levels and design a task consisting of J binary classification subtasks which individually predict whether a comment has karma of at least level-j for each level $j = 1, \ldots, J$ given the text of the comment and the structure of the full discussion thread. (All samples have karma at least level-0.)

Karma scores are quantized into 8 levels of community endorsement according to statistics computed over a large collection of comments in the subreddit. The quantization process is similar to the head-tail break rule described in (Jiang, 2013). First, comments with karma no more than 1 are labeled as level-0, indicating that these comments receive no more upvotes than downvotes.[3] Then, we compute the median karma score for the rest of the comments, and label those with below-than-median karma as level-1. This process is repeated through level-6, and the remaining comments are labeled as

level-7. The resulting data distributions are shown in Fig. 2. Note that the quantization is subreddit dependent, since the distribution and range of karma tends to vary for different subreddits.

Evaluation metric: Since we use a quantization scheme following a binary thresholding process, we can compute the F1 score for each level-j subtask ($j = 1, 2, \ldots, 7$) by treating comments whose predicted level is lower than j as negative samples and others as positive samples. To evaluate the overall prediction performance, the seven F1 scores are aggregated via a macro average, which effectively puts a higher weight on the higher endorsement levels.

4 Model Description

The proposed model utilizes two kinds of information for a comment to predict its quantized karma: (1) the submission context encoded by a set of graph and timing statistics, and (2) the textual content of the comment itself. Both sources of information are first embedded in a continuous space by a neural network as illustrated in Fig. 3, where $\mathbf{c} \in \mathbb{R}^C$ and $\mathbf{d} \in \mathbb{R}^D$ encode the submission context and the textual content, respectively. As described further below, the two vectors are transformed for use in the final decision function to $\tilde{\mathbf{c}}$, a linear combination of latent basis vectors, and $\tilde{\mathbf{d}}$, a context-dependent weighted version of the text features.

Submission context modes: Reddit discussions have a variety of conversation structures, including sections involving many contributors or just a few. Based on observations that high karma com-

---

[2] A prediction error of 50 is minimal for a comment with karma of 500 but substantial for a comment with karma of 1, and the low karma comments dominate the overall MSE.

[3] The inital karma score of a comment is 1.

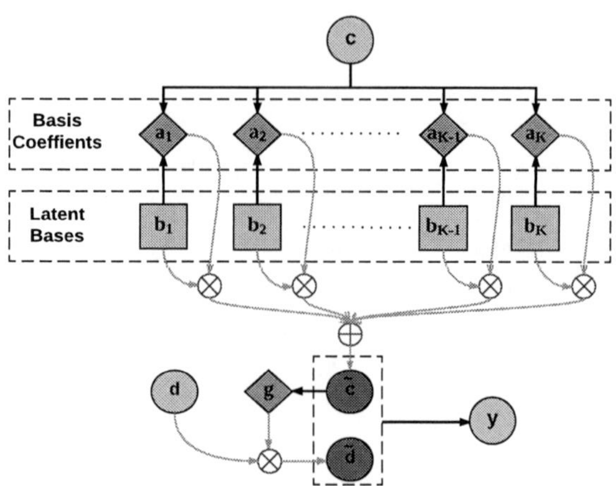

Figure 3: Proposed model: Gray circles **c** and **d** are the projected submission context features and the encoded textual content vector, respectively. Blue boxes $\mathbf{b}_1, \cdots, \mathbf{b}_K$ are latent basis vectors, which are learned by the neural network. Purple diamonds $\mathbf{a}_1, \cdots, \mathbf{a}_K$ and **g** represent scalers, i.e., the basis coefficients and context-dependent gate value. Red circles $\tilde{\mathbf{c}}$ and $\tilde{\mathbf{d}}$ are the context embedding (i.e., a linear combination of latent basis vectors) and the weighted text embedding, respectively. The yellow circle **y** is the output layer. Black arrows are connections carrying weight matrices. $\otimes$ and $\oplus$ indicate multiplication and element-wise addition, respectively.

ments seem to co-occur with active points of discussions, we identify a set of features to represent the submission context of a comment, specifically aiming to characterize relative timing of the comment within the discussion, participant response to the comment, and whether the comment author is the original poster (see Table 1 for the full list). The features are normalized to zero mean and unit variance based on the training set.

In this paper, instead of controlling for the submission context, we let the model learn latent modes of submission context and examine how the learned context modes relate to different levels of community endorsement. The proposed model learns K latent basis vectors $\mathbf{b}_1, \cdots, \mathbf{b}_K \in \mathbb{R}^C$ for characterizing the submission context of a particular comment in the discussion. Given the raw submission context feature vector $\mathbf{x} \in \mathbb{R}^N$, the model computes a vector $\mathbf{c} \in \mathbb{R}^C$ as $\mathbf{c} = \mathrm{LReL}(\mathbf{Px})$, where $\mathbf{P} \in \mathbb{R}^{C \times N}$ is a projection matrix, and $\mathrm{LReL}(\cdot)$ is the leaky rectified linear function (Mass et al., 2013) with 0.1 as the slope of the negative part. Coefficients for these

Range	Description
0/1	Whether the comment author is the user who initiated the thread.
$\mathbb{Z}_{\geq 0}$	Number of replies to the comment. Number of comments in the subtree rooted from the comment. Height of the subtree rooted from the comment. Depth of the comment in the tree rooted from the original post.
$\mathbb{R}_{\geq 0}$	Relative comment time (in hours) with respect to the original post. Relative comment time (in hours) with respect to the parent comment.

Table 1: Features for representing the conversation structure.

K latent bases are then estimated as

$$a_k = \mathrm{softmax}(\mathbf{v}^T \tanh(\mathbf{U}\,[\mathbf{c};\ \mathbf{b}_k])),$$

where $\mathbf{v} \in \mathbb{R}^C$ and $\mathbf{U} \in \mathbb{R}^{C \times 2C}$ are parameters to be learned. The final submission context embedding is obtained as $\tilde{\mathbf{c}} = \sum_{k=1}^{K} a_k \cdot \mathbf{b}_k \in \mathbb{R}^C$.

The computation of basis coefficients is similar to the attention mechanism that has been used in the context of machine translation (Bahdanau et al., 2015), constituency parsing (Vinyals et al., 2015), question answering and language modeling (Weston et al., 2015; Sukhbaatar et al., 2015). To the best of our knowledge, this is the first attempt to use the attention mechanism for latent basis learning.

Text embeddings: Recurrent neural networks (RNNs) have been widely used to obtain sequence embeddings for different applications in recent years (Sutskever et al., 2014; Cheng et al., 2015; Palangi et al., 2016). In this paper, we use a bi-directional RNN to encode each sentence, and concatenate the hidden layers at the last time step of each direction as the sentence embedding. For comments with multiple sentences, we average the sentence embeddings into a single vector as the textual content embedding $\mathbf{d} \in \mathbb{R}^D$.

For the t-th token in a sentence, the hidden layers of the bi-directional RNN are computed as

$$\mathbf{h}_t^{(l)} = \mathrm{GRU}(\mathbf{z}_t, \mathbf{h}_{t-1}^{(l)}), \quad \mathbf{h}_t^{(r)} = \mathrm{GRU}(\mathbf{z}_t, \mathbf{h}_{t+1}^{(r)}),$$

where $\mathbf{z}_t \in \mathbb{R}^D$ is the token input vector, $\mathbf{h}_t^{(l)} \in \mathbb{R}^D$ and $\mathbf{h}_t^{(r)} \in \mathbb{R}^D$ are the hidden layers for the left-to-right and right-to-left directions, respectively, and

$\text{GRU}(\cdot, \cdot)$ denotes the gated recurrent unit (GRU), which is proposed by Cho et al. (2014) as a simpler alternative to the long short-term memory unit (Hochreiter and Schmidhuber, 1997) for addressing the vanishing gradient issue in RNNs. For consistency of the model and consideration of computation speed, we replace the hyperbolic tangent function in the GRU with the LReL function. Although not shown in Fig. 3, weight matrices in the bi-directional RNN are jointly learned with all other parameters.

To generate the token input vector to the RNN, we utilize the lemma and part-of-speech (POS) tag of each token (obtained with the Stanford CoreNLP toolkit (Manning et al., 2014)), in addition to its word form. A token embedding $\mathbf{z}_t \in \mathbb{R}^D$ for the t-th token in a sentence is computed as

$$\mathbf{z}_t = \mathbf{E}^{\text{word}}\mathbf{e}_t^{\text{word}} + \mathbf{E}^{\text{pos}}\mathbf{e}_t^{\text{pos}} + \mathbf{E}^{\text{lemma}}\mathbf{e}_t^{\text{lemma}},$$

where $\mathbf{e}_t$'s are one-hot encoding vectors for the token, and $\mathbf{E}$'s are parameters to be learned. The dimensions of these one-hot encoding vectors are determined by the size of the corresponding vocabularies, which include all observed types except singletons. Thus, these embedding matrices $\mathbf{E}$'s have the same first dimension D but different second dimensions. This type of additive token embedding has been used in (Botha and Blunsom, 2014; Fang et al., 2015) to integrate various types of information about the token. Moreover, it reduces the tuning space since we only need to make a single decision on the dimensionality of the token embedding.

Gating mechanism: For estimating comment karma levels, the textual content should provide additional information beyond the submission context. However, we hypothesize that the usefulness of textual content may vary under different submission contexts since structure reflects size of the readership. Therefore, we design a context-dependent gating mechanism in the proposed model to weight the textual factors. A scalar gate value is estimated from the submission context embedding $\tilde{\mathbf{c}}$, i.e., $g = \text{sigmoid}(\mathbf{w}^T\tilde{\mathbf{c}})$, where $\mathbf{w} \in \mathbb{R}^C$ is the parameter to be learned. The textual content embedding $\mathbf{d} \in \mathbb{R}^D$ is scaled by the gate value g before being fed to the output layer, i.e., $\tilde{\mathbf{d}} = g \cdot \mathbf{d}$.

Decision function: The estimated probability distribution $\mathbf{y} = [y_0, \ldots, y_7]$ over all quantized karma levels is computed by the softmax output layer, i.e., $\mathbf{y} = \text{softmax}(\mathbf{Q}\left[\tilde{\mathbf{c}}; \tilde{\mathbf{d}}\right])$, where $\mathbf{Q} \in \mathbb{R}^{J \times (C+D)}$ is the weight matrix to be learned. The hypothesized level for a comment is $\hat{\mathcal{L}} = \text{argmax}_j y_j$. For each level-$j$ subtask, both the label $\mathcal{L}$ and the hypothesis $\hat{\mathcal{L}}$ are converted to binary values by checking the condition whether they are no less than j.

5 Parameter Learning

To train the proposed model, each comment is treated as an independent sample, and the objective is the maximum log-likelihood of these samples. We use mini-batch stochastic gradient descent with a batch size of 32, where the gradients are computed with the back-propagation algorithm (Rumelhart et al., 1986). Specifically, the Adam algorithm is used (Kingma and Ba, 2015). The initial learning rate is selected from the range of [0.0010, 0.0100], with a step size of 0.0005, according to the log-likelihood of the validation data at the first epoch. The learning rate is halved at each epoch once the log-likelihood of the validation data decreases. The whole training procedure terminates when the log-likelihood decreases for the second time.

Each comment is treated as a data sample, and assigned to a partition number in $\{0, 1, \ldots, 9\}$ according to the thread it belongs to. Each partition has roughly the same number of threads. We use partitions 4–9 as training data, partitions 2–3 as validation data, and partitions 0–1 as test data, The training data are shuffled at the beginning of each epoch.

As discussed in Section 3, there are many more low-level comments than high-level comments, and the evaluation metric effectively puts more emphasis on high-level comments. Therefore, rather than using the full training and validation sets, we subsample the low-level comments (level-0, level-1, level-2, level-3) such that each level has roughly the same number of samples as level-4. Since the three subreddits studied in this paper vary in their sizes, to eliminate the factor of training data size, we use similar amounts of training ($\sim$90K comments) and validation ($\sim$30K comments) data for these subreddits. Note that we do not subsample the test data, i.e., 192K for `AskMen`, 463K for `AskWomen`, and 1,167K for `Politics`.

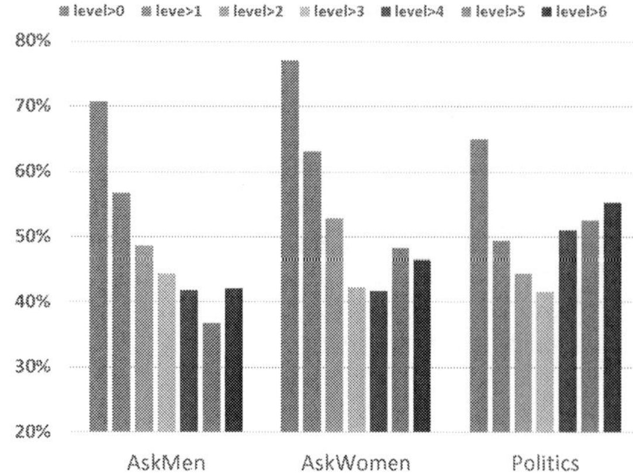

Figure 4: Individual F1 scores for the full model.

	AskMen	AskWomen	Politics
SubtreeSize	39.1	42.9	41.7
ConvStruct	43.9	41.4	42.0
Feedfwd-1	46.5	50.6	49.6
Feedfwd-2	46.8	50.9	49.8
Feedfwd-3	47.1	50.5	50.0
LatentModes	47.0	51.0	50.3

Table 2: Test macro F1 scores for models that do not use the textual content information.

	AskMen	AskWomen	Politics
No text	47.0	51.0	50.3
Un-gated	48.3	52.5	49.5
Gated	**48.7**	**53.1**	**51.3**

Table 3: Test macro F1 scores for models with and without the gating mechanism. All models use latent modes to represent the submission context information.

6 Experiments

In this section, we present the performance of the proposed model and conduct contrastive experiments to study model variants in two dimensions. For the submission context features, we compare representations obtained via feedforward neural networks to that obtained by a learned combination of latent basis vectors. In terms of textual features, we compare a model which uses no text, context-independent text features, and a context-depending gating mechanism. Finally, we analyze the learned latent submission context modes, as well as context-dependent gate values that reflect the amount of textual information used by the full model.

6.1 Model Configuration

All parameters in the neural networks except bias terms are initialized randomly according to the Gaussian distribution $\mathcal{N}(0, 10^{-2})$. We tune the number of latent bases K and the number of hidden layer neurons C and D based on the macro F1 scores on the validation data. For the full model, the best configuration uses $K = 8$, $C = 32$ and $D = 64$ for all subreddits, except Politics where $D = 32$.

6.2 Main Results

The performance of the full model on individual levels is presented in Fig. 4. As expected, the lowest level comments are easier to classify. Detection of high-level comments is most reliable in the Politics subreddit, but still difficult.

Table 2 compares models variants that only use the submission context features. The SubtreeSize baseline uses a multinominal logistic regression model to predict the level according to the subtree size feature alone, whereas the ConvStruct uses the same model but with all conversation structure features defined in Tabel 1. All baselines are stronger than predicting based on prior distributions, which has F1 scores in the 11-17 range. The model Feedfwd-n is a feedforward neural network with n hidden layers; it uses the submission context feature c in Fig. 3 for prediction. The model LatentBases represents the submission context information by a linear combination of latent bases; it uses $\tilde{c}$ in Fig. 3 for prediction. Compared with Feedfwd-1 in terms of the number of model parameters, Feedfwd-2, Feedfwd-3 and LatentBases have C^2, $2C^2$, and $(2C^2+K)$ extra parameters, respectively. These models have similar performance, but there is a slight improvement by increasing model capacity. While the proposed method does not give a significant performance gain, it leads to a more interpretable model.

Table 3 studies the effect of adding text and introducing the gating mechanism. The un-gated variant uses d instead of $\tilde{d}$ for prediction. Without the gating mechanism, textual information provides significant improvement for AskMen and AskWomen but not for Politics. With the introduced dynamic gating mechanism, the textual information is used more effectively for all three subreddits.

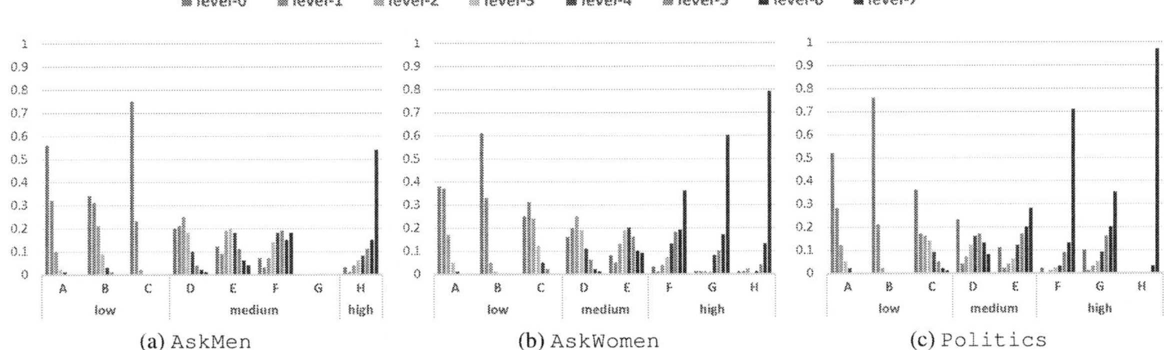

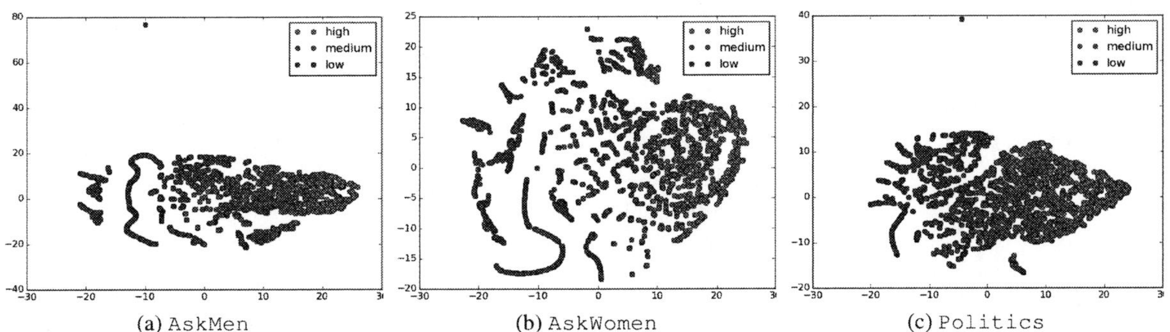

(a) AskMen (b) AskWomen (c) Politics

Figure 5: Empirical distributions of levels for each latent mode. Modes are grouped by dominating levels, i.e., level-0 and level-1 as `low`, level-6 and level-7 as `high`, and the rest as `medium`. Within each cluster, the modes are sorted by the number of samples.

(a) AskMen (b) AskWomen (c) Politics

Figure 6: Visualization of learned clusters.

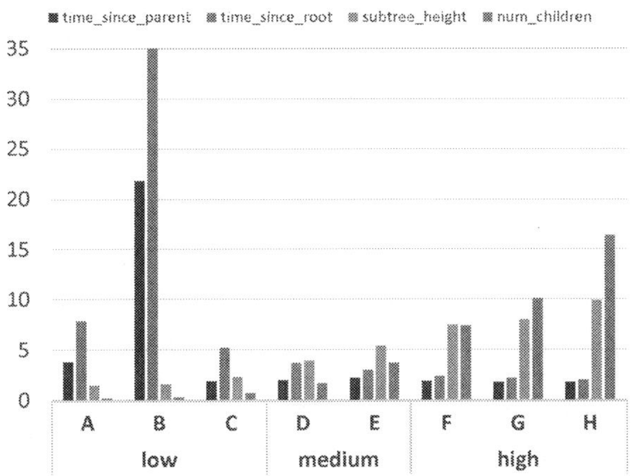

Figure 7: Mean values of four submission context features for each latent mode of `AskWomen`.

6.3 Analysis

In this subsection, we analyze the learned submission context modes and the gate values that control the amount of textual information to be used by the model for predicting comment karma level.

Submission context modes: To study the submission context modes, we assign each comment to a cluster according to which basis vector receives the highest weight: $\mathrm{argmax}_{k=1,\ldots,K} a_k$. The label distribution for each cluster is shown in Fig. 5. It can be observed that some clusters are dominated by level-0 comments, and others are dominated by level-7 comments. In Fig. 6, we visualize the learned clusters by projecting the raw conversation structure features $\mathbf{x}$ to a 2-dimensional space using the t-SNE algorithm (van der Maaten and Hinton, 2008). For purposes of illustrating cross-domain similarities, we group the clusters dominated by level-0 and level-1 comments into a low endorsement cluster, those dominated by level-6 and level-7 into a high endorsement cluster, and the rest as the medium endorsement cluster. It can be seen that the learned clusters split the comments with a consistent pattern, with the higher endorsement comments towards the

	AskMen	AskWomen	Politics
medium	0.87	0.87	0.85
high	0.67	0.66	0.76

Table 4: Text gate values relative to low karma modes.

right and the low endorsement comments to the left.

In Fig. 7, we show mean values of four selected submission context features for each latent mode of AskWomen, where units of time are in hours. High karma comments tend to be submitted early in the discussion, and the number of children (direct replies) is similar to or greater than the height of its subtree (corresponding to a broad subtree). Low and medium karma comments have a ratio of number of children to subtree height that is less than one. Low karma comments tend to come later in the discussion overall (time since root) but also later in terms of the group of responses to a parent comment (time since parent). These trends hold for all three subreddits. All subreddits have within-group differences in the mode characteristics, particularly the low-karma modes. For AskWomen, graph cluster B corresponds to comments made at the end of a discussion, which are more likely to be low karma because there are fewer readers and less opportunity for a new contribution. Cluster C comments come earlier in the discussion but have small subtrees compared to other early comments.

Text gate: In Table 4, we show the mean gate values g for each group of latent modes. Since gate values are not comparable across subreddits due to dynamic range of feature values, the values shown are scaled by the value for the low-level mode. We observe a consistent trend across all subreddits: lower gate values for higher karma. Recall that the high karma comments typically spawn active discussions. Thus, a possible explanation is that users may be biased to endorse comments that others are endorsing, making the details of the content less important.

7 Conclusion

In summary, this work has addressed the problem of predicting community endorsement of comments in a discussion forum using a new neural network architecture that integrates submission context features (including relative timing and response structure) with features extracted from the text of a comment. The approach represents the submission context in terms of a linear combination of latent basis vectors that characterize the dynamic conversation mode, which gives results similar to using a deep network but is more interpretable. The model also includes a dynamic gate for the text content, and analysis shows that when response structure is available to the predictor, the content of a comment has the most utility for comments that are not in active regions of the discussion. These results are based on characterizing quantized levels of karma with a series of binary classifiers. Quantized karma prediction could also be framed as an ordinal regression task, which would involve a straightforward change to the neural network learning objective.

This work differs from related work on popularity prediction in that the task does not control for content of a post/comment, nor limit the time window of the submission. With fewer controls, it is more difficult to uncover the aspects of textual content that contribute to endorsement, but by conditioning on submission context we can begin to understand herd effects of endorsement. The task described here also differs from previous work in that the full (or almost full) discussion thread is available in extracting features characterizing the response to the comment, but the modeling framework would also be useful with a limited window lookahead. The results using the full discussion tree also show the limits of using response volume to measure endorsement.

A limitation of this work is that the submission context is represented only in terms of the relative timing and graph structure in a discussion thread and does not use the text within earlier or responding comments. Prior work has shown that the relevance of a comment to the preceding discussion matters (Jaech et al., 2015), and clearly the sentiment expressed in responses should provide important cues. Capturing these different sources of information in a gated framework is of interest for future work.

Acknowledgments

This paper is based on work supported by the DARPA DEFT Program. Views expressed are those of the authors and do not reflect the official policy or position of the Department of Defense or the U.S. Government.

References

Dzmitry Bahdanau, Kyunghyun Cho, and Yoshua Bengio. 2015. Neural machine translation by jointly learning to align and translate. In *Proc. Int. Conf. Learning Representations (ICLR)*.

Roja Bandari, Sitaram Asur, and Bernardo Huberman. 2012. The pulse of news in social media: forecasting popularity. In *Proc. Int. AAAI Conf. Web and Social Media (ICWSM)*.

Jan A. Botha and Phil Blunsom. 2014. Compositional morphology for word representations and language modelling. In *Proc. Int. Conf. Machine Learning (ICML)*.

Justin Cheng, Lada Adamic, P. Alex Dow, Jon Michael Kleinberg, and Jure Leskovec. 2014. Can cascade be predicted? In *Proc. Int. Conf. World Wide Web (WWW)*, pages 925–936.

Hao Cheng, Hao Fang, and Mari Ostendorf. 2015. Open-domain name error detection using a multi-task RNN. In *Proc. Conf. Empirical Methods Natural Language Process. (EMNLP)*.

Kyunghyun Cho, Bart van Merriënboer, Caglar Gulcehre, Dzmitry Bahadanau, Fethhi Bougares, Holger Schwenk, and Yoshua Bengio. 2014. Learning phrase representations using RNN encoder-decoder for statistical machine translation. In *Proc. Conf. Empirical Methods Natural Language Process. (EMNLP)*, pages 1724–1734.

Hao Fang, Mari Ostendorf, Peter Baumann, and Janet Pierrehumbert. 2015. Exponential language modeling using morphological features and multi-task learning. *IEEE Trans. Audio, Speech, and Language Process.*, 23(12):2410–2421, December.

Sepp Hochreiter and Jürgen Schmidhuber. 1997. Long short-term memory. *Neural Computation*, 9(8):1735–1780, November.

Liangjie Hong, Ovidiu Dan, and Brian Davison. 2011. Predicting popular messages in Twitter. In *Proc. Int. Conf. World Wide Web (WWW)*, pages 57–58.

Aaron Jaech, Vicky Zayats, Hao Fang, Mari Ostendorf, and Hannaneh Hajishirzi. 2015. Talking to the crowd: What do people react to in online discussions? In *Proc. Conf. Empirical Methods Natural Language Process. (EMNLP)*, pages 2026–2031.

Bin Jiang. 2013. Head/tail break: A new classification scheme for data with a heavy-tailed distribution. *The Professional Geographer*, 65(3):482–494.

Diederik Kingma and Jimmy Ba. 2015. Adam: A method for stochastic optimization. In *Proc. Int. Conf. Learning Representations (ICLR)*.

Himabindu Lakkaraju, Julian McAuley, and Jure Leskovec. 2013. What's in a name? Understanding the interplay between titles, content, and communities in social media. In *Proc. Int. AAAI Conf. Web and Social Media (ICWSM)*.

Christopher D. Manning, Mihai Surdeanu, John Bauer, Jenny Finkel, Steven J. Bethard, and David McClosky. 2014. The Stanford CoreNLP natural language processing toolkit. In *Proc. Annu. Meeting Assoc. for Computational Linguistics: System Demonstrations*, pages 55–60.

Andrew L. Mass, Awni Y. Hannun, and Andrew Y. Ng. 2013. Rectifier nonlinearities improve neural network acoustic models. In *Proc. Int. Conf. Machine Learning (ICML)*.

Hamid Palangi, Li Deng, Yelong Shen, Jianfeng Gao, Xiaodong He, Jianshu Chen, Xinying Song, and Rabab Ward. 2016. Deep sentence embedding using long short-term memory networks: Analysis and application to information retrieval. *IEEE Trans. Audio, Speech, and Language Process.*, 24(4):694–707, April.

David E. Rumelhart, Geoffrey E. Hinton, and Ronald J. Williams. 1986. Learning representations by back-propogating errors. *Nature*, 323(6088):533–536, October.

B. Suh, L. Hong, P. Pirolli, and E. H. Chi. 2010. Want to be retweeted? large scale analytics on factors impacting retweet in twitter network. In *Proc. IEEE Inter. Conf. on Social Computing (SocialCom)*, pages 177–184.

Sainbayar Sukhbaatar, Arthur Szlam, Jason Weston, and Rob Fergus. 2015. End-to-end memory networks. In *Proc. Annu. Conf. Neural Inform. Process. Syst. (NIPS)*, pages 2431–2439.

Ilya Sutskever, Oriol Vinyals, and Quoc V. Le. 2014. Sequence to sequence learning with neural networks. In *Proc. Annu. Conf. Neural Inform. Process. Syst. (NIPS)*, pages 3104–3112.

Chenhao Tan, Lillian Lee, and Bo Pang. 2014. The effect of wording on message propagation: Topic- and author-controlled natural experiments on Twitter. In *Proc. Annu. Meeting Assoc. for Computational Linguistics (ACL)*, pages 175–186.

Manos Tasgkias, Wouter Weerkamp, and Maarten de Rijke. 2009. Predicting the volume of comments on online news stories. In *Proc. CIKM*, pages 1765–1768.

Alexandru Tatar, Jeremie Leguay, Panayotis Antoniadis, Arnaud Limbourg, Marcelo Dias de Amorim, and Serge Fdida. 2011. Predicting the polularity of online articles based on user comments. In *Proc. Inter. Conf. on Web Intelligence, Mining and Semantics (WIMS)*, pages 67:1–67:8.

Laurens van der Maaten and Geoffrey Hinton. 2008. Visualizing data using t-SNE. *Machine Learning Research*, 9, Nov.

Oriol Vinyals, Lukasz Kaiser, Terry Koo, Slav Petrov, Ilya Sutskever, and Geoffrey Hinton. 2015. Grammar as a foreign language. In *Proc. Annu. Conf. Neural Inform. Process. Syst. (NIPS)*, pages 2755–2763.

Jason Weston, Sumit Chopra, and Antoine Bordes. 2015. Memory networks. In *Proc. Int. Conf. Learning Representations (ICLR)*.

Tae Yano and Noah A. Smith. 2010. What's worthy of comment? content and comment volume in political blogs. In *Proc. Int. AAAI Conf. Weblogs and Social Media (ICWSM)*.

Qingyuan Zhao, Murat A. Erdogdu, Hera Y. He, Anand Rajaraman, and Jure Leskovec. 2015. SEISMIC: A self-exciting point process model for predicting Tweet popularity. In *Proc. ACM SIGKDD Conf. Knowledge Discovery and Data Mining*.

Witness Identification in Twitter

Rui Fang, Armineh Nourbakhsh, Xiaomo Liu, Sameena Shah, Quanzhi Li
Research & Development, Thomson Reuters
NYC, USA
{rui.fang, armineh.nourbakhsh, xiaomo.liu, sameena.shah, quanzhi.li}@thomsonreuters.com

Abstract

Identifying witness accounts is important for rumor debunking, crises management, and basically any task that involves on the ground eyes. The prevalence of social media has provided citizen journalism with scale and eye witnesses prominence. However, the amount of noise on social media also makes it likely that witness accounts get buried too deep in the noise and are never discovered. In this paper, we explore automatic witness identification in Twitter during emergency events. We attempt to create a generalizable system that not only detects witness reports for unseen events, but also on true out-of-sample "real time streaming set" that may or may not have witness accounts. We attempt to detect the presence or surge of witness accounts, which is the first step in developing a model for detecting crisis-related events. We collect and annotate witness tweets for different types of events (earthquake, car accident, fire, cyclone, etc.) explore the related features and build a classifier to identify witness tweets in real time. Our system is able to significantly outperform prior methods with an average F-score of 89.7% on previously unseen events.

1 Introduction

Citizen journalism or street journalism involves public citizens playing an active role in collecting, reporting, analyzing, and disseminating news and information. Apart from the fact that it allows bringing in a broader perspective, a key reason for its rise and influence is because of witness reports. Witnesses are able to share an eyewitness report, photo, or video of the event. Another reason is the presence of a common person's perspective, that may otherwise be intentionally or unintentionally hidden because of various reasons, including political affiliations of mass media. Also, for use cases involving time-sensitive requirements (for example, situational awareness, emergency response, and disaster management) knowing about people on the ground is crucial.

Some stories may call for identifying experts who can speak authoritatively to a topic or issue (also called cognitive authorities). However, in breaking-news situations that involve readily perceivable information (for example, fires, crimes) cognitive authorities are perhaps less useful than eyewitnesses. Since most of the use-cases that value citizen reports involve gaining access to information very quickly, it is important for the system to be real time and avoid extensive searches and manual screening of enormous volume of tweets.

Social media has provided citizen journalism with an unprecedented scale, and access to a real time platform, where once passive witnesses can become active and share their eyewitness testimony with the world, including with journalists who may choose to publicize their report. However, the same scalability is available to spam, advertisements, and mundane conversations that obscure these valuable citizen reports. It is clear that discovery of such witness accounts is important. However, presence of significant amount of noise, unrelated content, and mundane conversations about an event that may be not very useful for others, make such a task challenging.

In this paper, we address the problem of automated witness account detection from tweets. Our contributions include: (1) A method to automatically classify witness accounts on social media using only social media data. (2) A set of features (textual and numeric), spanning conversa-

Proceedings of The Fourth International Workshop on Natural Language Processing for Social Media, pages 65–73,
Austin, TX, November 1, 2016. ©2016 Association for Computational Linguistics

tions, natural language, and meta features suitable for witness identification. (3) A large scale study that evaluates the above methods on a diverse set of different event types such as accidents, natural disasters, and witnessable crimes. (4) Making available an annotated witness database. (5) A real time out-of-sample test on a stream of tweets. In many cases, the presence of witness reports may be the first indication of an event happening. We use the proposed method to determine if surge in witness accounts is related to potential witnessable events.

2   Related Work

A witness may be described as "a person who sees an event happening, especially a crime or an accident"[1]. WordNet defines a witness to be "someone who sees an event and reports what happens" (Miller, 1995), suggesting an expansion from being able to perceive an event to being able to provide a report. From a journalism perspective, witnesses may be defined as "people who see, hear, or know by personal experience and perception" (Diakopoulos et al., 2012).

The motivation behind our definition of witness accounts is that this paper is part of a bigger study on early identification of emergencies and crises through social media. The aim of the larger study is to detect such events prior to news media. In such cases, it is crucial to detect and verify witness accounts before the events are reported by news outlets, and therefore it is important to distinguish between first-hand accounts of the events, and those which are reflected by news reports. The latter type of messages would not be helpful to the study even if they conveyed situational awareness or provided insight into the event.

(Morstatter et al., 2014) explore the problem of finding tweets that originate from within the region of the crisis. Their approach relies only on linguistic features to automatically classify tweets that are inside the region of the crisis versus tweets that are outside the crisis region. The tweets inside the region of the crisis are considered as witness tweets in their experiment setting. However, this is incompatible with our definition of a witness tweet. In our definition, a witness has to be in the crisis region *and* report on having witnessed the event. Thus, we do not consider all the tweets

---

inside the crisis region as witness tweets.

(Cheng et al., 2010) explored the possibility of inferring user's locations based on their tweets. (Han et al., 2014) developed an approach that combines a tweet's text with its meta-data to estimate a user's location. The estimated user location, that is, if they are close to or within the crisis region is used as an indicator of witness tweets, but as discussed above, this is not sufficient for the purposes of our study.

There are few research studies that exclusively concentrate on *situational awareness*. (Verma et al., 2011) explore the automatic identification of tweets for situational awareness. They work on a related problem of finding potential witnesses by focusing on people who are in the proximity of an event. Such tweets may not contain content that demonstrates an awareness of the scope of the crisis and specific details about the situation. However, these tweets are not necessarily from a witness; they could be from a news report of the situation. Hence their problem is not equivalent to ours.

While computational models exist for situational awareness where all within region may be characterized as witness tweets but no real time system exists to identify eyewitness accounts; rather only characterizations of such accounts have been studied. For example, (Truelove et al., 2014) analyzed several characteristics of witness accounts in twitter from a journalistic perspective and developed a conceptual model of witness accounts. Their analysis is based on a case study event (a bushfire), without a computational model for witness identification. They found that witness accounts can be differentiated from non-witness accounts from many different dimensions, such as linguistic use and Twitter's meta data.

3   Data Collection and Annotation

We primarily concentrate on building a real-time system that is able to discover witness reports from tweets. To this purpose, we take a supervised classification approach. Preliminary data analysis revealed that different event types involved varied language specific to that event type, and varied temporal and spatial characteristics specific to the exact event. For example, words used in describing earthquakes might have phrases like 'tremors', 'shaking' but not 'saw suspect'. Also, witness characteristics depended on when and where an

Figure 1: An example witness tweet

event took place. In the next section, we begin by describing our event types.

3.1 Selection of Events

As discussed before, eyewitness accounts are perhaps most useful to journalists and emergency responders during disasters and crises. Therefore we focus on these type of events in building our dataset. These include natural disasters such as floods and earthquakes, accidents such as flight crashes, and witnessable criminal events such as acts of terrorism.

We formed an events list by evaluating the disaster and accident categories in news agency websites, for example, Fox news disasters category[2]. We found the following events: cyclones, (grass)fires, floods, train crash, air crash, car accidents, volcano, earthquake, landslide, shooting, and bombing. Note that the events (within or cross category) may be distinct on several integral characteristics, like different witness/non-witness ratios. This is mainly due to the varying spatial and temporal characteristics of the events. For example, the Boston Marathon Bombing happened in a crowded place and at daytime. This led to a large number of eye-witnesses, who reported hearing the blast, and the ensuing chaos. Figure 1 shows an example witness tweet from Boston marathon bombing. On the other hand for the landslide that occurred 4 miles east of Oso, Washington, there were very few people near the landslide site. Thus, most of the tweets related to that landslide actually originated from some news agency report.

3.2 Data Collection

In order to study the identification of eyewitnesses, we needed to identify some events and collect all related tweets for each event. Some previous studies(Yang et al., 2012; Castillo et al., 2011) used TwitterMonitor(Mathioudakis and Koudas, 2010) that detected sudden bursts of activity on Twitter and came up with an automatically generated Boolean query to describe those trends. The query could then be applied to Twitter's search interface to capture more relevant tweets about the topic. However, TwitterMonitor is no longer active. We formulated the required search queries manually, by following a similar approach.

3.3 Query Construction

Each query was a boolean string consisting of a subject, a predicate, and possibly an object. These components were connected using the AND operator. For instance,"2014 California Earthquake" was transformed to "(California) AND (Earthquake)". Each component was then replaced with a series of possible synonyms and replacements, all connected via the OR operator. For instance, the query may further be expanded to "(California OR C.A. OR CA OR Napa) AND (earthquake OR quake OR earthshock OR seism OR tremors OR shaking)". Finally, we added popular hashtags to the search query, as long as they didn't exceed Twitter's limit of 500 characters. For instance, the query would be expanded by hashtags such as "NapaEarthquake". As we read the retrieved tweets, more synonyms and replacements were discovered which we added them back to the query and searched in Twitter again. We repeat this process several times until the number of retrieved tweets is relatively stable. This process can help us find a good coverage of event tweets and witness tweets. However, we believe it is very hard to evaluate the accurate recall of our query results since we have to (1) have the complete twitter data of a specific time period and (2) label a huge amount of tweets.

3.4 Search

Each query was applied to Twitter to collect relevant tweets. Twitter offers a search API that provides a convenient platform for data collection. However, the search results are limited to one week. Since some of the items in our data-set

---

[2]http://www.foxnews.com/us/disasters/index.html

Table 1: Descriptive statistics of the events in the collected data-set

Event	# Witness tweets	# Total tweets
Cyclone	37	13,261
Grass fire	5	6,739
River flood	27	6,671
Flight crash	17	7,955
Train crash	5	7,287
Car accident	32	19,058
Volcano	2	3,096
Tornado	7	6,066
Earthquake	127	40,035
Landslide	1	3,318
Shooting	3	5,615
Bombing	138	31,313

spanned beyond a week's time, we could not rely on the search API to perform data collection. Instead, we decided to use Twitter's search interface, which offers a more comprehensive result set. We used an automated script to submit each query to the search interface, scroll through the pages, and download the resulting tweets.

For our event categories, we found 28 events with a total of 119,101 related tweets. If there were multiple events of either category then they were merged into their respective category. For example, tweets from 6 distinct grass fire events were merged into a single grass fire event. Similarly 3 train crashes, 3 cyclones, 3 flight crashes, 3 earthquakes, 2 river floods, 2 car accidents, and 2 tornadoes were merged. Table 1 provides further details on the different events.

3.5 Witness annotation

We first applied the following two filters to automatically label non-witness tweets.

1. If tweet text mentions a news agency's name or contains a news agency's url, it is not a witness tweet. For example, "Breaking: Injuries unknown after Asiana Airlines flight crash lands at San Francisco Airport - @AP"

2. If it is a retweet (since by definition it is not from a witness even if its a retweet of a witness account).

After the above filtering step, 46,249 tweets were labeled as non-witness tweets, while 72,852 tweets were left for manual annotation. Two annotators were assigned to manually label a tweet as a witness tweet in case it qualified as either of the following three categories(Truelove et al., 2014):

- Witness Account: Witness provides a direct observation of the event or its effects. Example: "Today I experienced an earthquake and a blind man trying to flag a taxi. I will never take my health for granted."

- Impact Account: Witness describes being impacted directly or taking direct action due to the event. Example: "Had to cancel my last home visit of the day due to a bushfire.".

- Relay Account: Micro-blogger relays a Witness Account or Impact Account of another person. Example: "my brother just witnessed a head on head car crash".

If neither of the above three, then the tweet was labeled as a non witness account. After the annotation (The kappa score for the inter-annotator agreement is 0.77), we obtained in 401 witness tweets and 118,700 non-witness tweets.

4 Methodology

In this section, we outline our methodology for automatically finding witness tweets using linguistic features and meta-data. We first discuss the features, and then the models used.

4.1 Linguistic Features

Linguistic features depend on the language of Twitter users. Currently we concentrate only on English. Previous related works have also shown the utility of a few linguistic features (Morstatter et al., 2014; Verma et al., 2011) such as N-grams of tweets, Part-of-Speech and syntactic constituent based features. The following describes our new features:

Crisis-sensitive features. Parts-of-speech sequences and preposition phrase patterns (e.g., "near me").

Expression: Personal/Impersonal. If the tweet is a description of personal observations it is more likely to be a witness report. We explore several features to identify personal experiences and perceptions. (1) If the tweet is expressed as a first person account (e.g., contains first personal pronoun such as "I") or (2) If the tweet contains words that are from LIWC[3] categories such as "see" and

____
[3]http://www.liwc.net/

"hear", it is indicative of a personal experience; (3) If the tweet mentions news agency names or references a news agency source, it is not about a personal experience and thus not a witness report.

Time-awareness. Many witness accounts frame their message in a time-sensitive manner, for example, "Was having lunch at union station when *all of a sudden* chaos!" We use a manually created list of terms that indicate time-related concepts of immediacy.

Conversational/Reply feature. Based on analysis of the collected witness and non-witness tweets, we observe that the responses to a tweet and the further description of the situation from that original user helps confirm a witness account. We extract the following features: (1) If the reply tweet is personal in expression; (2) If the reply tweet contains journalism-related users; (3) If the reply tweet is from friends/non-friends of the original user; (4) If the reply tweet is a direct reply (to the original tweet).

Word Embedding The recent breakthrough in NLP is the incorporation of deep learning techniques to enhance rudimentary NLP problems, such as language modeling (Bengio et al., 2003) and name entity recognition(Collobert et al., 2011). Word embeddings are distributed representations of words which are usually generated from a large text corpus. The word embeddings are proved to be able to capture nuanced meanings of words. That is why word embeddings are very powerful in NLP related applications. In this study, the word embedding for each word is computed using neural network and generated from billions of words from tweets, without any supervision.(more details in Section 4.4)

4.2 Meta features

In addition to linguistic features, there are a few other indicators which might help identify witness accounts. (1) **Client application**. We hypothesize that witness accounts are likelier to be posted using a cellphone than a desktop application or the standard web interface; (2) **Length of tweet**. The urgent expression of witness tweets might require more concise use of language. We measure the length of a tweet in terms of individual words used; (3) **Mentions or hashtags**. Another indication of urgency can be the absence of more casual features such as mentions or hashtags.

Table 2: Description of features

contains first-person pronoun, i.e. "I","we"
contains LIWC keywords,i.e."see","hear" ?
contains news agency URL or name?
is a retweet?
contains media (picture or video)?
contains time-aware keywords?
journalist account involved in conversation?
situated awareness keywords in conversation?
contains reply from friend/non-friend
contains direct/indirect reply
type of client application used to post the tweet
length of tweet in words
contains mentions or hashtags?
similarity to witnessable emergency topics
word embeddings

4.3 Topic as a feature

As mentioned previously, witness accounts are most relevant for reporting on *witnessable* events. These include accidents, crimes and disasters. Thus, we hypothesize that features that help identify the topic of the tweets may help measure their relevance. Therefore we incorporate topic as a feature. We use OpenCalais'[4] topic schema to identify witnessable events. The following sections describe how we use these categories to generate topic features.

Table 2 shows the set of new features we proposed in witness identification.

4.4 Feature Extraction

In addition to the features introduced above, we experimented with several other potential features such as objectivity vs. emotion, user visibility and credibility, presence of multimedia in the message, and other linguistic and network features. They did not improve the performance of the classifier, and statistical analysis of their distributions across witness and non-witness messages failed to show any significant distinctions. Due to space limit, we provide the feature extraction details for two features.

Topic Features: Using OpenCalais' topic-classification api, we classified about 33,000 tweets collected via Twitter's streaming API in January-June 2015. We then separated those classified as WAR_CONFLICT, LAW_CRIME, or DISASTER_ACCIDENT. This resulted in 7,943

---

[4]http://www.opencalais.com/opencalais-api/

Table 3: Description of data set for training word embeddings

# of Tweets	198 million
# of words in training data	2.9 billion
# of unique tokens	1.9 million

tweets. Three researchers manually cross-checked the classification for accuracy. For each topic, 500 tweets on which all researchers agreed were chosen to represent that topic. We calculated TF-IDF metrics on these tweets and represented each topic as a vector of terms and their TF-IDF values. When applying these features to the training data, we calculated the cosine similarity between the term vector of each tweet and the term vector of each topic.

Word Embeddings: To extract word embeddings for each word in tweet, we use the word2vec toolkit[5]. word2vec is an implementation of word embeddings developed by Mikolov et al.(Mikolov et al., 2013). This model has two training options, continuous bag of words (CBOW) and the Skip-gram model. The Skip-gram model is an efficient method for learning high-quality distributed vector representations that capture a large number of precise syntactic and semantic word relationships. Based on previous studies the Skip-gram model produces better results and we adopt it for training.

We train the model on tweet data. The tweets used in this study span from October 2014 to September 2015. They were acquired through Twitter's public 1% streaming API and Twitter's Decahose data (10% of Twitter streaming data) granted to us by Twitter for research purposes. Table 3 shows the basic statistics of the data set used in this study. Only English tweets are used, and about 200 million tweets are used for building the word embedding model. Totally, 2.9 billion words are processed. With a term frequency threshold of 5 (tokens with fewer than 5 occurrences in the data set are discarded), the total number of unique tokens (hashtags and words) in this model is 1.9 million. The word embedding dimension is 300 for each word.

Each tweet is preprocessed to get a clean version, which is then processed by the model building process.

---

[5]Available at https://code.google.com/p/word2vec/

Table 4: A case study of transfer learning for witness identification

Models	Test on earthquake event
Model 1: trained on non-earthquake events	83.3%
Model 2: trained on earthquake event	87.0%

5 Experiments and Evaluation

To classify tweets as witness or non-witness automatically, we take a machine learning approach, employing several models such as decision tree classifier, maximum entropy classifier, random forest and Support Vector Machine (SVM) classifier to predict whether a tweet is a witness tweet or not. (SVM classifier performed the best for our method as well as on baselines, we only report results using SVM). As input to the classifier, we vectorized the tweet by extracting the features from the tweet's text and meta-data. Each of our features are represented as whether they occur within the tweet, i.e. Boolean features. The model then outputs its prediction of whether the tweet is a witness account.

5.1 Transfer learning

We first perform a case study of transfer learning. We trained one model on all event-types and tested on a specific type of event (e.g. earthquake). We then trained a second model for that specific type of event and compared the performance of these two paradigms. We choose earthquake events in our dataset for case study. We trained two models on 1000 tweets with witness and non-witness accounts and test on an event with 500 tweets. *Model 1* is trained on all other types of events, while *Model 2* is trained on another earthquake event. Table 4 shows the results. The F-1 score of *Model 1* and 2 are 83.3%, 87.0% respectively. This suggests that event-based witness identifiers have better performance than general witness identifiers, but the model generalizes relatively well.

For the next experiment, we balanced the collected data by over-sampling the witness tweets by 10 times, and down-sampling the non-witness tweets to the same size accordingly. We then perform leave one out cross validation. For each event category, we use all tweets in other event categories to train the model. Once the training is done, we test the trained model on the tweets in the holdout event category. For example, for the cyclone category, we would use all tweets in all other 11 categories (grass fire, river flood, flight crash, train crash,....,) to train the model, and test the model on cyclone category tweets. This process was repeated for each event type.

5.2 Comparison of Prediction Models

We compared our proposed method with two baseline models from the literature(Diakopoulos et al., 2012; Morstatter et al., 2014).

- **Baseline 1**: A dictionary-based technique(Diakopoulos et al., 2012). The approach classifies potential witnesses based on 741 words from numerous LIWC categories including "percept", "see", "hear", and "feel". The approach applied one simple heuristic rule: If a tweet contained at least one keyword from the categories, then the tweet is classified as witness tweet.

- **Baseline 2**: A learning based approach(Morstatter et al., 2014). This method extracts linguistic features(as shown in Table 2) from each tweet and automatically classifies tweets that are inside the region of the crisis versus tweets that are outside the crisis region.

Table 5: Witness identification F-score for each event and model: Baseline

Testing Events	F-score	
	Baseline 1	Baseline 2
Cyclone	8.7%	75.1%
Grass fire	6.9%	**95.0%**
River flood	65.8%	83.3%
Flight crash	23.1%	77.2%
Train crash	39.9%	91.2%
Car accident	54.4%	86.1%
Volcano	46.0%	76.8%
Tornado	1.8%	83.9%
Earthquake	36.3%	77.3%
Landslide	46.1%	70.1%
Shooting	15.0%	80.9%
Bombing	34.5%	72.2%
Average	31.5%	80.8%

We experiment a set of models for witness identification:

- **Model i** (+Conversation) combines the new proposed 'conversational features' with all the features used in **Baseline 2**(Morstatter et al., 2014).

- **Model ii** (+Expression) combines the new proposed tweet 'expression features' with all features used in Baseline 2.

- **Model iii** (+Conversation+Expression) combines the new proposed conversational and tweet expression features with all features used in **Baseline 2**.

- **Model iv** (+Conversation+Expression+Meta) combines the previous classifier with meta features and topic-related features.

- **Model v (WE.)** uses only word embedding features which were obtained by an unsupervised learning process as described in subsection 4.4. As tweets are of various length, in order to get a fixed size feature vector representation of tweet to train the SVM, we explore min, average, and max convolution operators(Collobert et al., 2011). Specifically, we treat each tweet as a sequence of words $[w_1, ..., w_s]$. Each word is represented by a d-dimensional word vector $\mathbf{W} \in \mathfrak{R}^d$ (note that, $d = 300$ in our case). For each tweet s we build a sentence matrix $\mathbf{S} \in \mathfrak{R}^{d \times |s|}$, where each column k represents a word vector $\mathbf{W}_k$ in a sentence s. We can calculate the minimum, average, and max value of each row in the sentence matrix $\mathbf{S} \in \mathfrak{R}^{d \times |s|}$ and form a d x 1 vector, respectively. These d x 1 feature vector is used to train SVM classifier. Our empirical results shows that the max operator obtains the best results in a sample training data, so we only report this for the **WE.** model.

- **Model vi** (+Conversation+Expression+Meta+WE.) combines the handcrafted features used in **Model iv** with the word embedding features used in **Model v**.

For experiment and evaluation, we group similar events (for example, car accidents that happened in different times and locations) together, and perform a leave one out cross validation. More specifically, we used SVM classifier trained on

Table 6: Witness identification F-score for each event and model

Testing Events	F-score					
	Model i	**Model ii**	**Model iii**	**Model iv**	**Model v**	**Model vi**
Cyclone	75.5%	88.5%	**89.7%**	86.5%	87.0%	88.6%
Grass fire	94.7%	91.1%	93.6%	93.2%	93.1%	94.1%
River flood	83.3%	**91.5%**	91.4%	81.1%	82.2%	82.6%
Flight crash	77.5%	79.1%	81.5%	91.3%	85.7%	**91.5%**
Train crash	90.5%	90.9%	89.2%	92.8%	**92.9%**	**92.9%**
Car accident	88.1%	87.9%	88.5%	92.6%	90.7%	**92.7%**
Volcano	77.9%	81.0%	82.6%	**93.3%**	87.0%	93.1%
Tornado	85.9%	90.8%	**94.8%**	94.1%	93.8%	94.3%
Earthquake	78.8%	**80.8%**	80.7%	80.8%	80.5%	**80.9%**
Landslide	73.6%	80.7%	82.3%	85.7%	**85.9%**	85.5%
Shooting	82.8%	91.2%	92.2%	97.7%	93.0%	**97.8%**
Bombing	72.2%	72.8%	73.4%	82.0%	75.3%	**82.1%**
Average	81.7%	85.5%	86.7%	89.3%	87.2%	**89.7%**

data from all other types of events to classify tweet data from a new event. The F-score for each event as well as the average F-score are reported in Table 5, 6.

Table 5,6 show that our approaches were able to outperform previous two baseline approaches on categorizing witness tweets, with an average F-score of 81.0%, 85.5%, 86.7%, 87.2%, 89.3% and 89.7%, respectively.

The results indicate that our system is able to significantly outperform the two baseline approaches with an highest average F-score of 89.7% on previously unseen events.

It is interesting to observe that, the performance of **Model v** which uses only word embedding features obtained from unsupervised training on large tweet data-set, is comparable to the learning model (e.g. **Model iv**) that use hand-crafted features. Furthermore, when word embedding features are combined with handcrafted features (**Model vi**), the model's performance is further improved. One main reason is that the word embedding features explicitly encode many linguistic regularities and patterns which might not have been well captured by hand-made features. This result is in line with studies on other natural language processing task such as sentiment analysis (Tang et al., 2014).

We also observe that conversational features do not seem to improve performance to a considerable level (80.8% for Baseline 2 Versus 81.7% for **Model i**), we think that might be partially due to two reasons: (1) the fact that not all tweets lead to conversations (see statistics on Subsection 4.1); (2)the way we extract the conversational features is preliminary. In the future we will collect more data and explore more sophisticated features from conversations.

5.3 Witness identification on the real-time streaming Twitter data

In this section, we evaluate the hypothesis of whether detecting a witness accounts indicates that an event has taken place. We apply our witness identification model on streaming real-time Twitter data. For the time period that we tested in, the number of real-time tweets were 7,517,654 tweets. In the entire tweet collection, 47,254 tweets were identified as witness tweets. Based on a simple similarity measure, we clustered the tweets. If less than 3 tweets were found in a cluster, we eliminated that cluster. This led to 49,906 clusters or events. Of the 47,254 witness tweets, 1782 were from the clusters. Note that the proportion of witness tweets is 3.57% in the cluster events and only 0.63% in the streaming 1% sample. This suggests that there is a relationship between statistically finding more witness accounts and detection of events. In future, we aim to study this relationship in more detail.

6 Conclusion

We proposed a witness detection system for tweets. We studied characteristics of witness reports and proposed several diverse features. We show that the system is robust enough to work well on both in sample and true out of sample events.

References

[Bengio et al.2003] Yoshua Bengio, Réjean Ducharme, Pascal Vincent, and Christian Janvin. 2003. A neural probabilistic language model. *J. Mach. Learn. Res.*, 3:1137–1155, March.

[Castillo et al.2011] Carlos Castillo, Marcelo Mendoza, and Barbara Poblete. 2011. Information credibility on twitter. In *WWW*, pages 675–684.

[Cheng et al.2010] Zhiyuan Cheng, James Caverlee, and Kyumin Lee. 2010. You are where you tweet: A content-based approach to geo-locating twitter users. In *Proc. of the 19th ACM International Conference on Information and Knowledge Management*, CIKM '10, pages 759–768, New York, NY, USA. ACM.

[Collobert et al.2011] Ronan Collobert, Jason Weston, Léon Bottou, Michael Karlen, Koray Kavukcuoglu, and Pavel Kuksa. 2011. Natural language processing (almost) from scratch. *J. Mach. Learn. Res.*, 12:2493–2537, November.

[Diakopoulos et al.2012] Nicholas Diakopoulos, Munmun De Choudhury, and Mor Naaman. 2012. Finding and assessing social media information sources in the context of journalism. In *SIGCHI Conference on Human Factors in Computing Systems*, CHI '12, pages 2451–2460, New York, NY, USA. ACM.

[Han et al.2014] Bo Han, Paul Cook, and Timothy Baldwin. 2014. Text-based twitter user geolocation prediction. *J. Artif. Int. Res.*, 49(1):451–500, January.

[Mathioudakis and Koudas2010] Michael Mathioudakis and Nick Koudas. 2010. Twittermonitor: trend detection over the twitter stream. In *Proc. of the 2010 ACM SIGMOD International Conference on Management of Data*, pages 1155–1158. ACM.

[Mikolov et al.2013] Tomas Mikolov, Ilya Sutskever, Kai Chen, Greg Corrado, and Jeffrey Dean. 2013. Distributed representations of words and phrases and their compositionality. *CoRR*, abs/1310.4546.

[Miller1995] George A. Miller. 1995. Wordnet: A lexical database for english. *Communications of ACM*, 38(11):39–41, November.

[Morstatter et al.2014] Fred Morstatter, Nichola Lubold, Heather Pon-Barry, Jrgen Pfeffer, and Huan Liu. 2014. Finding eyewitness tweets during crises. In *ACL Workshop on Language Technology and Computational Social Science*.

[Tang et al.2014] Duyu Tang, Furu Wei, Nan Yang, Ming Zhou, Ting Liu, and Bing Qin. 2014. Learning sentiment-specific word embedding for twitter sentiment classification. In *Proceedings of the 52nd Annual Meeting of the Association for Computational Linguistics, ACL 2014, June 22-27, 2014, Baltimore, MD, USA, Volume 1: Long Papers*, pages 1555–1565.

[Truelove et al.2014] Marie Truelove, Maria Vasardani, and Stephan Winter. 2014. Towards credibility of micro-blogs: characterising witness accounts. *GeoJournal*, 80:339–359.

[Verma et al.2011] Sudha Verma, Sarah Vieweg, William Corvey, Leysia Palen, James H. Martin, Martha Palmer, Aaron Schram, and Kenneth Mark Anderson. 2011. Natural language processing to the rescue? extracting "situational awareness" tweets during mass emergency. In Lada A. Adamic, Ricardo A. Baeza-Yates, and Scott Counts, editors, *ICWSM*. The AAAI Press.

[Yang et al.2012] Fan Yang, Yang Liu, Xiaohui Yu, and Min Yang. 2012. Automatic detection of rumor on sina weibo. In *Proc. of the ACM SIGKDD Workshop on Mining Data Semantics*, page 13.

How Do I Look? Publicity Mining From Distributed
Keyword Representation of Socially Infused News Articles

Yu-Lun Hsieh

SNHCC, Taiwan International Graduate Program, Institute of Information Science,
Academia Sinica, and Department of Computer Science,
National Chengchi University, Taipei, Taiwan

Yung-Chun Chang, Chun-Han Chu, Wen-Lian Hsu

Institute of Information Science, Academia Sinica, Taipei, Taiwan
Email: {morphe,changyc,johannchu,hsu}@iis.sinica.edu.tw

Abstract

Previous work on opinion mining and sentiment analysis mainly concerns product, movie, or literature reviews; few applied this technique to analyze the publicity of person. We present a novel document modeling method that utilizes embeddings of emotion keywords to perform reader's emotion classification, and calculates a publicity score that serves as a quantifiable measure for the publicity of a person of interest. Experiments are conducted on two Chinese corpora that in total consists of over forty thousand users' emotional response after reading news articles. Results demonstrate that the proposed method can outperform state-of-the-art reader-emotion classification methods, and provide a substantial ground for publicity score estimation for candidates of political elections. We believe it is a promising direction for mining the publicity of a person from online social and news media that can be useful for propaganda and other purposes.

1 Introduction

The Internet has grown into a powerful medium for information dispersion and social interaction, on which one can easily share experiences and emotions instantly. It has become a popular source for sentiment analysis and opinion mining, e.g., movie reviews (Pang et al., 2002; Turney, 2002), product reviews (Hu and Liu, 2004), and other subjects (Turney, 2002; Wilson et al., 2009). Moreover, human feelings can be quickly identified through automatic emotion classification, as these emotions reflect an individual's feelings and experiences toward certain subject matters (Turney, 2002; Wilson et al., 2009). Emotion classification aims to predict the emotion categories (e.g., happy, angry, or worried) to which the given text belongs (Das and Bandyopadhyay, 2009; Quan and Ren, 2009). There are two aspects of emotions regarding a piece of text, namely, the writer's and the reader's emotion. The former consists of the emotions expressed by the author, while the latter refers to the emotions that the readers of the text may possess after reading the text. Recognition of reader-emotion is different from that of writer-emotion and may be even more complicated (Lin et al., 2008; Tang and Chen, 2012). In particular, writers can directly express their emotions through sentiment words; in contrast, reader-emotions possess a more complex nature, as even common words can evoke different types of reader-emotions depending on personal experiences and knowledge of the readers (Lin et al., 2007). For instance, a news article with the title "The price of crude oil will rise 0.5% next week" is just objectively reporting an event without any emotion, but it may invoke emotions like *angry* or *worried* in its readers. In addition, it is possible that more sponsorship opportunities can be obtained from companies or manufacturers if the articles describing a certain product are able to promote greater emotional resonance in the readers. As online commerce becomes more and more prominent nowadays, a growing amount of customers rely on online reviews to determine their purchases. Meanwhile, news organizations observe increasing traffic on their online websites as opposed to paper-based publications. We believe that reader's

Proceedings of The Fourth International Workshop on Natural Language Processing for Social Media, pages 74–83,
Austin, TX, November 1, 2016. ©2016 Association for Computational Linguistics

emotion analysis has a great potential in all domains and applications.

In light of the above rationale, in this work we attempt to capture the perception of readers toward public figures through recognizing reader's emotion from news articles. We propose a distributed emotion keyword vector (DEKV) representation for reader-emotion classification, from which we derive a novel method for publicity mining. It is a practice of monitoring the public opinion toward a certain human subject at a given period of time. Experiments show that DEKV outperforms other text categorization and reader-emotion classification methods; in turn, these results can be used to conduct publicity mining for propaganda and other public relations purposes.

2   Related Work

Articles are one of the most common medium for persons to convey their feelings. Identifying essential factors that affect emotion transition is important for human language understanding. With the rapid growth of computer mediated communication applications, such as social websites and micro-blogs, research on emotion classification has recently been attracting more attention from enterprises (Chen et al., 2010; Purver and Battersby, 2012). In general, a single piece of text may possess two types of emotions: writer-emotion and reader-emotion. The research of writer-emotion investigates the emotion expressed by the writer when writing the text. For example, Pang et al. (2002) pioneered the use of machine learning technique on sentiment classification of movie reviews into positive and negative emotions. Mishne (2005), and Yang and Chen (2006) used emoticons as tags to train SVM (Cortes and Vapnik, 1995) classifiers at the document or sentence level, respectively. In their studies, emoticons are taken as the answer, and textual keywords are considered as features. Wu et al. (2006) propose a sentence level emotion recognition method using dialogs as their corpus, in which "Happy", "Unhappy", or "Neutral" are assigned to each sentence as its emotion category. Yang et al. (2006) adopted Thayer's model (Thayer, 1989) to classify music emotions. Each music segment can be classified into four classes of moods. As for sentiment

analysis, Read (2005) used emoticons in newsgroup articles to extract relevant instances for training polarity classifiers.

On the other hand, the research of reader-emotion concerns the emotions expressed by a reader after reading the text. The writer and readers may view the same text from different perspectives, hence they do not always share the same emotion. Since the recent increase in the popularity of Internet, certain news websites, such as Yahoo! Kimo News, incorporate the Web 2.0 technologies that allow readers to express their emotions toward news articles. Classifying emotions from the readers' point of view is a challenging task, and research on this topic is relatively sparse as compared to those considering the writers' perspective. While writer-emotion classification has been extensively studied, only a few focused on reader-emotion classification. Lin et al. (2007) first described the task of reader-emotion classification on news articles and classified Yahoo! News articles into 8 emotion classes (e.g. happy, angry, or depressing) from the readers' perspectives. They combined unigram, bigram, metadata, and emotion categories to train a classifier for the reader-emotions toward news. Yang et al. (2009) automatically annotated reader-emotions on a writer-emotion corpus with a reader-emotion classifier, and studied the interactions between them. Furthermore, applications of reader-emotion categorization include learning linguistic templates for writing assistance (Chang et al., 2015). One can also collect public opinions toward political issues through emotion classification. Sarmento et al. (2009) used a rule-based method to collect a corpus of online comments for political opinion mining. Fang et al. (2012) extract contents from multiple sources on the same topic and quantify the differences within. An opinion formation framework was developed for content analysis of social media to conduct political opinion forecast (Sobkowicz et al., 2012).

What distinguishes this work from others is that we attempt to test the possibility of inferring publicity, or "likability", of a person by detecting the emotion of the public towards news about that person. Given enough unbiased data, this technique enables for propaganda and maintenance of good public image. Note that we do not aim to predict the probability of a person being elected, as such efforts

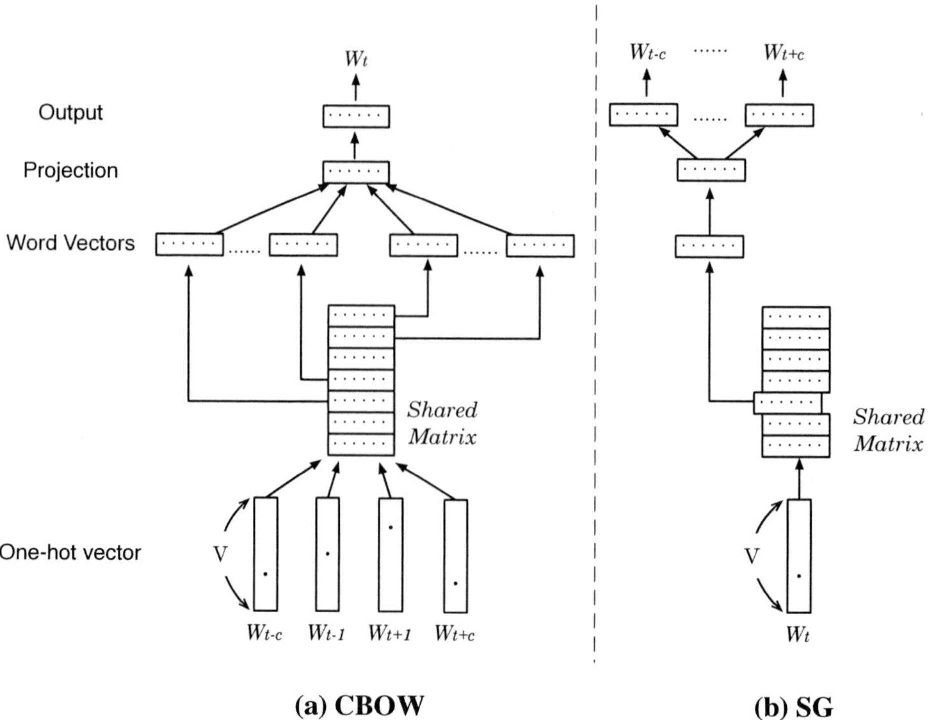

(a) CBOW **(b) SG**

Figure 1: (a) The CBOW model uses the context words $W_{t-c}, \cdots, W_{t+c}$ in the window as inputs to predict the current word W_t. (b) The SG model predicts words $W_{t-c}, \cdots, W_{t+c}$ in the context using the current word W_t as the input.

had already been made without showing promising results (Gayo-Avello, 2012).

3 Method

3.1 Distributed Word Representation

Bengio et al. (2003) proposed a neural network-based language model that motivated recent advances in natural language processing (NLP), including two word embedding learning strategies continuous bag-of-word (CBOW) and skip-gram (SG) (Mikolov et al., 2013a). The CBOW method is based on the distributional hypothesis (Miller and Charles, 1991), which states that words occur in similar contexts often possess similar meanings. This method attempts to learn a word representation that can capture the context information for each word. In contrast to traditional bag-of-word models, the CBOW model tries to obtain a dense vector representation (embedding) of each word directly (Mikolov et al., 2013a). The structure of the CBOW model is similar to a feed-forward neural network without non-linear hidden layers, as illustrated in

Fig. 1. It has been proven that this model can learn powerful representation of words and be trained on a large amount of data efficiently (Mikolov et al., 2013a). The SG model, being a simplified feed-forward neural network as well, differs from CBOW in that SG employs an inverse training objective instead for learning word representations (Mikolov et al., 2013a; Mikolov et al., 2013b; Le and Mikolov, 2014). The concept of SG model is illustrated in Fig. 1b. It attempts to predict words in the context by using the current words. In practice, SG tends to be more effective than CBOW when larger datasets are available (Lai et al., 2015).

3.2 Distributed Emotion Keyword Vectors for Reader-Emotion Classification

Building on top of the success of word embeddings, we propose the Distributed Emotion Keyword Vectors (DEKV) to model the reader-emotion of news articles. Chang et al. (2015) demonstrated that keywords are crucial in emotion classification, and motivated us to incorporate the distributed representation approach in the reader-emotion classification

$$LLR(w, E) = 2log \left(\frac{p(w|E)^k (1 - p(w|E))^m p(w|\neg E)^l (1 - p(w|\neg E))^n}{p(w)^{k+l}(1 - p(w))^{m+n}} \right) \qquad (1)$$

task. To begin, word embeddings are learned from the corpus using the CBOW method. We then find a set of keywords for each emotion category using log likelihood ratio (LLR) (Manning and Schütze, 1999), which is related to the probability of a keyword being specific to this category. LLR value of each word w is calculated as follows. Given a training set with emotion categories, we first define $k = N(w \wedge E), l = N(w \wedge \neg E), m = N(\neg w \wedge E)$, and $n = N(\neg w \wedge \neg E)$, where $N(w \wedge E)$ denotes the number of documents that contain w and belong to emotion E, $N(w \wedge \neg E)$ denotes the number of documents that contain w but does not belong to emotion E, and so on. Then, we employ Eq. (1) to calculate LLR for w in the emotion E.

Finally, a document is represented as illustrated in Fig. 2, in which D_t is a weighted average of keyword vectors, and the weight λ_i for a keyword KW_i is its scaled LLR value. Note that if there is no keyword in a document, we use the average of all word embeddings in this document and compute cosine similarity against all keyword vectors to find the closest ones to represent this document. In this case, the number of keywords that are used to represent this unknown document is the same as that of each category. In essence, each document is projected onto a semantic space constructed by keyword vectors as illustrated in Fig. 3.

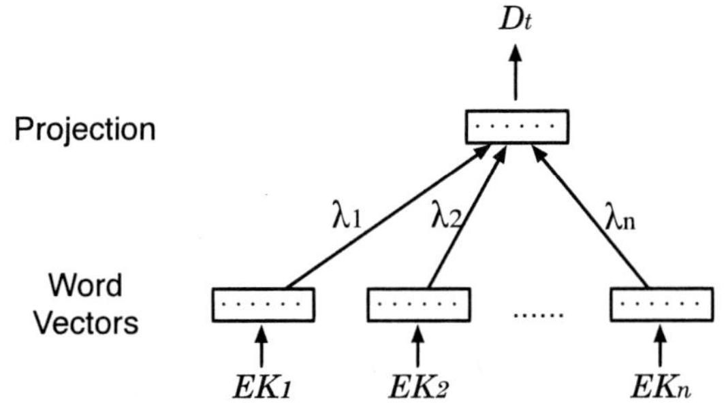

Figure 2: The DEKV model represents each target document D_t as emotion keyword vectors EK_i that are present in this document, weighted by scaled LLR scores λ_i.

4 Mining Publicity from Reader-Emotion

Our approach for mining publicity is by collecting online news articles centered around k specific public figures and determine the reader-emotion towards each of them, with the goal of identifying the public image of these people that can potentially affect how much the general population is willing to support them. We formulate the publicity of a person as a publicity score (PS) with positive or negative notion that can be summarized from identification of reader's emotion of articles. For this purpose, we only consider coarse-grained emotion categories (i.e., *positive* and *negative*). Thus, fine-grained emotion categories like *happy*, *warm*, and *odd* are considered to be "positive", while *angry*, *boring*, *depressing*, and *worried* being "negative". Moreover, PS is not only directly related to the public opinion towards an individual, but also affected by how his or her opponents are viewed. Hence, PS should jointly consider both directions of emotion. We define publicity score PS_i of a person i as:

$$PS_i = (P_i - N_i) + \sum_{j=1, j \neq i}^{k} (\frac{N_j - P_j}{k - 1}), \qquad (2)$$

where P_i and N_i denotes the number of documents with positive and negative reader's emotion, respectively. Meanwhile, there are P_j and N_j articles with positive and negative reader-emotion for another person j. We postulate that PS_i also benefits from the negative publicity of other opposing people. However, since the negativity of the person j does not guarantee that the same amount of positivity from the public will automatically divert to a specific person, we divide the negative score of person j by the number of remaining candidates, $k - 1$, before adding that to PS_i. This way, we can quantify the publicity of, e.g. presidential candidates, and examine its relationship with other measurable metrics such as polls.

5 Experiments

We conduct two experiments to test the effectiveness of DEKV. The goal of the first one is detecting the

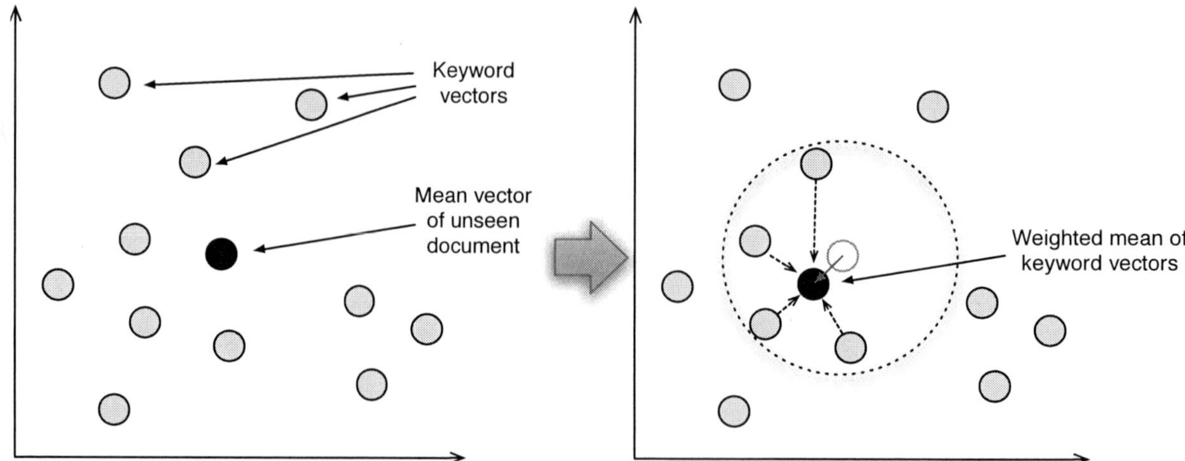

Figure 3: DEKV transforms a document with no keywords as a weighted average of closest keyword vectors.

reader-emotion of a news article, and the second one is inferring the publicity of famous public figures. Details are explained in the following sections.

5.1 Exp. I: Reader-emotion Classification

5.1.1 Dataset

We use a corpus containing 47,285 Chinese news articles[1] for evaluation. It is a very suitable testbed because it contains a socially infused feature of community voting. In particular, a reader of a news article can cast a vote expressing his or her feelings after reading this article with the emotion categories include *angry, worried, boring, happy, odd, depressing, warm*, and *informative*. Furthermore, only those with a clear statistical distinction between the highest vote and others determined by a *t*-test with 95% confidence level are included to ensure the validity of our experiments. The dataset is divided into training and test sets, containing 11,681 and 35,604 articles, respectively. Detail statistics of the corpus is listed in Table 1. Note that the evaluation excludes *informative* for it is not considered as an emotion (Lin et al., 2007; Lin et al., 2008).

5.1.2 Experimental Settings

DEKV is based on embeddings learned from the training set using CBOW with default settings in the toolkit (Řehůřek and Sojka, 2010), and LLR for keywords in each emotion category as weights. Each

____
[1]Collected from `http://tw.news.yahoo.com`

Category	#Train	#Test	Total
Angry	2,001	4,326	6,327
Worried	261	261	522
Boring	1,473	1,473	2,946
Happy	2,001	7,344	9,345
Odd	1,526	1,526	3,052
Depressing	1,573	1,573	3,146
Warm	835	835	1,670
Informative	2,001	18,266	20,267
Total	11,681	35,604	47,285

Table 1: Descriptive statistics of the reader-emotion dataset.

article is represented as a weighted average of keywords and classified by linear SVM (Chang and Lin, 2011). Different combinations of the dimension in embeddings and number of keywords are tested, and the best one (500-dimension embeddings with 2,000 keywords/emotion) is compared with other methods described below. First, Naïve Bayes (McCallum et al., 1998) is used as baseline (denoted as NB). Next, we include LDA (Blei et al., 2003) as document representation and an SVM classifier (denoted as LDA). To examine the effect of our keyword extraction approach, an emotion keyword-based model that represents each article as a sparse vector and uses SVM as its classifier, denoted as KW, is also compared. In addition, we implement a method (denoted as CF) in (Lin et al., 2007) that uses extensive features including bigrams, words, metadata, and emotion category words. To inspect the effect of weighting, we also use the average of keyword vectors trained using the same parameters as DEKV, denote as *mean*.

Details of the implementations of these methods are as follows. We employ CKIP (Hsieh et al., 2012) for Chinese word segmentation. The dictionary required by Naïve Bayes and LDA is constructed by removing stop words according to a Chinese stop word list provided by Zou et al. (2006), and retaining tokens that make up 90% of the accumulated frequency. In other words, the dictionary can cover up to 90% of the tokens in the corpus. As for unseen events, we use Laplace smoothing in Naïve Bayes, and an LDA toolkit is used to perform the detection of LDA. Regarding the CF, the words output by the segmentation tool are used. The information related to news reporter, news category, location of the news event, time (hour of publication) and news agency are treated as the metadata features. The extracted emotion keywords are used in place of the emotion category words, since the emotion categories was not released in (Lin et al., 2007).

To evaluate the effectiveness of these systems, we adopt the accuracy measures used by Lin et al. (2007); macro-average (avg_M) and micro-average (avg_μ) are selected to compute the average performance. These measures are defined based on a contingency table of predictions for a target emotion E_k. The accuracy $acc(E_k)$, macro-average avg_M, and micro-average avg_μ are defined as follows:

$$acc(E_k)$$

$$= \frac{TP(E_k) + TN(E_k)}{TP(E_k) + FP(E_k) + TN(E_k) + FN(E_k)}, \quad (3)$$

$$avg_M = \frac{1}{m} \sum_{k=1}^{m} acc(E_k), \quad (4)$$

$$avg_\mu = \frac{acc(E_k) \times N(E_k)}{\sum_{k=1}^{m} N(E_k)}, \quad (5)$$

where $TP(E_k)$ is the set of test documents correctly classified to the emotion E_k, $FP(E_k)$ is the set of test documents incorrectly classified to the emotion, $FN(E_k)$ is the set of test documents wrongly rejected, $TN(E_k)$ is the set of test documents correctly rejected, and $N(E_k)$ is the total number of documents in this emotion category.

5.1.3 Results

Table 2 lists performances of all methods. As a baseline, the Naïve Bayes classifier is a keyword statistics-based system which can only accomplish a mediocre performance. Since it only considers surface word weightings, it is difficult to represent inter-word relations. The overall accuracy of the Naïve Bayes classifier is 56.13%, with the emotion "Warm" only achieving 15.09% accuracy. On the contrary, the LDA yields a macro average accuracy of 74.12%, indicating its ability to select important topics for some emotion categories. However, KW is more effective in finding representative keywords using LLR as weights, obtaining 80.79% accuracy overall. Furthermore, it exhibits a more evenly distributed performance among categories than LDA. Next, CF achieves an overall accuracy of 85.69%, which may be attributed to its extensive feature engineering. It also obtains the highest accuracy for the category *boring*. Finally, when comparing *mean* and DEKV, it is clear that using a simple average of embeddings is inferior to weighting by LLR. DEKV obtains the best macro average accuracy of 89.21%, and six out of seven best per-category accuracy. For the purpose of our next task, we combine fine-grained emotions *happy, warm, odd* into "*positive*", and *angry, boring, depressing, worried* into "*negative*".

Emotion	Accuracy(%)					
	NB	LDA	KW	CF	mean	DEKV
angry	47.00	74.21	79.21	83.71	79.47	**86.31**
worried	69.56	92.83	81.96	87.50	98.33	**98.46**
boring	75.67	76.21	84.34	**87.52**	83.81	85.62
happy	37.90	67.59	80.97	86.27	87.70	**90.86**
odd	73.90	85.40	77.05	84.25	85.41	**86.17**
depressing	73.76	81.43	85.00	87.70	88.28	**91.05**
warm	15.09	87.09	79.59	85.83	92.95	**95.20**
avg_M	56.13	74.12	80.79	85.69	85.58	**89.21**
avg_μ	23.95	80.68	81.16	86.11	87.99	**90.50**

Table 2: Comparison of accuracies from five reader-emotion classification methods. Bold numbers indicate the best performance in each emotion category (row).

To better visualize the effectiveness of our keyword selection method, we present these keywords as a word cloud in Fig. 4. Each keyword is color-coded by its corresponding emotion category, and scaled in size by its LLR score. Through this method, we can easily identify features within each group. For example, as stated in the previous section, we observed that keywords related to "Happy" (in green) are mostly about sports, including terms

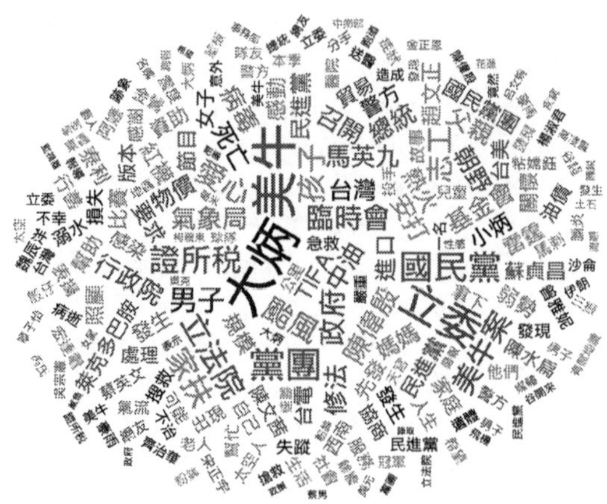

Figure 4: The word cloud generated from reader-emotion keywords. Colors and their corresponding emotion: Red—Angry, Green—Happy, Orange—Warm, Brown—Worried, Dark Blue—Depressed, Magenta—Boring, Light blue—Odd.

such as team names (e.g., "熱火 (Miami Heat)" and "紅襪 (Boston Red Sox)") and player names (e.g., "陳偉殷 (Wei-Yin Chen)", a pitcher for the baseball team Baltimore Orioles). Similar findings had also been revealed previously (Lin et al., 2007). On the contrary, "Angry"-related keywords (in red) consist largely of political parties or issues. For instance, the most noticeable word "美牛 (United States beef)" indicates the controversy of importing beef from the United States to Taiwan, which has been an issue that affects the Taiwan-U.S. relations and causes domestic political unrest. Simultaneously, numerous political terms such as "國民黨 (Kuomintang)", "立法院 (Legislative Yuan)", and "立委 (legislator)" are also keywords that provoke anger. The figure highlights the fact that the extracted emotion keywords are highly correlated with reader-emotions, and including them in the DEKV determine precise reader-emotions. As for the "Depressing" category, keywords are mostly related to social events that involve severe weathers or casualties. The most prevalent word, "大炳 (Da Bing)", refers to a Taiwanese actor who died in 2012, coinciding the time span of our retrieved data. Names of athletes might also show up in this category, owing to the readers' concerns about their performance in major sports events. In addition, the "Warm" category contains words associated with social care, volunteering, and charity.

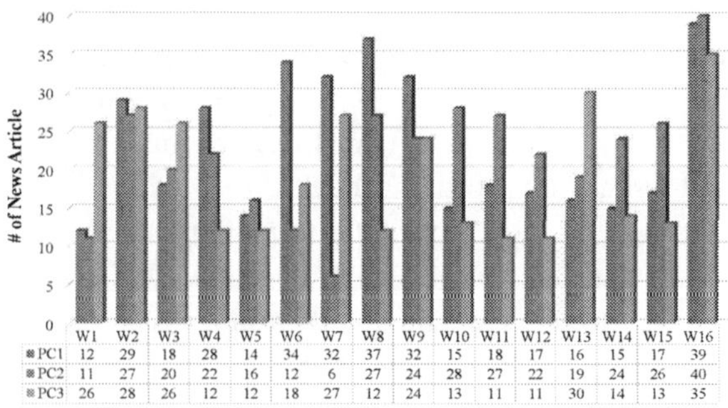

Figure 5: Descriptive statistics of the presidential election dataset. Numbers indicate the amount of news articles about a presidential candidate (PC) per week.

	W1	W2	W3	W4	W5	W6	W7	W8	W9	W10	W11	W12	W13	W14	W15	W16
PC1	12	29	18	28	14	34	32	37	32	15	18	17	16	15	17	39
PC2	11	27	20	22	16	12	6	27	24	28	27	22	19	24	26	40
PC3	26	28	26	12	12	18	27	12	24	13	11	11	30	14	13	35

5.2 Exp. II: From Reader-Emotion to Publicity

The purpose of this experiment is to test the effectiveness of publicity score (PS) of a person based on our reader-emotion categorization method to estimate the trend of the poll. We collected 1,036 news articles from October 2015 to January 2016 regarding three presidential candidates (PC) from the same source as the previous experiment. Descriptive statistics about how many articles per PC by week are listed in Fig. 5. Note that they do not overlap with the previous corpus. We used the poll data from the first week as the initial value, and incremented it with PS obtained for each PC every week. These articles are first categorized into "*positive*" and '*negative*' using DEKV, and PS is calculated using (2) defined in Section 4.

	PC 1	PC 2	PC 3
poll/PS	0.20	0.50	0.72
poll/%Positive	-0.44	-0.42	-0.46

Table 3: Comparison of Pearson's r between the poll, publicity score (PS), and the ratio of positive emotion in news articles.

5.2.1 Results

We first examine the Pearson correlation coefficients in Table 3 between the poll and PS as well as the amount of positive emotion in the news articles, defined as the number of positive articles subtracted by that of the negative ones. It shows that the degree of correlation between PS and the poll number is positive and higher than that between a simpler metric, namely, the count of positive and negative articles. As a result, PS can serve as a more suitable measure of the publicity of a certain subject. Still, we also observe that there is a considerable difference in the coefficients among different candidates. PS for PC 1 appears to be the least correlated, while PC 3 shows a high correlation between PS and poll. Further analysis is required to unveil the reason behind this phenomenon, but we suspect it may be related to the amount of documents for each PC.

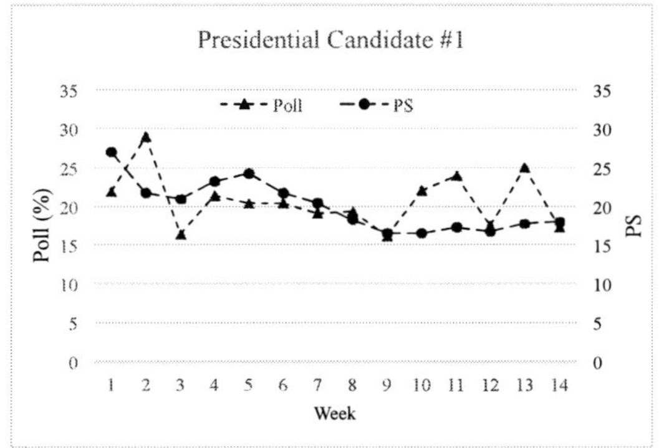

Figure 6: Timeline of the trend in publicity score (PS) and poll for presidential candidate (PC) #1.

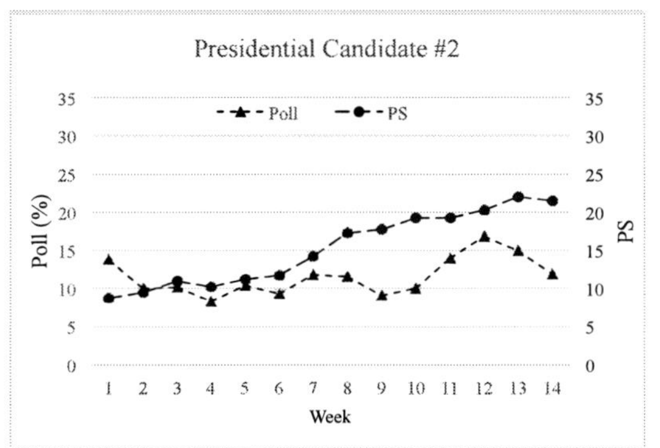

Figure 7: Timeline of the trend in publicity score (PS) and poll for presidential candidate (PC) #2.

Next, we plot PS for each PC in Fig. 6 to 8 for a subjective evaluation. We can see that the direction of increase and decrease (i.e., ups and downs) of the curves roughly align with those of the poll, validating our initial assumption of using the reader's emotion of a news article to quantify the publicity of a person. It also shows that there exists a positive correlation between the poll and PS. In general, PS does not experience sharp turns like the trend we witnessed in the curves of poll, showing that the publicity score is more robust due to its immunity to

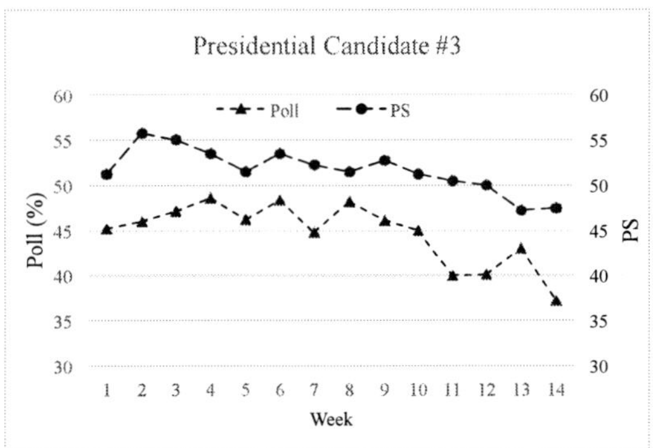

Figure 8: Timeline of the trend in publicity score (PS) and poll for presidential candidate (PC) #3.

the temporary surge in news articles. However, PS is less than optimal for predicting the polls for PC#1, illustrated by the curves in PC#1 being more random than others (e.g., in weeks 2 and 11) and the results in Table 3. Thus, a more sophisticated modeling of the interaction between reader's emotion and a candidate's publicity is worthy of further research.

In sum, our method objectively induce the publicity score through classification of readers' emotion on news events, preserving its accuracy from the fluctuation of sampling bias in non-official polling institutions. Our approach for mining the publicity of public figures through reader's emotion classification provides a promising direction for automated collection of such information online.

6 Conclusion

We propose a novel document representation model, DEKV, for reader-emotion classification, as well as a publicity mining method. Experiments on two Chinese news corpora demonstrate that DEKV outperforms well-known models for reader-emotion detection and can subsequently be related to the publicity of a person. We believe it is an emerging direction for automated collection of social and emotional information online. We also envision its applications on numerous academic as well as business domains. In the future, we will explore different ways to integrate deeper semantics and further investigate the relation between emotion and publicity.

Acknowledgments

We are grateful to the anonymous reviewers for their insightful comments. This research was supported by the Ministry of Science and Technology of Taiwan under grant number MOST105-2221-E-001-008-MY3.

References

Yoshua Bengio, Réjean Ducharme, Pascal Vincent, and Christian Janvin. 2003. A neural probabilistic language model. *The Journal of Machine Learning Research*, 3:1137–1155.

David M Blei, Andrew Y Ng, and Michael I Jordan. 2003. Latent Dirichlet allocation. *Journal of Machine Learning Research*, 3:993–1022.

Chih-Chung Chang and Chih-Jen Lin. 2011. LIBSVM : a library for support vector machines. *ACM Transactions on Intelligent Systems and Technology*, 2(3):27:1–27:27.

Yung-Chun Chang, Cen-Chieh Chen, Yu-lun Hsieh, Chien Chin Chen, and Wen-Lian Hsu. 2015. Linguistic template extraction for recognizing reader-emotion and emotional resonance writing assistance. In *Proceedings of the 53rd ACL and the 7th IJCNLP (Volume 2: Short Papers)*, pages 775–780.

Ying Chen, Sophia Yat Mei Lee, Shoushan Li, and Chu-Ren Huang. 2010. Emotion cause detection with linguistic constructions. In *Proceedings of the 23rd International Conference on Computational Linguistics*, pages 179–187.

Corinna Cortes and Vladimir Vapnik. 1995. Support-vector networks. *Machine learning*, 20(3):273–297.

Dipankar Das and Sivaji Bandyopadhyay. 2009. Word to sentence level emotion tagging for bengali blogs. In *Proceedings of the ACL-IJCNLP 2009 Conference*, pages 149–152.

Yi Fang, Luo Si, Naveen Somasundaram, and Zhengtao Yu. 2012. Mining contrastive opinions on political texts using cross-perspective topic model. In *Proceedings of the fifth ACM international conference on Web search and data mining*, pages 63–72. ACM.

Daniel Gayo-Avello. 2012. I wanted to predict elections with twitter and all i got was this lousy paper – a balanced survey on election prediction using twitter data. *arXiv preprint arXiv:1204.6441*.

Yu-Ming Hsieh, Ming-Hong Bai, Jason S Chang, and Keh-Jiann Chen. 2012. Improving PCFG chinese parsing with context-dependent probability re-estimation. *CLP 2012*, page 216.

Minqing Hu and Bing Liu. 2004. Mining and summarizing customer reviews. In *Proceedings of the 10th ACM SIGKDD International Conference on Knowledge Discovery and Data Mining*, pages 168–177. ACM.

Siwei Lai, Kang Liu, Liheng Xu, and Jun Zhao. 2015. How to generate a good word embedding? 07.

Quoc Le and Tomas Mikolov. 2014. Distributed representations of sentences and documents. In *Proceedings of the 31st International Conference on Machine Learning (ICML-14)*, pages 1188–1196.

Kevin Hsin-Yih Lin, Changhua Yang, and Hsin-Hsi Chen. 2007. What emotions do news articles trigger in their readers? In *Proceedings of the 30th Annual International ACM SIGIR Conference on Research and Development in Information Retrieval*, pages 733–734.

Kevin Hsin-Yih Lin, Changhua Yang, and Hsin-Hsi Chen. 2008. Emotion classification of online news articles from the reader's perspective. In *Proceedings of the 2008 IEEE/WIC/ACM International Conference on Web Intelligence and Intelligent Agent Technology*, volume 1, pages 220–226.

Christopher D Manning and Hinrich Schütze. 1999. *Foundations of statistical natural language processing*. MIT press.

Andrew McCallum, Kamal Nigam, et al. 1998. A comparison of event models for naive bayes text classification. In *AAAI-98 workshop on learning for text categorization*, volume 752, pages 41–48.

Tomas Mikolov, Kai Chen, Greg Corrado, and Jeffrey Dean. 2013a. Efficient estimation of word representations in vector space. In *Proceedings of Workshop at ICLR*.

Tomas Mikolov, Ilya Sutskever, Kai Chen, Greg S Corrado, and Jeff Dean. 2013b. Distributed representations of words and phrases and their compositionality. In *Advances in neural information processing systems*, pages 3111–3119.

George A Miller and Walter G Charles. 1991. Contextual correlates of semantic similarity. *Language and cognitive processes*, 6(1):1–28.

Gilad Mishne. 2005. Experiments with mood classification in blog posts. In *Proceedings of the 1st Workshop on Stylistic Analysis Of Text For Information Access (Style 2005)*.

Bo Pang, Lillian Lee, and Shivakumar Vaithyanathan. 2002. Thumbs up?: sentiment classification using machine learning techniques. In *Proceedings of the ACL-02 conference on Empirical methods in natural language processing-Volume 10*, pages 79–86. Association for Computational Linguistics.

Matthew Purver and Stuart Battersby. 2012. Experimenting with distant supervision for emotion classification. In *Proceedings of the 13th Conference of the European Chapter of the Association for Computational Linguistics*, pages 482–491.

Changqin Quan and Fuji Ren. 2009. Construction of a blog emotion corpus for chinese emotional expression analysis. In *Proceedings of the 2009 Conference on Empirical Methods in Natural Language Processing*, volume 3, pages 1446–1454.

Jonathon Read. 2005. Using emoticons to reduce dependency in machine learning techniques for sentiment classification. In *Proceedings of the ACL Student Research Workshop*, pages 43–48. Association for Computational Linguistics.

Radim Řehůřek and Petr Sojka. 2010. Software Framework for Topic Modelling with Large Corpora. In *Proceedings of the LREC 2010 Workshop on New Challenges for NLP Frameworks*, pages 45–50, Valletta, Malta, May. ELRA.

Luís Sarmento, Paula Carvalho, Mário J Silva, and Eugénio De Oliveira. 2009. Automatic creation of a reference corpus for political opinion mining in user-generated content. In *Proceedings of the 1st international CIKM workshop on Topic-sentiment analysis for mass opinion*, pages 29–36. ACM.

Pawel Sobkowicz, Michael Kaschesky, and Guillaume Bouchard. 2012. Opinion mining in social media: Modeling, simulating, and forecasting political opinions in the web. *Government Information Quarterly*, 29(4):470–479.

Yi-jie Tang and Hsin-Hsi Chen. 2012. Mining sentiment words from microblogs for predicting writer-reader emotion transition. In *Proceedings of the 8th International Conference on Language Resources and Evaluation (LREC)*, pages 1226–1229.

Robert E Thayer. 1989. *The biopsychology of mood and arousal*. Oxford University Press.

Peter D Turney. 2002. Thumbs up or thumbs down?: semantic orientation applied to unsupervised classification of reviews. In *Proceedings of the 40th Annual Meeting of the Association for Computational Linguistics*, pages 417–424.

Theresa Wilson, Janyce Wiebe, and Paul Hoffmann. 2009. Recognizing contextual polarity: An exploration of features for phrase-level sentiment analysis. *Computational Linguistics*, 35(3):399–433.

Chung-Hsien Wu, Ze-Jing Chuang, and Yu-Chung Lin. 2006. Emotion recognition from text using semantic labels and separable mixture models. 5(2):165–183.

Changhua Yang and Hsin-Hsi Chen. 2006. A study of emotion classification using blog articles. In *Proceedings of Conference on Computational Linguistics and Speech Processing*.

Yi-Hsuan Yang, Chia-Chu Liu, and Homer H. Chen. 2006. Music emotion classification: A fuzzy approach. In *Proceedings of the 14th Annual ACM International Conference on Multimedia*, MULTIMEDIA '06, pages 81–84, New York, NY, USA. ACM.

Changhua Yang, Kevin Hsin-Yih Lin, and Hsin-Hsi Chen. 2009. Writer meets reader: Emotion analysis of social media from both the writer's and reader's perspectives. In *Proceedings of the 2009 IEEE/WIC/ACM International Joint Conference on Web Intelligence and Intelligent Agent Technology-Volume 01*, pages 287–290. IEEE Computer Society.

Feng Zou, Fu Lee Wang, Xiaotie Deng, Song Han, and Lu Sheng Wang. 2006. Automatic construction of chinese stop word list. In *Proceedings of the 5th WSEAS International Conference on Applied Computer Science*, pages 1010–1015.

Hierarchical Character-Word Models for Language Identification

Aaron Jaech[1] **George Mulcaire**[2] **Shobhit Hathi**[2] **Mari Ostendorf**[1] **Noah A. Smith**[2]
[1]Electrical Engineering [2]Computer Science & Engineering
University of Washington, Seattle, WA 98195, USA
ajaech@uw.edu, gmulc@uw.edu, shathi@uw.edu
ostendor@uw.edu, nasmith@cs.washington.edu

Abstract

Social media messages' brevity and unconventional spelling pose a challenge to language identification. We introduce a hierarchical model that learns character and contextualized word-level representations for language identification. Our method performs well against strong baselines, and can also reveal code-switching.

1 Introduction

Language identification (language ID), despite being described as a solved problem more than ten years ago (McNamee, 2005), remains a difficult problem. Particularly when working with short texts, informal styles, or closely related language pairs, it is an active area of research (Gella et al., 2014; Wang et al., 2015; Baldwin and Lui, 2010). These difficult cases are often found in social media content. Progress on language ID is needed especially since downstream tasks, like translation and semantic parsing, depend on correct language ID.

This paper brings continuous representations for language data, which have produced new states of the art for language modeling (Mikolov et al., 2010), machine translation (Bahdanau et al., 2015), and other tasks, to language ID. We adapt a hierarchical character-word neural architecture from Kim et al. (2016), demonstrating that it works well for language ID. Our model, which we call C2V2L ("character to vector to language") is hierarchical in the sense that it explicitly builds a continuous representation for each word from its character sequence, capturing orthographic and morphology-related patterns, and then combines those word level representations in context, finally classifying the full word

sequence. Our model does not require any special handling of casing or punctuation nor do we need to remove URLs, usernames, or hashtags, and it is trained end-to-end using standard procedures.

We demonstrate the model's state-of-the-art performance in experiments on two datasets consisting of tweets. This hierarchical technique works well compared to classifiers using character or word n-gram features as well as a similar neural model that treats an entire tweet as a single character sequence. We find further that the model can benefit from additional out-of-domain data, unlike much previous work, and with little modification can annotate word-level code-switching. We also confirm that smoothed character n-gram language models perform very well for language ID tasks.

2 Model

Our model has two main components trained together, end-to-end.[1] The first, "char2vec," applies a convolutional neural network (CNN) to a whitespace-delimited word's Unicode character sequence, providing a word vector.[2] The second is a bidirectional LSTM recurrent neural network (RNN) that maps a sequence of such word vectors to a language label.

2.1 Char2vec

The first layer of char2vec is an embedding learned for each Unicode code point that appears at least twice in the training data, including punctuation, emoji, and other symbols. If C is the set of characters then we let the size of the character embed-

---

[1]Code available here: http://github.com/ajaech/twitter_langid
[2]For languages without word segmentation, e.g., Chinese, the entire character sequence is treated as a single word. This still works well (see Section 3.2.)

Proceedings of The Fourth International Workshop on Natural Language Processing for Social Media, pages 84–93,
Austin, TX, November 1, 2016. ©2016 Association for Computational Linguistics

ding layer be $d = \lceil \log_2 |C| \rceil$. (If each dimension of the character embedding vector holds one bit of information then d bits should be enough to uniquely encode each character.) The character embedding matrix is $\mathbf{Q} \in \mathbb{R}^{d \times |C|}$. Words are given to the model as a sequence of characters. When each character in a word of length l is replaced by its embedding vector we get a matrix $\mathbf{C} \in \mathbb{R}^{d \times (l+2)}$. There are $l + 2$ columns in C because padding characters are added to the left and right of each word.

The char2vec architecture uses two sets of filter banks. The first set is comprised of matrices $\mathbf{H}_{a_i} \in \mathbb{R}^{d \times 3}$ where i ranges from 1 to n_1. The matrix $\mathbf{C}$ is narrowly convolved with each $\mathbf{H}_{a_i}$, a bias term b_a is added and an ReLU non-linearity, $\mathrm{ReLU}(x) = \max(0, x)$, is applied to produce an output $\mathbf{T}_1 = \mathrm{ReLU}(\mathrm{conv}(\mathbf{C}, \mathbf{H}_a) + \mathbf{b}_a)$. $\mathbf{T}_1$ is of size $n_1 \times l$ with one row for each of the filters and one column for each of the characters in the input word. Since each of the $\mathbf{H}_{a_i}$ is a filter with a width of three characters, the columns of $\mathbf{T}_1$ each hold a representation of a character trigram. During training, we apply dropout on $\mathbf{T}_1$ to regularize the model. The matrix $\mathbf{T}_1$ is then convolved with a second set of filters $\mathbf{H}_{b_i} \in \mathbb{R}^{n_1 \times w}$ where b_i ranges from 1 to $3n_2$ and n_2 controls the number of filters of each of the possible widths, $w = 3, 4,$ or 5. Another convolution and ReLU non-linearity is applied to get $\mathbf{T}_2 = \mathrm{ReLU}(\mathrm{conv}(\mathbf{T}_1, \mathbf{H}_b) + \mathbf{b}_b)$. Max-pooling across time is used to create a fix-sized vector $\mathbf{y}$ from $\mathbf{T}_2$. The dimension of $\mathbf{y}$ is $3n_2$, corresponding to the number of filters used.

Similar to Kim et al. (2016) who use a highway network after the max-pooling layer, we apply a residual network layer. Both highway and residual network layers allow values from the previous layer to pass through unchanged but the residual layer is preferred in our case because it uses half as many parameters (He et al., 2015). The residual network uses a matrix $\mathbf{W} \in \mathbb{R}^{3n_2 \times 3n_2}$ and bias vector $\mathbf{b}_3$ to create the vector $\mathbf{z} = \mathbf{y} + f_R(\mathbf{y})$ where $f_R(\mathbf{y}) = \mathrm{ReLU}(\mathbf{W}\mathbf{y} + \mathbf{b}_3)$. The resulting vector $\mathbf{z}$ is used as a word embedding vector in the word-level LSTM portion of the model.

There are three differences between our version of the model and the one described by Kim et al. (2016). First, we use two layers of convolution instead of just one, inspired by Ling et al. (2015a)

who used a 2-layer LSTM for character modeling. Second, we use the ReLU function as a nonlinearity as opposed to the tanh function. ReLU has been highly successful in computer vision applications in conjunction with convolutional layers (Jarrett et al., 2009). Finally, we use a residual network layer instead of a highway network layer after the max-pooling step, to reduce the model size.

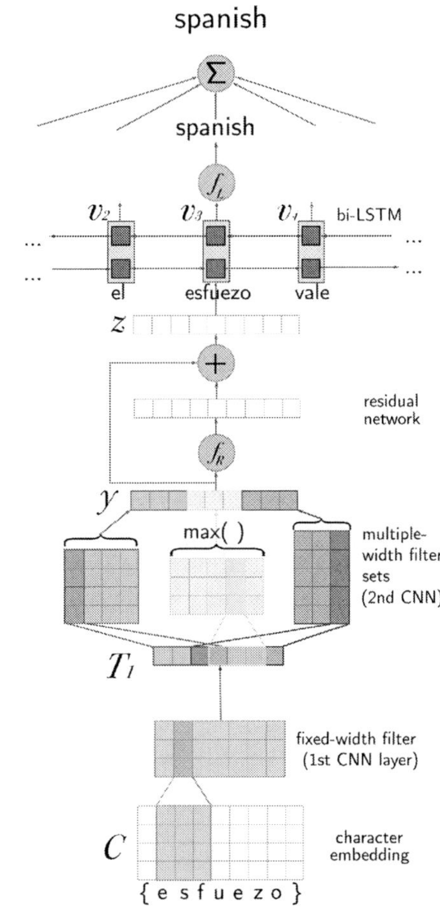

Figure 1: C2V2L model architecture. The model takes the (misspelled) word "esfuezo," and produces a word vector via the two CNN layers and the residual layer. The word vectors are then combined via the LSTM, and the words' predictions averaged for a tweet prediction.

It is possible to use bi-LSTMs instead of convolutional layers in char2vec as done by Ling et al. (2015a). We did explore this option in preliminary experiments but found that using convolutional layers has several advantages, including a large improvement in speed for both the forward and backward pass, many fewer parameters, and improved language ID accuracy.

2.2 Sentence-level Language ID

The sequence of word embedding vectors is processed by a bi-LSTM, which outputs a sequence of vectors, $[\mathbf{v}_1, \ldots \mathbf{v}_T]$ where T is the number of words in the tweet. All LSTM gates are used as defined by Sak et al. (2014). Dropout is used as a regularizer on the inputs to the LSTM, as in Pham et al. (2014). The output vectors $\mathbf{v}_i$ are transformed into probability distributions over the set of languages by applying an affine transformation followed by a softmax:

$$\mathbf{p}_i = f_L(\mathbf{v}_i) = \frac{\exp(\mathbf{A}\mathbf{v}_i + b)}{\sum_{t=1}^{T} \exp(\mathbf{A}\mathbf{v}_t + b)}$$

(These word-level predictions, we will see in §5.4, are useful for annotating code-switching.) The sentence-level prediction $\mathbf{p}_S$ is then given by averaging the word-level language predictions.

The final affine transformation can be interpreted as a language embedding, where each language is represented by a vector of the same dimensionality as the LSTM outputs. The goal of the LSTM then is (roughly) to maximize the dot product of each word's representation with the language embedding(s) for that sentence. The only supervision in the model comes from computing the loss of sentence-level predictions.

3 Tasks and Datasets

We consider two datasets: TweetLID and Twitter70. Summary statistics for each of the datasets are provided in Table 1.

3.1 TweetLID

The TweetLID dataset (Zubiaga et al., 2014) comes from a language ID shared task that focused on six commonly spoken languages of the Iberian peninsula: Spanish, Portuguese, Catalan, Galician, English, and Basque. There are approximately 15,000 tweets in the training data and 25,000 in the test set. The data is unbalanced, with the majority of examples being in the Spanish language. The "undetermined" label ('und'), comprising 1.4% of the training data, is used for tweets that use only non-linguistic tokens or belong to an outside language.

Additionally, some tweets are ambiguous ('amb') among a set of languages (2.3%), or code-switch between languages (2.4%). The evaluation criteria take into account all of these factors, requiring prediction of at least one acceptable language for an ambiguous tweet or all languages present for a code-switched tweet. The fact that hundreds of tweets were labeled ambiguous or undetermined by annotators who were native speakers of these languages reveals the difficulty of this task.

For tweets labeled as ambiguous or containing multiple languages, the training objective distributes the "true" probability mass evenly across each of the languages, e.g., 50% Spanish and 50% Catalan.

The TweetLID shared task had two tracks: one that restricted participants to only use the official training data and another that was unconstrained, allowing the use of any external data. There were 12 submissions in the constrained track and 9 in the unconstrained track. Perhaps surprisingly, most participants performed worse on the unconstrained track than they did on the constrained one.

As supplementary data for our unconstrained-track experiments, we collected data from Wikipedia for each of the six languages in the TweetLID corpus. Participants in the TweetLID shared task also used Wikipedia as a data source for the unconstrained track. We split the text into 25,000 sentence fragments per language, with each fragment of length comparable to that of a tweet. The Wikipedia sentence fragments are easily distinguished from tweets. Wikipedia fragments are more formal and are more likely to use complex words; for example, one fragment reads "ring homomorphisms are identical to monomorphisms in the category of rings." In contrast, tweets tend to use variable spelling and more simple words, as in "Haaaaallelu-jaaaaah http://t.co/axwzUNXk06" and "@justin-bieber: Love you mommy http://t.co/xEGAxBl6Cc http://t.co/749s6XKkgK awe ♡". Previous work confirms that language ID is more challenging on social media text than sentence fragments taken from more formal text, like Wikipedia (Carter, 2012). Despite the domain mismatch, we find in §5.2 that additional text in training helps our model.

The TweetLID training data is too small to divide into training and validation sets. We created a tuning set by adding samples taken from Twitter70

	TweetLID	Twitter70
Tweets	14,991	58,182
Character vocab.	956	5,796
Languages	6	70
Code-switching?	Yes	Not Labeled
Balanced?	No	Roughly

Table 1: Dataset characteristics.

and from the 2014 Workshop on Computational Approaches to Code Switching (Solorio et al., 2014) to the official TweetLID training data. We used this augmented dataset with a 4:1 train/development split for hyperparameter tuning.[3]

3.2 Twitter70

The Twitter70 dataset was published by the Twitter Language Engineering Team in November 2015.[4] The languages come from the Afroasiatic, Dravidian, Indo-European, Sino-Tibetan, and Tai-Kadai families. Each person who wants to use the data must redownload the tweets using the Twitter API. In between the time when the data was published and when it is downloaded, some of the tweets can be lost due to account deletion or changes in privacy settings. At the time when the data was published there were approximately 1,500 tweets for each language. We were able to download 82% of the tweets but the amount we could access varied by language with as many as 1,569 examples for Sindhi and as few as 371 and 39 examples for Uyghur and Oriya, respectively. The median number of tweets per language was 1,083. To our knowledge, there are no published benchmarks on this dataset.

Unlike TweetLID, the Twitter70 data has no unknown or ambiguous labels. Some tweets do contain code-switching but it is not labeled as such; a single language is assigned. There is no predefined test set so we used the last digit of the identification number to partition them. Identifiers ending in zero

---

[3]We used this augmented data to tune hyperparameters for both constrained and unconstrained models. However, after setting hyperparameters, we trained our constrained model using only the official training data, and the unconstrained model using only the training data + Wikipedia. Thus, no extra data was used to learn actual model parameters for the constrained case.

[4]For clarity, we refer to this data as "Twitter70" but it can be found in the Twitter blog post under the name "recall oriented." See `http://t.co/EOVqA0t79j`

(15%) were used for the test set and those ending in one (5%) were used for tuning.

When processing the input at the character level, the vocabulary for each data source is defined as the set of Unicode code-points that occur at least twice in the training data: 956 and 5,796 characters for TweetLID and Twitter70, respectively. A small number of languages, e.g. Mandarin, are responsible for most characters in the Twitter70 vocabulary.

Gillick et al. (2016) processed the input one byte at a time instead of by character. In early experiments, we found that when using bytes the model would often make mistakes that should have been obvious from the orthography alone. We do not recommend using the byte sequence for language ID.

4 Implementation Details

4.1 Preprocessing

An advantage of the hybrid character-word model is that only limited preprocessing is required. The runtime of training char2vec is proportional to the longest word in a minibatch. The data contains many long and repetitive character sequences such as "hahahaha..." or "arghhhhh...". To deal with these, we restricted any sequence of repeating characters to at most five repetitions where the repeating pattern can be from one to four characters. There are many tweets that string together large numbers of Twitter usernames or hashtags without spaces between them. These create extra long "words" that cause our implementation to need more memory and computation during training. To solve this we enforce the constraint that there must be a space before any URL, username, or hashtag. To deal with the few remaining extra-long character sequences, we force word breaks in non-space character sequences every 40 bytes. This primarily affects languages that are not space-delimited like Chinese. We do not perform any special handling of casing or punctuation nor do we need to remove the URLs, usernames, or hashtags as has been done in previous work (Zubiaga et al., 2014). The same preprocessing is used when training the n-gram models.

4.2 Training and Tuning

Training is done using minibatches of size 25 and a learning rate of 0.001 using the Adam method for

Parameter	TweetLID	Twitter70
1st Conv. Layer (n_1)	50	59
2nd Conv. Layer (n_2)	93	108
LSTM	23	38
Dropout	25%	30%
Total Params.	193K	346K

Table 2: Hyperparameter settings for selected models.

optimization (Kingma and Ba, 2015). For the Twitter70 dataset we used 5% held out data for tuning and 15% for evaluation. To tune, we trained 15 models with random hyperparameters and selected the one that performed the best on the development set. Training is done for 80,000 and 100,000 mini-batches for TweetLID and Twitter70 respectively.

The only hyperparameters to tune are the number of filters in each of the two convolutional layers, the size of the word-level LSTM vector, and the dropout rate. The selected values are listed in Table 2.

5 Experiments

For all the studies below on language identification, we compare to two baselines: i) `langid.py`, a popular open-source language ID package, and ii) a classifier using n-gram character language models. For the TweetLID dataset, additional comparisons are included as described next. In addition, we test our model's word-level performance on a code-switching dataset.

The first baseline, based on the `langid.py` package, uses a naïve Bayes classifier over *byte* n-gram features (Lui and Baldwin, 2012). The pre-trained model distributed with the package is designed to perform well on a wide range of domains, and achieved high performance on "microblog messages" (tweets) in the original paper. `langid.py` uses feature selection for domain adaptation and to reduce the model size; thus, retraining it on in-domain data as we do in this paper does not provide an entirely fair comparison. However, we include it for its popularity and importance.

The second baseline is built from character n-gram language models. It assigns each tweet according to language $\ell^* = \arg\max_\ell p(\text{tweet} \mid \ell)$, i.e., applying Bayes' rule with a uniform class prior (Dunning, 1994). For TweetLID, the rare 'und' was handled with a rejection model. Specifically, after ℓ^* is

chosen, a log likelihood ratio test is applied to decide whether to reject the decision in favor of the 'und' class, using the language models for ℓ^* and 'und' with a threshold chosen to optimize F_1 on the development set. The models were trained using Witten-Bell smoothing (Bell et al., 1989), but otherwise the default parameters of the SRILM toolkit (Stolcke, 2002) were used.[5] N-gram model training ignores tweets labeled as ambiguous or containing multiple languages, and the unconstrained models use a simple interpolation of TweetLID and Wikipedia component models. The n-gram order was chosen to minimize perplexity with 5-fold cross validation, yielding n=5 for TweetLID and Twitter70, and n=6 for Wikipedia.

Note that both of these baselines are generative, learning separate models for each language. In contrast, the neural network models explored here are trained on all languages, so parameters may be shared across languages. In particular, a character sequence corresponding to a word in more than one language (e.g., "no" in English and Portuguese) has a language-independent word embedding.

5.1 TweetLID: Constrained Track

In the constrained track of the 2014 shared task, Hurtado et al. (2014) attained the highest performance (75.2 macroaveraged F_1). They used a set of one-vs-all SVM classifiers with character n-gram features, and returned all languages for which the classification confidence was above a fixed threshold. This provides our third, strongest baseline.

In the unconstrained track, the winning team was Gamallo et al. (2014), using a naïve Bayes classifier on word unigrams. They incorporated Wikipedia text to train their model, and were the only team in the competition whose unconstrained model outperformed their constrained one. We compare to their constrained-track result here.

We also consider a version of our model, "C2L," which uses only the char2vec component of C2V2L, treating the entire tweet as a single word. This tests the value of the intermediate word representations in C2V2L; C2L has no explicit word representations. Hyperparameter tuning was carried out separately for C2L.

---

[5]Witten-Bell works well with small character vocabularies.

Results The first column of Table 3 shows the aggregate results across all labels. Our model achieves the state of the art on this task, surpassing the shared task winner, Hurtado et al. (2014). As expected, C2L fails to match the performance of C2V2L, demonstrating that there is value in the hierarchical representations. The performance of the n-gram LM baseline is notably strong, beating eleven out of the twelve submissions to the TweetLID shared task. We also report category-specific performance for our models and baselines in Table 3. Note that performance on underrepresented categories such as 'glg' and 'und' is much lower than the other categories. The category breakdown is not available for previously published results.

One important advantage of our model is its ability to handle special categories of tokens that would otherwise require special treatment as out-of-vocabulary symbols, such as URLs, hashtags, emojis, usernames, etc. Anecdotally, we observe that the input gates of the word-level LSTM are less likely to open for these special classes of tokens. This is consistent with the hypothesis that the model has learned to ignore tokens that are non-informative with respect to language ID.

5.2 TweetLID: Unconstrained Track

We augmented C2V2L's training data with 25,000 fragments of Wikipedia text, weighting the TweetLID training examples ten times more strongly. After training on the combined data, we "fine-tune" the model on the TweetLID data for 2,000 minibatches, which helped to correct for bias away from the undetermined language category, not covered in the Wikipedia data. The same hyperparameters were used as in the constrained experiment.

For the n-gram baseline, we interpolate the models trained on TweetLID and Wikipedia for each language. Interpolation weights given to the Wikipedia language models, set by cross-validation, ranged from 16% for Spanish to 39% for Galician, the most and least common labels respectively.

We also compare to unconstrained-track results of Hurtado et al. (2014) and Gamallo et al. (2014).

Results The results for these experiments are given in Table 4. Like Gamallo et al. (2014), we see a benefit from the use of out-of-domain data, giving a new state of the art on this task as well. Overall, the n-gram language model does not benefit from Wikipedia, but we observe that if the undetermined category, which is not found in the Wikipedia data, is ignored, then there is a net performance gain.

In Table 5, we show the top seven neighbors to selected input words based on cosine similarity. In the left column we see that words with similar features, such as the presence of the "n't" contraction, can be grouped together by char2vec. In the middle column, an out-of-vocabulary username is supplied and similar usernames are retrieved. When working with n-gram features, removing usernames is common, but some previous work demonstrates that they still carry useful information for predicting the language of the tweet (Jaech and Ostendorf, 2015). The third example, "noite" (Portuguese for "night"), shows that the word embeddings are largely invariant to changes in punctuation and capitalization.

5.3 Twitter70

We compare C2V2L to `langid.py` and the 5-gram language model on the Twitter70 dataset; see Table 6. Although the 5-gram model achieves the best performance, the results are virtually identical to those for C2V2L except for the closely-related Bosnian-Croatian language pair.

The lowest performance for all the models is on closely related language pairs. For example, using the C2V2L model, the F_1 score for Danish is only 62.7 due to confusion with the mutually intelligble Norwegian (Van Bezooijen et al., 2008). Distinguishing Bosnian and Croatian, two varieties of a single language, is also difficult. Languages that have unique orthographies such as Greek and Korean are identified with near perfect accuracy.

A potential advantage of the C2V2L model over the n-gram models is the ability to share information between related languages. In Figure 2 we show a T-SNE plot of the language embedding vectors taken from the softmax layer of our model trained with a rank constraint of 10 on the softmax layer.[6] Many languages appear close to related languages, although a few are far from their *phonetic* neighbors due to *orthographic* dissimilarity.

---

[6]The rank constraint was added for visualization; without it, the model makes all language embeddings roughly orthogonal to each other, making T-SNE visualization difficult.

Model	Avg. F_1	eng	spa	cat	eus	por	glg	und	amb
n-gram LM	75.0	74.8	94.2	82.7	74.8	**93.4**	49.5	**38.9**	87.0
`langid.py`	68.9	65.9	92.0	72.9	70.6	89.8	52.7	18.8	83.8
C2L	72.7	73.0	93.8	82.6	75.7	89.4	57.0	18.0	92.1
C2V2L	**76.2**	**75.6**	**94.7**	**85.3**	**82.7**	91.0	**58.5**	27.2	**94.5**

Table 3: F_1 scores on the TweetLID language ID task (constrained track), averaged and per language category (including undetermined and ambiguous). The scores for Hurtado et al. (2014) and Gamallo et al. (2014) are 75.2 and 75.6 respectively, as reported in Zubiaga et al. (2014); per-language scores are not available.

Model	F_1	Δ
Hurtado et al. (2014)	69.7	−4.5
Gamallo et al. (2014)	75.3	+2.7
n-gram LM	74.7	−0.3
C2V2L	**77.1**	+0.9

Table 4: F_1 scores for the unconstrained data track of the TweetLID language ID task. Δ measures change in absolute F_1 score from the constrained condition.

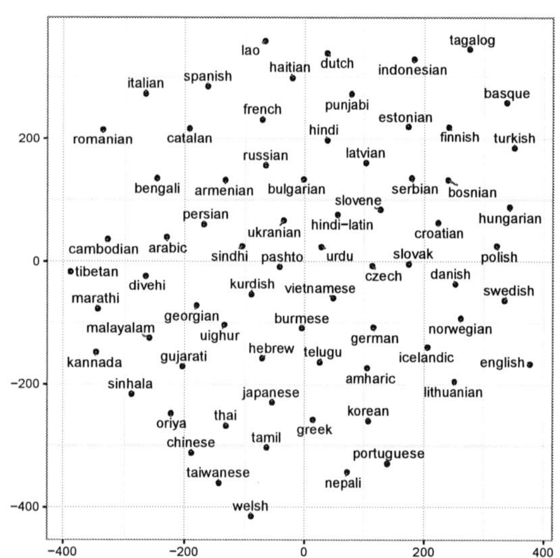

Figure 2: T-SNE plot of language embeddings.

5.4 Code-Switching

Because C2V2L produces language predictions for every word before making the tweet-level prediction, the same architecture can be used in word-level analysis of code-switched text, switching between multiple languages. Training a model with token level code-switching predictions requires a dataset that has token level labels. We used the Spanish-English dataset from the EMNLP 2014 shared task on Language Identification in Code-Switched Data (Solorio et al., 2014): a collection of monolingual and code-switched tweets in English and Spanish.

To train and predict at the word level, we remove the final average over the word predictions, and calculate the loss as the sum of the cross-entropy between each word's prediction and the corresponding gold label. Both the char2vec and word LSTM components of the model are unaffected, other than retraining their parameters.[7] To tune hyperparameters, we trained 10 models with random parameter settings on 80% of the data from the training set, and chose the settings from the model that performed best on the remaining 20%. We then retrained on the full training set with these settings.

C2V2L performed well at this task, scoring 95.1 F_1 for English (which would have achieved second place in the shared task, out of eight entries), 94.1 for Spanish (second place), 36.2 for named entities (fourth place) and 94.2 for Other (third place).[8] While our code-switching results are not quite state-of-the-art, they show that our model learns to make accurate word-level predictions. For other results on code-switched data, see Jaech et al. (2016b).

6 Related Work

Language ID has a long history both in the speech domain (House and Neuburg, 1977) and for text (Cavnar and Trenkle, 1994). Previous work on the text domain mostly uses word or character n-gram features combined with linear classifiers (Hurtado et al., 2014; Gamallo et al., 2014).

Recently published work by Radford and Gallé (2016) showed that combining an n-gram language model classifier (similar to our n-gram baseline)

---

[7]Both sentence and word-level supervision could be used to train the same model, but we leave that for future work.

[8]Full results for the 2014 shared task are omitted for space but can be found at `http://emnlp2014.org/workshops/CodeSwitch/results.php`.

couldn't		@maria_sanchez		noite	
can't	0.84	@Ainhooa_Sanchez	0.85	Noite	0.99
'don't	0.80	@Ronal2Sanchez:	0.71	noite.	0.98
ain't	0.80	@maria_lsantos	0.68	noite?	0.98
don't	0.79	@jordi_sanchez	0.66	noite..	0.96
didn't	0.79	@marialouca?	0.66	noite,	0.95
Can't	0.78	@mariona_g9	0.65	noitee	0.92
first	0.77	@mario_casas_	0.65	noiteee	0.90

Table 5: Top seven most similar words from the training data and their cosine similarities for inputs "couldn't", "@maria_sanchez", and "noite".

Model	F_1
langid.py	87.9
5-gram LM	93.8
C2V2L (ours)	91.2

Table 6: F_1 scores on the Twitter70 dataset.

with information from the Twitter social graph improves language ID on TweetLID from 74.7 to 76.6 F_1, only slightly better than our result of 76.2.

Bergsma et al. (2012) created their own multilingual Twitter dataset and tested both a discriminative model based on n-grams plus hand-crafted features and a compression-based classifier. Since the Twitter API requires researchers to re-download tweets based on their identifiers, published datasets quickly go out of date when the tweets in question are no longer available online, making it difficult to compare against prior work.

Several other studies have investigated the use of character sequence models in language processing. These techniques were first used only to create word embeddings (dos Santos and Zadrozny, 2015; dos Santos and Guimaraes, 2015) and then later extended to have the word embeddings feed directly into a word-level RNN. Applications include part-of-speech tagging (Ling et al., 2015b), language modeling (Ling et al., 2015a), dependency parsing (Ballesteros et al., 2015), translation (Ling et al., 2015b), and slot filling text analysis (Jaech et al., 2016a). The work is divided in terms of whether the character sequence is modeled with an LSTM or CNN, though virtually all now leverage the resulting word vectors in a word-level RNN. We are not aware of prior results comparing LSTMs and CNNs on a specific task, but the reduction in model size compared to word-only systems is reported to be much higher for LSTM architectures. All analyses report that the greatest improvements in performance from character sequence models are for infrequent and previously unseen words, as expected.

Chang and Lin (2014) outperformed the top results for English-Spanish and English-Nepali in the EMNLP 2014 Language Identification in Code-Switched Data (Solorio et al., 2014), using an RNN with skipgram word embeddings and character n-gram features. Word-level language ID has also been studied by Mandal et al. (2015) in the context of question answering and by King and Abney (2013). Both used primarily character n-gram features, which are well motivated for code-switching tasks since the presence of multiple languages increases the odds of encountering a previously unseen word.

7 Conclusion

We present C2V2L, a hierarchical neural model for language ID that outperforms previous work on the challenging TweetLID task. We also find that smoothed character n-gram language models can work well as classifiers for language ID for short texts. Without feature engineering, our n-gram baseline beat eleven out of the twelve submissions in the TweetLID shared task, and gives the best performance on the Twitter70 dataset, where training data for some languages is quite small. In future work, we plan to further adapt C2V2L to analyze code-switching, having shown that the current architecture already performs well.

Acknowledgments

This work is supported in part by a subcontract with Raytheon BBN Technologies Corp. under DARPA Prime Contract No. HR0011-15-C-0013 and by a gift to the University of Washington by Google. Views expressed are those of the authors and do not reflect the official policy or position of the Department of Defense or the U.S. government.

References

Dzmitry Bahdanau, Kyunghyun Cho, and Yoshua Bengio. 2015. Neural machine translation by jointly learning to align and translate. In *Proc. Int. Conf. Learning Representations (ICLR)*.

Timothy Baldwin and Marco Lui. 2010. Language identification: The long and the short of the matter. In *Proc. Conf. North American Chapter Assoc. for Computational Linguistics: Human Language Technologies (NAACL-HLT)*, pages 229–237. Association for Computational Linguistics.

Miguel Ballesteros, Chris Dyer, and Noah Smith. 2015. Improved transition-based parsing by modeling characters instead of words with LSTMs. In *Proc. Conf. Empirical Methods Natural Language Process. (EMNLP)*, pages 349–359.

Timothy Bell, Ian H Witten, and John G Cleary. 1989. Modeling for text compression. *ACM Computing Surveys (CSUR)*, 21(4):557–591.

Shane Bergsma, Paul McNamee, Mossaab Bagdouri, Clayton Fink, and Theresa Wilson. 2012. Language identification for creating language-specific Twitter collections. In *Proc. Workshop on Language in Social Media (LSM)*, pages 65–74. Association for Computational Linguistics.

Simon Christopher Carter. 2012. *Exploration and exploitation of multilingual data for statistical machine translation*. Ph.D. thesis, University of Amsterdam.

William B. Cavnar and John M. Trenkle. 1994. N-gram-based text categorization. In *In Proc. of SDAIR-94, 3rd Annual Symposium on Document Analysis and Information Retrieval*, pages 161–175.

Joseph Chee Chang and Chu-Cheng Lin. 2014. Recurrent-neural-network for language detection on Twitter code-switching corpus. *CoRR*, abs/1412.4314.

Cicero dos Santos and Victor Guimaraes. 2015. Boosting named entity recognition with neural character embeddings. In *Proc. ACL Named Entities Workshop*, pages 25–33.

Cicero dos Santos and Bianca Zadrozny. 2015. Learning character-level representations for part-of-speech tagging. In *Proc. Int. Conf. Machine Learning (ICML)*.

Ted Dunning. 1994. Statistical identification of language. Technical report, Computing Research Laboratory, New Mexico State University, March.

Pablo Gamallo, Marcos Garcia, and Susana Sotelo. 2014. Comparing ranking-based and naive Bayes approaches to language detection on tweets. In *TweetLID@ SEPLN*.

Spandana Gella, Kalika Bali, and Monojit Choudhury. 2014. "ye word kis lang ka hai bhai?": Testing the limits of word level language identification. In *Proc. Int. Conf. Natural Language Processing (ICON)*.

Dan Gillick, Cliff Brunk, Oriol Vinyals, and Amarnag Subramanya. 2016. Multilingual language processing from bytes. In *Proc. Conf. North American Chapter Assoc. for Computational Linguistics (NAACL)*.

Kaiming He, Xiangyu Zhang, Shaoqing Ren, and Jian Sun. 2015. Deep residual learning for image recognition. *arXiv preprint arXiv:1512.03385*.

Arthur S House and Edward P Neuburg. 1977. Toward automatic identification of the language of an utterance. *The Journal of the Acoustical Society of America*, 62(3):708–713.

Lluís F Hurtado, Ferran Pla, and Mayte Giménez. 2014. ELiRF-UPV en TweetLID: Identificación del idioma en Twitter. In *TweetLID@ SEPLN*.

Aaron Jaech and Mari Ostendorf. 2015. What your username says about you. *Proc. Conf. Empirical Methods Natural Language Process. (EMNLP)*.

Aaron Jaech, Larry Heck, and Mari Ostendorf. 2016a. Domain adaptation of recurrent neural networks for natural language understanding. In *Proc. Conf. Int. Speech Communication Assoc. (INTERSPEECH)*.

Aaron Jaech, George Mulcaire, Shobhit Hathi, Mari Ostendorf, and Noah A. Smith. 2016b. A neural model for language identification in code-switched Tweets. In *Proc. Int. Workshop on Computational Approaches to Linguistic Code Switching (CALCS)*.

Kevin Jarrett, Koray Kavukcuoglu, Marc'Aurelio Ranzato, and Yann Lecun. 2009. What is the best multi-stage architecture for object recognition? In *2009 IEEE 12th International Conference on Computer Vision*, pages 2146–2153. IEEE.

Yoon Kim, Yacine Jernite, David Sontag, and Alexander Rush. 2016. Character-aware neural language models. In *Proc. AAAI*, pages 2741–2749.

Ben King and Steven Abney. 2013. Labeling the languages of words in mixed-language documents using weakly supervised methods. In *Proc. Conf. North American Chapter Assoc. for Computational Linguistics: Human Language Technologies (NAACL-HLT)*, pages 1110–1119.

Diederik Kingma and Jimmy Ba. 2015. Adam: A method for stochastic optimization. In *Proc. Int. Conf. Learning Representations (ICLR)*.

Wang Ling, Tiago Luís, Luís Marujo, Ramón Fernandez Astudillo, Silvio Amir, Chris Dyer, Alan W Black, and Isabel Trancoso. 2015a. Finding function in form: Compositional character models for open vocabulary word representation. *Proc. Conf. Empirical Methods Natural Language Process. (EMNLP)*.

Wang Ling, Isabel Trancoso, Chris Dyer, and Alan Black. 2015b. Character-based neural machine translation. *arXiv preprint arXiv:1511.04586v1*.

Marco Lui and Timothy Baldwin. 2012. langid. py: An off-the-shelf language identification tool. In *Proc. of the ACL 2012 system demonstrations*, pages 25–30. Association for Computational Linguistics.

Soumik Mandal, Somnath Banerjee, Sudip Kumar Naskar, Paolo Rosso, and Sivaji Bandyopadhyay. 2015. Adaptive voting in multiple classifier systems for word level language identification. In *the Working Notes in Forum for Information Retrieval Evaluation (FIRE)*.

Paul McNamee. 2005. Language identification: A solved problem suitable for undergraduate instruction. *J. Comput. Sci. Coll.*, 20(3):94–101, February.

Tomas Mikolov, Martin Karafiát, Lukas Burget, Jan Cernockỳ, and Sanjeev Khudanpur. 2010. Recurrent neural network based language model. In *Proc. Conf. Int. Speech Communication Assoc. (INTERSPEECH)*, volume 2, page 3.

V. Pham, T. Bluche, C. Kermorvant, and J. Louradour. 2014. Dropout improves recurrent neural networks for handwriting recognition. In *Proc. Int. Conf. on Frontiers in Handwriting Recognition*, pages 285–290.

Will Radford and Matthias Gallé. 2016. Discriminating between similar languages in Twitter using label propagation. *arXiv preprint arxiv:1607.05408*.

Hasim Sak, Andrew W Senior, and Françoise Beaufays. 2014. Long short-term memory recurrent neural network architectures for large scale acoustic modeling. In *Proc. Conf. Int. Speech Communication Assoc. (INTERSPEECH)*, pages 338–342.

Thamar Solorio, Elizabeth Blair, Suraj Maharjan, Steven Bethard, Mona Diab, Mahmoud Gohneim, Abdelati Hawwari, Fahad AlGhamdi, Julia Hirschberg, Alison Chang, et al. 2014. Overview for the first shared task on language identification in code-switched data. In *Proc. Int. Workshop on Computational Approaches to Linguistic Code Switching (CALCS)*, pages 62–72.

Andreas Stolcke. 2002. SRILM-An extensible language modeling toolkit. In *Proc. Conf. Int. Speech Communication Assoc. (INTERSPEECH)*, volume 2002, page 2002.

Renée Van Bezooijen, Charlotte Gooskens, Sebastian Kürschner, and Anja Schüppert. 2008. Linguistic factors of mutual intelligibility in closely related languages. In *Article presented at the Symposium on Receptive Multilingualism, part II (organized by JD ten Thije), AILA 2008 conference'Multilingualism: Challenges and Opportunities', Essen*, pages 24–29.

Pidong Wang, Nikhil Bojja, and Shivasankari Kannan. 2015. A language detection system for short chats in mobile games. In *Proc. Int. Workshop on Natural Language Processing for Social Media (SocialNLP)*, pages 20–28, Denver, Colorado, June. Association for Computational Linguistics.

Arkaitz Zubiaga, Inaki San Vicente, Pablo Gamallo, José Ramom Pichel Campos, Iñaki Alegría Loinaz, Nora Aranberri, Aitzol Ezeiza, and Víctor Fresno-Fernández. 2014. Overview of TweetLID: Tweet language identification at SEPLN 2014. In *TweetLID@ SEPLN*, pages 1–11.

Human versus Machine Attention in Document Classification:
A Dataset with Crowdsourced Annotations

Nikolaos Pappas and **Andrei Popescu-Belis**
Idiap Research Institute
Centre du Parc, Rue Marconi 19
CH-1920 Martigny, Switzerland
{nikolaos.pappas, andrei.popescu-belis}@idiap.ch

Abstract

We present a dataset in which the contribution of each sentence of a review to the review-level rating is quantified by human judges. We define an annotation task and crowdsource it for 100 audiobook reviews with 1,662 sentences and 3 aspects: story, performance, and overall quality. The dataset is suitable for intrinsic evaluation of explicit document models with attention mechanisms, for multi-aspect sentiment analysis and summarization. We evaluated one such document attention model which uses weighted multiple-instance learning to jointly model aspect ratings and sentence-level rating contributions, and found that there is positive correlation between human and machine attention especially for sentences with high human agreement.

1 Introduction

Classifying the sentiment of documents has moved past global categories to target finer-grained ones, such as specific aspects of an item – a task known as multi-aspect sentiment analysis. An important challenge for this task is that target categories have "weak" relations to the input documents, as it is unknown which parts of the documents convey information about each category refer to. Using supervised learning to solve this task requires labeled data. Several previous studies have adopted a strongly-supervised approach using *sentence-level* labels (McAuley et al., 2012; Zhu et al., 2012), obtained with a significant human annotation effort. However, *document-level* labels are often available in social media, but learning from them requires

Overall (5/5)	Perf. (5/5)	Story (5/5)	Document (audiobook review)
			Narrated by one of my favorite narrators, Scott Brick, I found this offering by (...)
			I found it very difficult to "put this down".
			It is one of those no-brainer 5 star thrillers!

Figure 1: Human attention to sentences when attributing aspect ratings (overall, performance, or story) to an audiobook review.

a weakly-supervised approach. Recently, attention mechanisms for document modeling, either using hierarchical neural networks (Yang et al., 2016) or weighted multiple-instance learning (Pappas and Popescu-Belis, 2014), have proved superior in classification performance and are also able to quantify the contribution of each sentence to the document-level category.

While explicit document models can be indirectly evaluated on aspect rating prediction or document segmentation, a more direct way to estimate their qualities is to compare the sentence-level weights or attention scores that they assign with those assigned by human judges. In this paper, we present a dataset[1] containing human estimates of the contribution of each sentence of an audiobook review to the review-level aspect rating, along three aspects: story, performance, and overall quality.

Following a pilot experiment (Sec. 2), the annotation task was fully specified and crowdsourced. Statistics about the resulting dataset are given in Sec. 3. We show how the dataset can be used to evaluate a document attention model based on multiple-instance learning (outlined in Sec. 4), by comparing

---

[1]Available at www.idiap.ch/paper/hatdoc/.

Proceedings of The Fourth International Workshop on Natural Language Processing for Social Media, pages 94–100,
Austin, TX, November 1, 2016. ©2016 Association for Computational Linguistics

In this task we ask you to rate the explanatory power of sentences in a user review of an audiobook with respect to the user's opinion about the following aspects of the audiobook (recorded reading of a paper book):

Overall: General rating based on all aspects, including also author attributes (writing style, imagination, etc.)
Performance: Rating based on narrator attributes (acting, voice, role, etc.)
Story: Rating based on the story attributes (plot, characters, setting, etc.)

We provide: the sentence under examination highlighted in the entire user review; the user's rating on a five-star scale towards an aspect of the audiobook (namely, 1: very negative, 2: negative, 3: neutral, 4: positive, 5: very positive). The question and possible answers are displayed for each required rating.

The question is: *"How much does the highlighted sentence explain the given aspect rating?"* or in other words "How much does the highlighted sentence carry the user's opinion about each aspect?" The answer is one of the following choices of how much each sentence explains the displayed aspect rating: 'not at all', 'a little', 'moderately', 'rather well', and 'very well'.

Figure 2: Main annotation instructions given to human judges in the crowdsourced task.

the sentence attention scores with those obtained by humans (Sec. 5). We find a positive correlation between human and machine attention for high confidence annotations and show that the system is more reliable than some of the qualified annotators.

2   Pilot Annotation

We defined the requirements for a pilot experiment to reflect our interest in capturing sentence-level justifications of the aspect ratings indicated in a review. The focus is on the sentiment of a sentence, and not merely its topic. For example, in an audiobook review, a sentence that lists the main characters of the book is about the story, but it is factual and does not explain the reviewer's sentiment with respect to the story, i.e whether they liked it or not.

Definition. We recruited three annotators with good command of English among our colleagues. They were given ten audiobook reviews in self-contained files, along with the aspect rating scores (1–5 stars for 3 aspects) assigned by the authors of the reviews. The aspects, namely 'overall', 'performance' and 'story' were briefly defined, e.g. as "about plot, characters or setting" for the latter. The annotators had to answer on a 5-point scale the following question for each sentence and aspect: *"How much does the sentence explain why the user rated the aspect as they did?"* We instructed the annotators to assign explanatory scores only when they met opinionated sentences (expressing sentiment) and to ignore factual sentences about the aspects, as well as subtle or indirect expressions of opinions.

Results. We obtained 684 sentence-level scores for 3 aspects in 10 reviews. The agreement between each pair of annotators was computed using Pearson's correlation coefficient r (Pearson, 1895) and Cohen's kappa coefficient κ (Cohen, 1960). For the

latter, since we do not want to treat two different labels as a complete disagreement, we incorporated a distance measure, namely the absolute differences of normalized values between annotators.

The pairwise scores between annotators a, b and c are listed in Table 1. When computed over all rating dimensions, the average r coefficient is 0.72 (strong positive linear relationship) and the average κ is 0.79 (substantial agreement). Both values show that the obtained sentence labels are to a great extent reliable. When considering each aspect separately, the largest agreement was achieved on 'performance', followed by 'story', and then 'overall'. This is most likely due to our definition of the latter aspect to include all other aspects as well as author attributes.

	$a \leftrightarrow b$		$b \leftrightarrow c$		$c \leftrightarrow a$	
	r	κ	r	κ	r	κ
Ov.	0.80	0.81	0.44	0.60	0.48	0.64
Pr.	0.96	0.97	0.87	0.92	0.89	0.92
St.	0.73	0.79	0.63	0.72	0.72	0.78
All	0.84	0.86	0.64	0.75	0.70	0.78

Table 1: Pearson's correlation (r) and Kohen's kappa (κ) scores computed for each aspect (Ov: overall, Pr: performance, St: story) and each pair of annotators (a, b and c) in the pilot study.

3   Crowdsourced Task

Definition. For the definitive task, we wrote detailed instructions to annotators, providing a precise definition of the explanatory value of each sentence with respect to the aspect rating of the review. The main instructions are shown in Fig. 2, and they were complemented with additional tips and observations, as well as two fully-annotated sample reviews. The annotation interface showed for each task the question and possible answers (listed at the bottom of Fig. 2), along with the target sentence, highlighted within

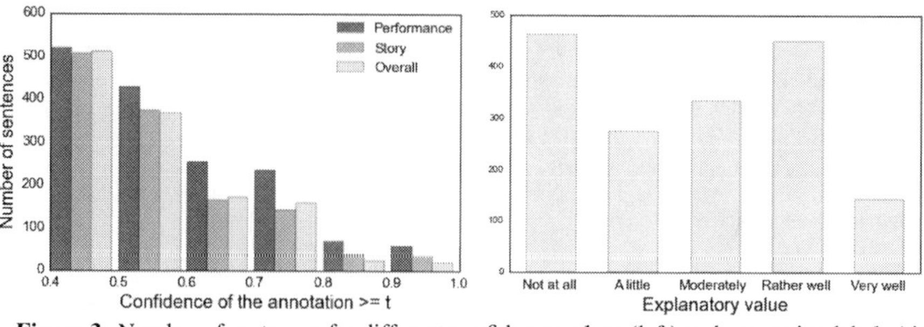

Figure 3: Number of sentences for different confidence values (left) and annotation labels (right).

the review. Each of the three aspects was annotated separately, to avoid confusion.

Results. We collected 100 reviews of audiobooks from Audible (`www.audible.com`) with 1,662 sentences. There are 20 reviews for each rating value of the 'overall' aspect (1–5 stars), to balance the distribution of positive vs. negative reviews. We obtained human judgments over the set of 100 reviews by crowdsourcing the task via Crowdflower (`www.crowdflower.com`).

The reliability of the judges was controlled by randomly inserting test questions with known answers ("gold" questions). Using these questions, Crowdflower computed a confidence score for each judge and then used it to compute the confidence for each annotated example. We only kept the answers of judges who achieved at least 70% success rate on the gold questions. For each non-gold question, we collected answers from at least four reliable annotators, and the majority answer was considered as the gold truth.

We obtained 7,121 judgments of the 1,662 sentences, on the entire spectrum of the rating distributions, as shown in Fig. 3, right side. The confidence of the annotations was computed by Crowdflower as 57% for the 'overall' and 'story' aspects, and 63% for 'performance'. The percentages of sentences with a confidence ≥ 0.8 were quite low, at respectively 4%, 7% and 12% for each aspect. Still, a substantial proportion of sentences have a confidence above 0.5, as shown in Fig. 3, left side. These numbers suggest that the task was the most difficult for the 'overall' aspect, followed by the 'story' and 'performance' aspects.

For evaluating an automatic system, high-confidence annotations (e.g. above 0.6) can be directly compared with labels assigned by a system. An alternative evaluation approach keeps all annotations, but replaces some of the human ratings with system ones, and examines the variation of inter-annotator agreement.

4 System: A Model of Document Attention

We use the data to evaluate a document attention model (Pappas and Popescu-Belis, 2014) which uses multiple-instance regression (MIR, Dietterich et al., 1997) to deal with coarse-grained input labels. The input is a set of bags (here, reviews), each of which contains a variable number of instances (here, sentences). The labels used for training (here, the aspect ratings) can be at the bag level (weak supervision), and not at the instance level. Our system learns to assign importance scores to individual instances, and to predict the labels of unseen bags.

In past models, the influence of instance labels on bag labels has been modeled with simplifying assumptions (e.g. averaging), whereas our system learns to aggregate instances of a bag according to their importance, like attention-based neural networks (Luong et al., 2015). To jointly learn instance weights and target labels, the system minimizes a regularized least squares loss. While in our 2014 paper this was done using alternating projections (as in Wagstaff and Lane, 2007), we use here stochastic gradient descent (Bottou, 1998) with the efficient ADAGRAD implementation (Duchi et al., 2011). In particular, the attention is modeled by a normalized exponential function, namely a softmax and a linear activation between a contextual vector and the document matrix (sentence vectors). Essentially, this formulation enables learning with stochastic gradient descent while preserving the initial instance relevance assumption in the MIR framework and the constraints in our 2014 paper.

The system is trained on a uniform sample of 50,000 audiobook reviews from Audible, with

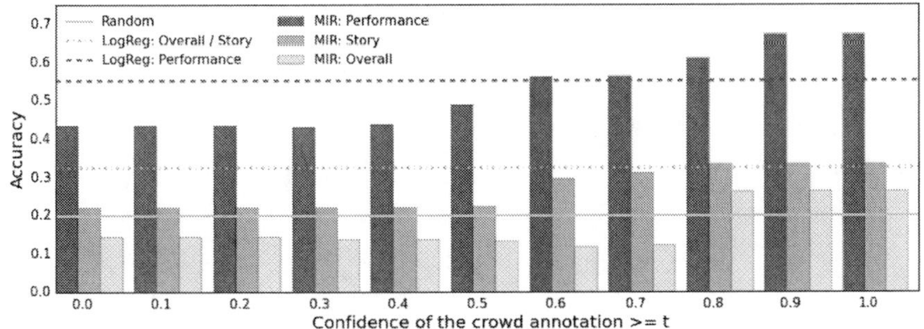

Figure 4: Accuracy of the evaluated system (MIR) on predicting the explanatory value of sentences with respect to review-level ratings of the three aspects, for subsets of increasing crowd confidence values. The accuracy of a supervised system, Logistic Regression, trained on the attention labels with 10-fold cross-validation, is noted LogReg. Random accuracy is 1 out of 5 (20%).

10,000 reviews for each value of the 'overall' aspect (1–5 stars). The training set does not include the 100 annotated reviews, used for testing only.

5 Comparison of System to Humans

Attention prediction. To evaluate the system's estimates of the contribution of each sentence to the review rating, a first and simple metric is the number of sentences for which system and human labels are identical, i.e. *accuracy*. Identity of labels is however hard to achieve, given that even humans do not have perfect agreement. Fig. 4 displays the accuracy of the system, for each aspect, for test subsets of increasing crowd confidence, from the entire test set to only the most reliable labels. Our MIR system appears to achieve the highest accuracy on the 'performance' aspect, exceeding 60% for labels assigned with at least 0.8 confidence by humans. The accuracy for 'story' is 33%, while for 'overall' it is the lowest, at 26%. The system outperforms the random baseline at 20% for 'performance' and 'story'. When compared with the expected accuracy of a supervised system (10-fold cross-validation over the ground-truth labels), namely Logistic Regression, our system achieves similar accuracy on sentences with confidence greater or equal to 0.6.

When relaxing the constraints of exact label matching, i.e. accepting as matches neighboring labels as well (distance 1), the accuracies at the 0.8 confidence level increase to 71%, 43% and 52% respectively for each aspect. Interestingly, the 'overall' aspect benefits the most from this relaxation, showing that many predictions were actually close to the gold label. The MIR performance is greater for higher crowd confidence values, which shows that both the system and the humans find similar difficulties in assigning importance scores to sentences wrt. document-level aspects.

While accuracy gives an indication of a system's quality, it is not entirely informative in the absence of a direct comparison term, such as a better baseline than random guesses. A second evaluation metric enabled by our dataset compares the system's quality with that of human annotators.

Reliability analysis. This more nuanced evaluation places the system on the same scale of qualification, from the most reliable judges (those who most agree with the average) to the least reliable ones. We consider the average standard deviation (STD) among humans, which decreases when the answers of the least reliable judges are removed, and ask: what happens if certain judges are replaced by our system? Fig. 5 displays the difference obtained from the STD of all judges for three replacement strategies:

Random: Select a random label per sentence and replace it with a random value.

Human: Replace the least reliable human judge for each sentence (i.e. largest distance to the average) with the average label of each sentence.

Model: Replace at random an annotator label per sentence with a system one.

As shown in Fig. 5, 'Model' consistently outperforms 'Random' for all aspects and confidence levels, as it leads to a larger decrease (or a smaller increase) in STD. The system performs better than the least agreeing judges on the 'story' and 'overall' aspects, as it leads to a smaller STD than the 'Human' configuration, sometimes even smaller than the initial STD of all judges. Given the qualification

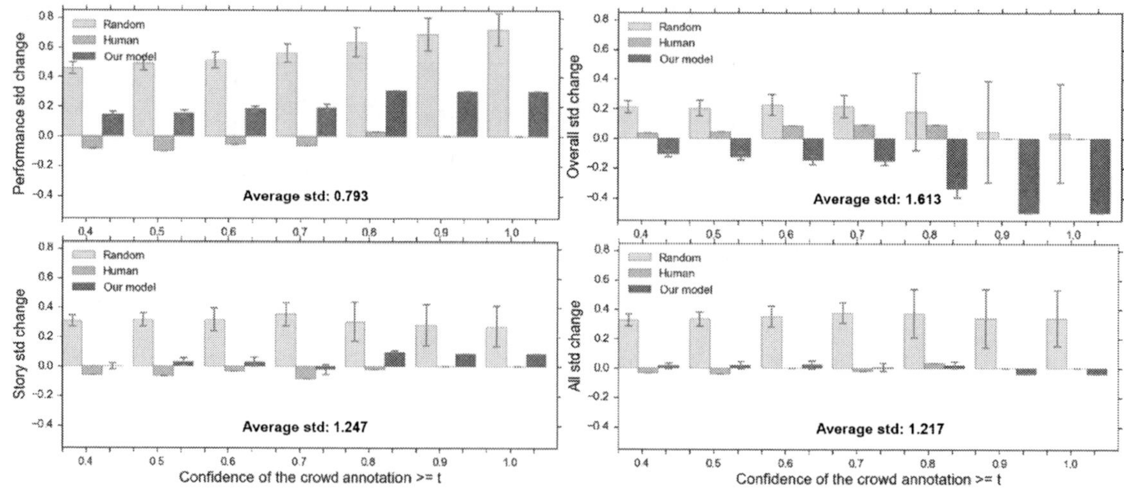

Figure 5: Changes in average STD of the explanatory sentence labels in three replacement experiments (color coded), for each of the three aspects separately and then jointly for all of them.

controls enforced by the Crowdflower, we conclude that the labels assigned by the system are comparable to those of qualified human judges for 'story' and 'overall'. For 'performance', however, the high agreement of judges cannot be matched by the system, according to this metric. Still, these results provide evidence that the weights found by the system capture the explanatory value of sentences in a way that is similar to humans.

6 Related Work

Multi-aspect sentiment analysis. This task usually requires aspect segmentation, followed by prediction or summarization (Hu and Liu, 2004; Zhuang et al., 2006). Most related studies have engineered various feature sets, augmenting words with topic or content models (Mei et al., 2007; Titov and McDonald, 2008; Sauper et al., 2010; Lu et al., 2011), or with linguistic features (Pang and Lee, 2005; Qu et al., 2010; Zhu et al., 2012). McAuley et al. (2012) proposed an interpretable probabilistic model for modeling aspect reviews. Kim et al. (2013) proposed an hierarchical model to discover the review structure from unlabeled corpora. Previous systems for rating prediction were trained on segmented texts (Zhu et al., 2012; McAuley et al., 2012), while our system (Pappas and Popescu-Belis, 2014) used weak supervision on unsegmented text. Here, we introduced a new evaluation of such models on sentiment summarization considering human attention.

Document classification. Recent studies have shown that attention mechanisms are beneficial to machine translation (Bahdanau et al., 2014), question answering (Sukhbaatar et al., 2015), text summarization (Rush et al., 2015), and document classification (Pappas and Popescu-Belis, 2014). Most recently, Yang et al. (2016) introduced hierarchical attention networks for document classification. Despite the improvements, it is yet unclear what exactly this attention mechanism captures for the task at hand. Our dataset enables the direct comparison of such mechanism and human attention scores for document classification, thus contributing to a better understanding of the document attention models.

7 Conclusion

We presented a new dataset with human attention to sentences triggered when attributing aspect ratings to reviews. The dataset enables the evaluation of attention-based models for document classification and the explicit evaluation of sentiment summarization. Our crowdsourcing task is sound and can be used for larger-scale annotations. In the future, statistical properties of the data (e.g. numeric scale), should be exploited even further to provide more accurate evaluations, for instance by relaxing the exact match rule to tolerate marginal mismatches.

Acknowledgments

We are grateful to the European Union for support in the Horizon 2020 SUMMA project n. 688139.

References

Dzmitry Bahdanau, Kyunghyun Cho, and Yoshua Bengio. 2014. Neural machine translation by jointly learning to align and translate. *CoRR* abs/1409.0473.

Léon Bottou. 1998. On-line learning and stochastic approximations. In David Saad, editor, *On-line Learning in Neural Networks*, Cambridge University Press, New York, pages 9–42.

Jacob Cohen. 1960. A coefficient of agreement for nominal scales. *Educational and Psychological Measurement* 20(1):37–46.

Thomas G. Dietterich, Richard H. Lathrop, and Tomás Lozano-Pérez. 1997. Solving the multiple instance problem with axis-parallel rectangles. *Artificial Intelligence* 89(12):31 – 71.

John C. Duchi, Elad Hazan, and Yoram Singer. 2011. Adaptive subgradient methods for online learning and stochastic optimization. *Journal of Machine Learning Research* 12:2121–2159.

Minqing Hu and Bing Liu. 2004. Mining and summarizing customer reviews. In *Proceedings of the 10th ACM SIGKDD International Conference on Knowledge discovery and data mining*. Seattle, WA, KDD '04, pages 168–177.

Suin Kim, Jianwen Zhang, Zheng Chen, Alice Oh, and Shixia Liu. 2013. A hierarchical aspect-sentiment model for online reviews. In *Proceedings of the 27th AAAI Conference on Artificial Intelligence*. Bellevue, WA, AAAI'13, pages 526–533.

Bin Lu, Myle Ott, Claire Cardie, and Benjamin K. Tsou. 2011. Multi-aspect sentiment analysis with topic models. In *Proc. of the 11th IEEE Int. Conf. on Data Mining Workshops*. Washington, DC, ICDMW '11, pages 81–88.

Minh-Thang Luong, Hieu Pham, and Christopher D. Manning. 2015. Effective approaches to attention-based neural machine translation. In *Proceedings of the 2015 Conference on Empirical Methods in Natural Language Processing*. Lisbon, EMNLP '15, pages 1412–1421.

Julian McAuley, Jure Leskovec, and Dan Jurafsky. 2012. Learning attitudes and attributes from multi-aspect reviews. In *Proceedings of the 12th IEEE International Conference on Data Mining*. Brussels, ICDM '12, pages 1020–1025.

Qiaozhu Mei, Xu Ling, Matthew Wondra, Hang Su, and ChengXiang Zhai. 2007. Topic sentiment mixture: modeling facets and opinions in weblogs. In *Proceedings of the 16th International Conference on the World Wide Web*. Banff, Canada, WWW '07, pages 171–180.

Bo Pang and Lillian Lee. 2005. Seeing stars: Exploiting class relationships for sentiment categorization with respect to rating scales. In *Proceedings of the 43rd Annual Meeting on Association for Computational Linguistics*. Ann Arbor, MI, ACL '05, pages 115–124.

Nikolaos Pappas and Andrei Popescu-Belis. 2014. Explaining the stars: Weighted multiple-instance learning for aspect-based sentiment analysis. In *Proceedings of the 2014 Conference on Empirical Methods in Natural Language Processing*. Doha, Qatar, EMNLP '14, pages 455–466.

Karl Pearson. 1895. Note on regression and inheritance in the case of two parents. *Proceedings of the Royal Society of London* 58:240–242.

Lizhen Qu, Georgiana Ifrim, and Gerhard Weikum. 2010. The bag-of-opinions method for review rating prediction from sparse text patterns. In *Proceedings of the 23rd International Conference on Computational Linguistics*. Beijing, China, COLING '10, pages 913–921.

Alexander M. Rush, Sumit Chopra, and Jason Weston. 2015. A neural attention model for abstractive sentence summarization. *CoRR* abs/1509.00685.

Christina Sauper, Aria Haghighi, and Regina Barzilay. 2010. Incorporating content structure into text analysis applications. In *Proceedings of the 2010 Conference on Empirical Methods in Natural Language Processing*. Cambridge, MA, EMNLP '10, pages 377–387.

Sainbayar Sukhbaatar, Arthur Szlam, Jason Weston, and Rob Fergus. 2015. Weakly supervised memory networks. *CoRR* abs/1503.08895.

Ivan Titov and Ryan McDonald. 2008. Modeling online reviews with multi-grain topic models. In *Proceedings of the 17th International Conference on World Wide Web*. Beijing, China, WWW '08, pages 111–120.

Kiri L. Wagstaff and Terran Lane. 2007. Salience assignment for multiple-instance regression. In *Proceedings of the ICML 2007 Workshop on Constrained Optimization and Structured Output Spaces*. Corvallis, OR.

Zichao Yang, Diyi Yang, Chris Dyer, Xiaodong He, Alex Smola, and Eduard Hovy. 2016. Hierarchical attention networks for document classification. In *Proceedings of the 15th Annual Conference of the North American Chapter of the Association for Computational Linguistics: Human Language Technologies*. San Diego, California, NAACL'16.

Jingbo Zhu, Chunliang Zhang, and Matthew Y. Ma. 2012. Multi-aspect rating inference with aspect-based segmentation. *IEEE Transactions on Affective Computing* 3(4):469–481.

Li Zhuang, Feng Jing, and Xiao-Yan Zhu. 2006. Movie review mining and summarization. In *Proceedings of the 15th ACM International Conference on Information and Knowledge Management*. Arlington, VA, CIKM '06, pages 43–50.

Author Index

Anderson, Kenneth, 1
Andrews, Nicholas, 20
Augenstein, Isabelle, 48

Bethard, Steven, 14
Bosnjak, Matko, 48
Boulard Masson, Cécile, 26
Brun, Caroline, 26

Cantarero, Alejandro, 7
Chang, Yung-Chun, 74
Cheng, Hao, 55
Chu, Chun-Han, 74

DeYoung, Jay, 20
Doggett, Erika, 7
Dredze, Mark, 20

Eisner, Ben, 48

Fang, Hao, 55
Fang, Rui, 65

Hathi, Shobhit, 84
Hsieh, Yu-Lun, 74
Hsu, Wen-Lian, 74

Jaech, Aaron, 84
Jain, Siddharth, 41

Kim, Sunghwan Mac, 34

Li, Quanzhi, 65
LIU, XIAOMO, 65

Mulcaire, George, 84

Navindgi, Amit, 26
Nourbakhsh, Armineh, 65
Nowson, Scott, 26

Ostendorf, Mari, 55, 84

Palen, Leysia, 1
Palmer, Martha, 1
Pappas, Nikolaos, 94
Paris, Cecile, 34
Paul, Michael J., 1
Pedersen, Ted, 14
Popescu-Belis, Andrei, 94

Rey-Villamizar, Nicolas, 14
Riedel, Sebastian, 48
Rocktäschel, Tim, 48

Sadeque, Farig, 14
Shah, Sameena, 65
Shrestha, Prasha, 14
Smith, Noah A., 84
Solorio, Thamar, 14
Stowe, Kevin, 1

Wan, Stephen, 34